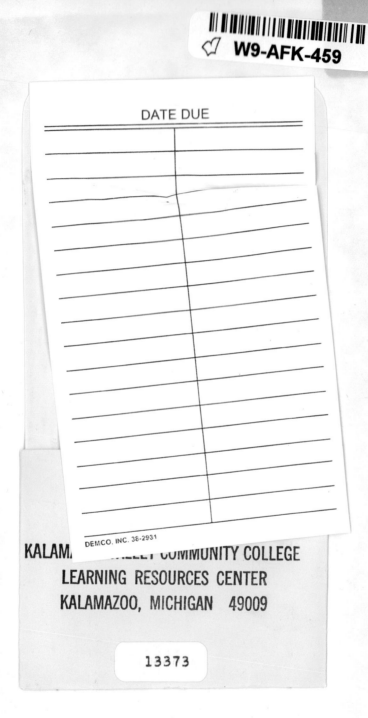

DATE DUE

AMERICAN WOMEN

images and realities

AMERICAN WOMEN
Images and Realities

Advisory Editors
ANNETTE K. BAXTER
LEON STEIN

A Note About This Volume

In 1909, sociologist Mary Elizabeth Burroughs
Roberts Smith Coolidge (1860-1945), published her
study of Chinese immigration, still the foremost study
of its kind. She also wrote about the Indians of Ari-
zona and New Mexico. In this book, she provides
valuable insights into the development of feminine behavior, seeking to distinguish what is innate in female
character from what has been shaped by the social
coercion of masculine preferences. Her book is a
scrupulously honest assessment of "the domestic
type"–the most commonly recognized female personality of middle-class America.

WHY WOMEN ARE SO

By

MARY ROBERTS COOLIDGE

ARNO PRESS

A New York Times Company

New York • 1972

Reprint Edition 1972 by Arno Press Inc.

Reprinted from a copy in The University of
Illinois Library

American Women: Images and Realities
ISBN for complete set: 0-405-04445-3
See last pages of this volume for titles.

Manufactured in the United States of America

- - - - - - - - - - - -

Library of Congress Cataloging in Publication Data

Coolidge, Mary Elizabeth Burroughs (Roberts)
    Smith, 1860-1945.
    Why women are so.

    (American women: images and realities)
    1. Woman--Social and moral questions. 2. Woman--
History and condition of women. I. Title.
II. Series.
HQ1206.C7 1972   301.41'2   72-2595
ISBN 0-405-04452-6

WHY WOMEN ARE SO

By

MARY ROBERTS COOLIDGE, Ph. D.

Author of *Chinese Immigration, Almshouse Women,* etc.

NEW YORK

HENRY HOLT AND COMPANY

1912

THE QUINN & BODEN CO. PRESS
RAHWAY, N. J.

TO

𝕯. 𝕮.

AND OTHER NEW MEN

WHO SET HUMAN QUALITY ABOVE FEMININITY

IN WOMEN

THE HYPOTHESIS

THESE chapters are neither a defense nor an arraignment of womankind; they are, rather, a first-hand study of the ordinary, orthodox, middle-class women who have constituted the domestic type for more than a century; the exotic great lady and the morbid woman with a grievance have alike been omitted. They try to answer the query: why are women so? Is the characteristic behavior which is called feminine an inalienable quality or merely an attitude of mind produced by the coercive social habits of past times?

As a working hypothesis it is assumed that the women of the nineteenth century in America were for the most part what men expected them to be; modified only by the disintegrating, and at the same time reconstructive, forces of modern society. In other words, sex traditions rather than innate sex character have produced what is called " feminine " as distinguished from womanly behavior.

CONTENTS

vii

CONTENTS

SECTION IV

FROM FEMININITY TO WOMANHOOD

SECTION I
THE DOMESTIC TRADITIONS

CHAPTER I

THE CONVENTIONS OF GIRLHOOD

"Creatures of circumstance who waited to be fallen in love with. . . . We stood and waited—on approval. And then came life itself and tore our mother's theories to tatters."—CICELY HAMILTON.

"The chief element of a good time . . . as these countless rich young women judge it, are a petty eventfulness, laughter, and to feel you are looking well and attracting attention. Shopping is one of its chief joys. . . . My cousins were always getting and giving, my uncle caressed them with parcels and checks. . . . So far as marriage went, the married state seemed at once very attractive and dreadfully serious to them, composed in equal measure of becoming important and becoming old. I don't know what they thought about children. I doubt if they thought about them at all."—H. G. WELLS.

"Fine girls sittin' like shopkeepers behind their goods, waitin' and waitin' and waitin'. . . ."—OLIVER WENDELL HOLMES.

FEMININE life in the middle Nineteenth Century, and to a degree now almost inconceivable, was permeated with the current traditions of what good women had been, and by the assumption that these stood for the pattern of what they should still be. From the moment of birth their sex was outwardly marked by the color of their ribbons, which became the embodiment, as it were, of their discreet and pallid characteristics. Throughout

3

the weeks that followed the mother watched impatiently to see whether the baby's hair would be
curly—" for curly hair is so pretty in a girl, you
know." By the time the infant could walk and
talk, she had learned that there were things taboo
for her which were perfectly proper for the little
male creatures of her kind: *she* might not yell, nor
romp, nor scuffle, nor, in short, " be a tomboy,"
because it was not nice for a little girl.

While the little boys of her age were gradually
emancipated from lingerie garments, she still remained the charming baby-doll of the household.
Her clothes continued to be made of light-colored
and fragile materials, which she was constantly
adjured not to soil. Her complexion, her hair,
her tiny hands and feet were discussed in her
presence as if they were marketable assets. Almost the first words in her vocabulary were
" nice " and " pretty; " the one subtly stimulating
sex-consciousness, the other associated with her
physical limitations and the good looks which
were to be a chief end of her existence. For her
alone was coined the phrase: pretty is that pretty
does. Boys did not have to be pretty, only good
and smart; and, therefore, in the initial rivalry of
the sexes she instinctively learned to lay her emphasis on prettiness. As a consequence, while
she was still in knee-length dresses, clothing, manners, and appearance became of superlative im-

portance. Her guardians need not have been surprised, when, a few years later, she became a vain
and self-conscious creature, already measuring her
beauty against that of other girls, and prematurely
trying it on the males of her acquaintance.

But alas for her if her hair did not curl—if she
turned out plain, or " not so pretty as her mother
was "! She heard from grandmothers and other
ladies of fading complexions and charms, over
their needlework and tea, a chorus of pity. Many
a little girl has cried her eyes out in secret because she had straight hair, large ears, or a muddy
skin. This constant emphasis upon appearance
had the effect, upon one temperament, of concentrating the desire of her whole nature on the
attainment of conventional prettiness; upon another more sensitive one to create a morbid embarrassment amounting to tragedy; and sometimes upon stronger natures, to turn their aspirations toward some form of practical efficiency or
to intellectual pursuits. However it turned out,
before the girl-child was ten years old she had received an indelible impression that beauty, particularly a purely physical and luscious loveliness
—such as would have been a disadvantage to a
boy—was the most important attainment of a
young girl's life.

Very early in this process of inculcating femininity it was necessary to check and pervert her-

physical impulses. Like the racing-horse, she must be trained while yet a colt never to break her gait. The goal of conventional prettiness permitted no indulgence in dirt or sunburn, therefore she could not run or play freely out-of-doors nor develop her muscles in competitive games that required speed and wind, a quick eye and a sure aim. Being a lively animal, her natural energy would try to find outlet somewhere at first, according to her temperament and coerced by her parents' ideals of woman's sphere. If she had a robust body and a strong-willed, original personality, she would kick over the traces and break through the corral fence a good many times before the habits of domestication became ingrained. Such a temperament was always a source of trouble until she submitted to the life predestined for her by the traditions of her foremothers. She was, indeed, fortunate if her temper was not embittered, her health undermined, or her life made unhappy by the thwarting of her natural character.

But if she were born not too vigorous, and both docile and pretty, her path was smooth for her from the very beginning. Before she had mastered her letters she learned the horror of dirt, and set out on that approved career of dainty fastidiousness which is the glory of womankind. Instead of developing her muscles in large, free movements, she spent her placid girlhood in dressing girl-dolls that were models of ladylikeness; in giving little girls' tea-parties, where the social game of their elders was imitated in the exhibition of best clothes, the practice of polite, conversational gossip, and the rehearsal of the attractive arts; and in learning to make patchwork and her own clothes, prize cakes and fancy jellies—if her mother were of the older school; or, at a later date, in doing monstrous fancywork and embroidering her undergarments.

While her brothers played baseball and shinny or went swimming, she sat on a piano-stool, with her feet a few inches from the floor, practising the hour or two a day necessary to attain a meager proficiency. For in that day the ideal young lady must play the piano; not at all because she had musical talent worthy of serious cultivation, or because it was a necessary equipment for life—one scarcely knows why, unless to keep her out of mischief, or, perhaps, to make her more alluring to that future husband who might like a little music in the evenings now and then to soothe his nerves.

Nor was her domestic training of a much more thorough sort, although the tradition that the women of the household should be cooks and manufacturers was still widespread. Among middle-class American families the domestic habits of Europe persisted long after manufactured goods were to be had in stores, and even at the beginning of a new century country women are still canning fruit, making bedding, crocheting lace— still clinging to the handicrafts of a by-gone industrial period. But the daughters of the latter half of the Nineteenth Century have had, on the one hand, slight respect for these homely accomplishments; and, on the other, scant opportunity for training in the more serious duties of administration of the household.

The feminine training of the Eighteenth Century was purely domestic; that of our generation purely academic; and thus there has been at least sixty years in the interim when girls were brought up almost without education for domestic life, and wholly without practical preparation for any other kind of life. During this period the manufacture of cotton and woolen goods in factories was superseding domestic processes; and even the preparation of food products was being transferred from the home to large collective agencies. As the processes of production were taken out of the house the physically stronger girls and women without male support followed it into the factory, there to become producers again, or into great department stores, to be distributors. But the great body of mothers and daughters left behind in homes still clung instinctively to the convention that domestic life was the economic sphere of women, although the necessary handicrafts which had made it so were all but gone.

The housewife of the Eighteenth Century earned her own living, and often quite half that of the family, by her labor, beside bearing and rearing children; and many women in our time, on the other hand, are rapidly acquiring economic independence; but, in the century between, thousands of women in America scarcely earned their salt. Not because they were lazy or incapable, but because the older ideal did not permit any but a serving-woman to go outside the home to earn money, and the occupations which had formerly made the home both a workshop and a storehouse no longer demanded their service.

So when our docile young girl in her immaculate frock had tired of playing with dolls and giving mannerly parties, she occupied herself in painting on velvet, in embroidery, crochet, or tatting, and in piano practice, in the intervals of a very polite education. In school she learned the common branches and, if she kept on long enough, acquired a superficial knowledge of English and American literature, made a painful reading-acquaintance with classical French, absorbed a little political history of by-gone European states, and, occasionally, a little mathematical astronomy and polite, herbarium botany. In those days, no knowledge of physiology, no discoveries of the laws of life in the biological laboratory, ever disturbed the guarded decency of the mind of any potential mother of the race.

This purely cultural and well-intentioned, but misdirected, education for young girls was one of the early by-products of the theories of democracy. In the Old World men and women had been born to a definite status in society, in which economic opportunities, duties, training, and even costume, were predetermined; but in the newer world, when the pioneers of the Colonial period had established their families with a competence, it became their ambition to lift their descendants into a higher social class. While the father was earning the money to fulfil their ambition, and the mother continued to practise the traditional handicrafts of the household, the daughters went to school and expressed, by their white-handedness and all but useless accomplishments, the rising social status of the family.

As domestic manufactures were superseded by factory-made products, there was less and less for girls to do at home, and there arose a kind of spurious feminine craft in the shape of inartistic and perfectly useless fancy-work. When the patchwork quilt, the hand-woven bed-cover and linen sheet had been replaced by the manufactured comforter and cheap cotton, women began to devise pillow shams, bedspreads of cloth cut into crazy-shaped pieces, or knitted of a thousand tiny shells. When the feather pillow, which once cost the housewife so much labor, came to be made in quantities by machinery, she turned her ambition into baby-pillows, pine-pillows, head-rests, throws, tidies, feather and hair flowers, sofa cushions, and rag rugs—in short, into a vast variety of quasi-ornamental, altogether hideous, and generally useless articles. The tradition that the woman should be a manufacturer—a tradition handed down from the dim ages when the female tanned the skins, wove the mats and blankets, and built the tepee—died slowly, and is not yet wholly vanished.

It may seem very strange that girls did not learn at least to cook, that being the oldest and most universal of women's occupations; and all the more as the chief pride of their mothers lay in housewifery, the center of which lay in the kitchen. As other handicrafts became less imperative, the housewife of the earlier period concentrated her whole mind on feeding her men-folks lavishly. Imbued with the colonial-English tradition of good eating, and spurred on by the rivalry of neighbor women equally energetic, she piled cake, pie, doughnuts, preserved fruit, and pancakes, with meat and vegetables, on the creaking table. She would doubtless have insisted on her pretty daughter learning to make all these elaborate dishes as she had learned them from her own mother, but for the arrival of thousands of immigrant Irish and German servants to give her cheap and willing assistance.

Nobody, not even a sturdy pioneer woman, continues to do hard manual labor when it is no longer either compulsory or admirable. The highly-skilled house-mother, remembering the hot stove, the aching feet, and the never-ending "woman's work," wanted her daughters to have an easier life than she had had, and was glad to accept the help of clumsy peasant hands in order to release them from such hardship. Moreover, the plain American fathers and mothers still associated gentle-hood with freedom from manual labor of an obligatory kind, and would not permit their soft-handed daughters to compete with foreign servant girls.

During the years of adolescence girls went to school, not because they expected to use the education they were getting in any practical way, but largely to fill up the time in a ladylike manner until they should be courted and married. If now and then some girl—too plain to join in the beauty contest, or too vital and ambitious to be contented with so tame a program of life—attempted to break through the meshes of the feminine cult into a larger sphere, she found few opportunities for solid education or occupation

open to her, and was greeted with general disapproval. If she had a sturdy, fighting temper,
and a love of learning or achievement, she sometimes threw away her pack of feminine traditions
and took the trail in pursuit of the ideal. It was,
indeed, a desert that they traveled—those first,
few, strong-minded young women—and, however
the adventure turned out, the effect of opposition,
of lack of sympathy and opportunity, the starva-
tion of the natural human soul hungering for
justice and for the approval of its kind, could
only be to pervert character. Some came out of
the struggle strong creatures, but masculine imitations rather than fully developed women;
others, maddened by injustice or misunderstanding, set their hands against every man, champion-
ing wild or premature causes; but the larger number disappeared from history, merely defeated
feminine souls carrying too great a handicap.

During all those years when plain and pretty
girls alike were growing up, they came somehow
to know that their destiny was to be married. Not
that any one asked them what they were going
to be or do—that would have been quite improper
or might have precipitated questions which girls
should not ask. Their brothers, even before they
left the grammar school, were encouraged to talk
of their future occupations, and to make prepara-

tion for them. But while girls heard from the pulpit and the rostrum, and read in the harmless romances of Sunday-school books or ladies' magazines, that marriage and motherhood were the inevitable and only admirable career of woman, nothing was ever said to them, except by way of a joke, about either. Indirectly, some conscientious mother might approach it shamefacedly, suggesting that the daughter should learn some household task, " because you may have a home of your own, some day; " but never a serious word was said about wifehood and motherhood. The atmosphere of prudery surrounding marriage and child-bearing, which was all but universal a century ago, is still common enough among ignorant women, who will never discuss before a spinster of any age, not even before a charity visitor, the facts incident to pregnancy. While boys were learning in the farmyard and from other men the facts and processes of reproduction, girls walked in a mist of secrecy and innuendo. When their mothers were bearing children they were sent away from home on some pretense, lest they should witness the great travail and be afraid; or, perhaps, because their parents were ashamed; or, it may be, solely because the convention was that young girls must be kept " innocent."

But girls are no more fools than boys, and the atmosphere of prudish or vulgar suggestion aroused in the keen-witted ones a determination to know how babies came, and what marriage meant. Many a young girl, not daring to ask what she wanted to know of older women, got a perverted knowledge from vulgar-minded servants, or from the medical dictionaries in the library; or puzzled out the obscene advertisements and tragedies of the half-world covertly described in the news-papers; or pored over the sexual horrors of the ancient scriptures, to satisfy her curiosity.

In the less curious and less original type of girl the conventional silence about her future career created a shrinking disgust from the facts of reproductive life.   She became ashamed of her functions without knowing why.   She could not help seeing that the figures of women were not beautiful during gestation, and that pregnancy and childbirth were a period of inconvenience, if not of semi-invalidism.   While the " glory " of motherhood was constantly preached at her, she heard women criticising the indecency of wives who appeared in public in the later months of pregnancy, and sometimes saw the lascivious smiles, or overheard the comments of men upon them.   Nor could she escape knowing that some men were wild beasts, nor the suggestion that men in general were not to be trusted in the dark. Thus everything in her own nature and everything in the social influences about her tended to produce repulsion, if not terror, for the only approved destiny held out before her.

Meanwhile, during the adolescent years of both the inquisitive and the acquiescent young woman, her mind was being colored by the effeminate fiction of the day, whose chief note was love and lovers, with a happy ending in marriage. That the experiences of the heroine did not seem to correspond with the lives of the women she knew, made it all the more alluring. In this dream-world there were no puzzling and inevitable facts of nature—the lover was always pure and brave and considerate; the heroine beautiful and adored. There was no baby even, as in real life, to precipitate difficulties, except on the last page, when he might arrive to fulfil the hope of an heir to some great property.

Somewhere along this road of female destiny the girl received a shock; from the newspapers, perhaps, or more often through some tragedy in her own community, she heard that some unhappy girl had murdered her baby or ended her unwedded romance in suicide. Then, suddenly, if she were capable of reasoning at all, she would realize that motherhood was only considered sacred when licensed by the State and by the Church.

At last, when she had filled in a few years following her schooldays with "helping her

mother," " going into society," playing the piano,
and teaching a Sunday-school class, and in modestly trying out her charms on the young men of
her acquaintance, *The Lover* arrived. It is not
without reason that the period of courtship has
been depicted from time immemorial as the happiest of life. The exhilaration of quickening instinct, the zest of the game of advance and re-
treat, the grateful mutual flattery, are full of joy
to the woman even more than to the man. For
while to the man it might become the highest
experience of his life if the ending were happy,
it seldom had the full allurement of novelty.
Very few men, probably, brought to their final
courtship an unvulgarized mind, a chaste person,
and an entire ignorance of the other sex, such as
girls are expected to have. To the woman courtship and marriage were the culmination of a long
dream, in which her natural instincts and hunger
for life—a real life of her own—overcame her
fear of men and her innocent dread of the travail
of motherhood. Whether their temperaments
were really domestic and maternal or not, passion,
romance, and a desire for a career, combined with
the tradition that marriage is the highest if not
the only destiny to make young women take the
path of least resistance.

It used to be said that childhood was the happiest time of life, and girlhood, even more than

boyhood, full of joy.   Certainly it was so when the parents were wise and sympathetic, and the children born with a harmonious temperament in a normal body.   But the unconscious joy usually attributed to childhood has not so often existed in fact.   Not even yet are parents wise enough to restrain without arbitrary coercion; to make the path of discipline and duty more alluring than that of self-indulgence; and to provide a wholesome outlet for physical energy.   Nor are they sympathetic enough to enter into the fearsome questions of the young soul, and, out of the richness of adult experience, guide it till it attains courage and self-poise.   In a girlhood such as I have been describing, happiness was only possible to the girl who submitted to the conventional mold.   The more vigorous she was, the more potential character she had, the less easy she would find it to conform to the pattern laid before her.   And if she did conform she was likely to arrive at womanhood physically undeveloped, and robbed of a part of her bodily vigor; prudish and ignorant, yet eager to be married; without preparation for domestic and maternal cares, and incapable of earning a fair living wage by any other means; and with an abnormally feminized conscience, which had no conception of men or the moral issues of their lives.   The girl of the middle Nineteenth Century was fortunate if, by the grace of God and the accident of heedless parents, she sometimes arrived at the goal of marriage a little less docile, pretty, anemic, conscientious, and incompetent than the ideals of her time would have had her become.

CHAPTER II

THE GREAT ADVENTURE

" As the vine which has long twined in graceful foliage about
the oak, and has been lifted by it into sunshine, will, when the
hardy plant has been rifled by the thunderbolt, cling around it
with its caressing tendrils, and bind up its shattered boughs, so
it is beautifully ordained by Providence that woman, who is the
ornament and dependent of man in his happier hours, should
be his stay and solace when smitten with sudden calamity, wind-
ing herself into the sudden recesses of his nature, tenderly sup-
porting the drooping head, and binding up the broken heart."—
From *The Lady's Album,* 1848.

" Woman has a better, a holier vocation. She works in the
elements of human nature. Her orders of architecture are
formed in the human soul—Obedience, Temperance, Truth, Love,
Piety—these she must build up in the character of her children;
often she is called upon to repair the ravages which sin, care,
and the desolating storms of life leave in the mind and heart
of her husband, whom she reverences and obeys. This task she
should perform faithfully but with humility; remembering that
it was for woman's sake Eden was forfeited, because Adam
loved his wife more than his Creator."—Mrs. S. J. HALE in
Woman's Record, 1872.

" But the woman is the glory of the man. . . . Neither was
the man created for the woman; but the woman for the man."—
PAUL *to the Corinthians.*

THE truest things are the platitudes which
everybody speaks, but which few ever think of
practising. The sensible men and women of the

20

past century knew then—as they do now—that the betrothal and wedding customs in vogue were preposterous, injurious, and even vulgar; and that the prospective bride and bridegroom were rendered unfit for parenthood by the fatigue of the wedding preparations and the abnormality of their situation. Every father and mother, out of their own experience, could have warned and advised—on matters of housekeeping and property settlements they did so—but on the purposes and consequences of marriage, the one great central relation which concerned the engaged pair and posterity, nothing was said.

It was as if each generation should begin without receiving any cumulated information on the subject of house-building, and should therefore be obliged to try all the experiments and make all the mistakes of previous generations over again. Because of the "conspiracy of silence," young lovers were deprived of every safeguard of knowledge in respect to sex and parenthood. It is impossible to understand the woman's attitude toward marriage, domesticity, and motherhood, unless one visualizes the ignorance and perversion of ideas with which girls came to the great event of their lives. At the risk of tediousness it is necessary to present the material phases of marriage in order that their consequences in diverting attention from the

aspects most significant to society, may be comprehended.

To the young girl the engagement ring was the
symbol both of obligation and individuality, for by
virtue of it she became for the first time in her
life a person of importance. To her school-
mates she was an object of envy because she was
peeping through the door which they all desired to
enter. If the young man were acceptable to
her parents, her father was frankly glad to trans-
fer the economic burden of a daughter to another
man; while her mother began to treat her with a
mixture of respect and solicitude which she could
not comprehend. Theoretically she knew that
she had incurred an obligation to her betrothed
which would some day demand wifely surrender
and devotion; but the more protected and innocent she was, the less did she understand what
lay behind the veil of marriage. To think
definitely of her future relation to her husband
and to prepare herself for its consequences would
have been as gross an impropriety as to expose her
person to his gaze.

Nor was she conscious that she would be expected to submit her will and her opinions as
well as her body to his control. Although she
heard on Sunday from the pulpit that wives were
to obey their husbands; and although she knew
that her mother, in all essential matters, sub-

mitted to her father, however unwillingly, she
trusted that her own charm and shrewdness
would prove as potent after marriage as it seemed
to be before. For during the spell of unrealized
desire the two young lovers idealized each other;
and the lover, who had, perhaps, only lately
ceased from bullying his mother, and would take
it for granted that his wife should defer to him
as his mother had yielded to his father, during this
one interval deferred to his betrothed. She could
not but suppose that a lover so tender and devoted,
who brought her gifts and did whatever her whims
commanded, would be less dominant than other
women's husbands.

Yet if the betrothal were prolonged enough,
the lovers would find that golden ring the beginning of a chain against which both would chafe.
According to the customs of the time, neither
could properly show an interest in any other unmarried person of the opposite sex without giving cause for justifiable jealousy. Although jealousy was generally regarded as a testimony of affection, it was—if the lovers had but known it—
merely a mean exhibition of that suspicious, pro-
prietary attitude which would make the marriage
a bondage rather than the highest expression of
mutual confidence.

The segregation of lovers from the rest of the
community, and the taboo surrounding them, was

symptomatic of the isolation in which they were to live the rest of their lives. From this time the man must never show any admiration for another woman; and the girl must conceal whatever interest she might have in any other man. In village communities, in church gatherings, in temperance and missionary societies, men herded with men and women flocked with women, losing the stimulus of the social and intellectual comradeship enjoyed by the sexes in modern life. Aside from the monotony of such a society its worst aspect lay in the in-and-in breeding of sex characteristics. Men, associating constantly with men, perpetuated the standards and habits inherited from their fathers; women, corraled by themselves, gossiped of their narrower experiences, perpetuating their own pettiness. Between boy and girl, between lover and maiden, between adult man and woman, stood always the menacing figure of sex with the sword of chastity, lest propriety and property be violated. Not a little of the lack of comprehension of each sex by the other arose from this survival of the ownership of woman, which resulted in a general assumption that neither could have any decent pleasure in the society of any person of the other sex except their own life partner.

The engaged girl, however, was not likely to question or to resent the flattering jealousy of a man whose preference set her for the first time upon a pedestal, even had she not been diverted by the conventional preparations for the marriage. Indeed, the man often became quite subordinate in her mind to the trousseau and the wedding display. Her parents were the more inclined to indulge her extravagant notions—for the last time —because it would reflect credit upon themselves. In the early part of the Nineteenth Century the ordinary bride's outfit followed the traditions of the European peasant woman, and consisted chiefly of the chest of linen and household furnishings made by her own hand; but, as manufactures supplanted home-made articles, the bride devoted more and more attention to the personal trousseau. For months before the wedding-day she cut and fitted and sewed; crocheted and tatted and embroidered; in order that she might be able to exhibit to her female friends and, incidentally, to the bewildered lover, so many dozens of elaborate, hand-made chemises, nightgowns, petticoats; tablecloths, napkins, and towels. And while the bride was working night and day harder than ever before in her life, the proud mother, with scarcely less enthusiasm, assisted the ambitious dressmaker of the neighborhood to contrive as many and as elaborate dresses as possible from the money provided by a father whose pride it was to give his daughter a suitable outfit.

If it be thought that all this was only mere girlish extravagance, let us remember that for the domestic woman the wedding-day was not only the first, but the sole time that she would ever be a person of public interest.   Not even if she should bear a son to become the savior of his country, would she be the principal in her family, or so conspicuous a figure in a solemn ceremony.   For a day of such importance nothing was quite good enough.   The trousseau was as essential to the prospective bride as an outfit to the explorer of arctic or tropical wilds; or, rather, it was like the equipment of a traveler who sets out for an unknown Oriental country—for who knew what might be needed and yet unattainable in the great adventure upon which she was about to embark!

Like other adventurers, she might be taking many inappropriate things.   The girl who married a young instructor attached to one of the best colleges might find it necessary to lay away the dozens of delicate undergarments, replacing them with plain, stout materials to be washed with her own hands.   The trousseau, at the end of the first year, might be quite useless in view of prospective motherhood; and might be laid away in lavender, never to be resurrected, perhaps, except for some old-folks masquerade devised by her grown-up daughter.

No small part of the enjoyment of the ante-wedding preparations lay in the receiving of presents. While cities were few in America, and the bulk of the population lived in villages and rural neighborhoods, the custom of bridal gifts was seldom overdone; but, after the war, the increase of wealth and the growth of urban communities gave women, particularly, leisure and excuse for excessive emphasis on the ornamental side of life. The habit of giving wedding presents—as is the tendency of such conventions—became an exaggerated social obligation which has only recently begun to diminish in force. The friends of both families vied with each other in expressing not so much their affection as their social status by the elegance of their contribution to the display. Day after day the bride and her fiancé received them, discussing their beauty, usefulness, and cost in view of the future ménage. In a country town, where the neighbors clubbed together to fit out completely the new kitchen, the friendly practicality of the gift was a fit expression of the attitude of the village toward a popular young couple. But more often the gifts were a showy agglomeration of more or less useless or unsuitable articles, in the polite acknowledgment of which the overworked bride spent all her spare time for weeks before and after marriage. All the pleasant excitement attendant upon

giving and receiving was likely to be destroyed by
the numerous duplications—no bride could accept
enthusiastically a sixth cut-glass bowl or a sev-
enth butter-knife. When the wedding etiquette
reached the stage where all the presents must be
displayed to the givers and the guests in a room
set apart for them, the custom had degenerated
into undisguised commercialism.

As the great day drew near the bride and her
family were usually engaged in a whirl of fever-
ish preparations: the house must be prepared for
a wedding breakfast, supper, or reception, the
church decorated for the ceremony, the wedding
attendants schooled in their parts—even the bride
and groom must " rehearse " the pageant in which
they were to be the chief figures. Even for a
" simple " wedding the fatigue and the expense
were invariably greater than had been anticipated,
and the higher emotions of all concerned were
drowned in the effort to make as much " splurge "
as possible, and in anxiety about petty, material
details. Thus the parents and the household
went to bed on the bridal eve utterly exhausted,
and with last admonitions to the young girl to
sleep that her beauty might not be dimmed on the
morrow.

The wedding-day itself would probably remain
forever, in the memories of both bride and groom,
a nightmare of jumbled impressions—the con-

fusion and haste of last preparations, the full-
dress parade, the blur of curious spectators, even
the solemn vows and prayers; the congratula-
tions, tears, and kisses; the eating, drinking, and
going away—all alike, to the chief actors in the
spectacle, could only be a series of perfunctory
performances to be lived through in order that
they might be allowed to attain the joy of permanent companionship.   It was as if the King's
trumpeters had announced from the city towers:
" Behold this man and woman about to enter
upon the most intimate human relation!   See how
correct, how respectable they are! "

Meanwhile, during all this furor, the groom
had been quite a minor figure, occupied in waiting
on the bride, assisting in the preparations, and
privately cursing the social traditions which had
involved him in so irksome a tangle of splurge and
etiquette.   If he were a simple, clean-minded fellow, the irritation and the strain of his abnormal
position were likely to put him in anything but a
loverlike frame of mind; if he were the " average
young man," he would probably accept the invitation of his bachelor friends to celebrate the
last days of his freedom with an orgy of eating,
drinking, and unprintable jests.

The facetious attitude toward marriage was
often, in country neighborhoods, carried to the
height of a vulgar practical joke in the custom of

the " shivaree." Upon the wedding-night or upon the return of the newly-wedded pair from the honeymoon, the men friends surrounded the house, let loose a pandemonium of hideous noises, demanding a sight of the bride and a speech from the groom. The custom was, in fact, so general in many places that the bridal pair provided refreshments in advance for the invading party.

It was certainly only by the grace of God and much mutual affection that the young married couple kept their respect for each other through these preliminaries of marriage. After this nerve-racking performance the bridegroom not infrequently found himself the guardian of a shrinking child, who was on the verge of hysterics through exhaustion and fear. To many a man there must have been a shock of astonishment, if not of dismay, on discovering that his wife was afraid of him, and had only the vaguest notion of their inevitable marital relation. The convention of absolute ignorance in which the young girl had usually been brought up, made of the sex relation an experience scarcely less terrible than bodily assault. Girls whose persons since their childhood had been sacred even from their mother's eyes, who had been taught not to look at their own bodies, and to bathe in the dark, found themselves in the keeping of men to whom the sex relation was already a commonplace. The husband, as a rule, entered upon marriage with slight illusions and with the natural impulses of a healthy animal. The young wife had been taught to ignore the very idea of passion, and, in proportion as she was physically delicate and modest, received a shock which was intensified if she immediately became pregnant. After a honeymoon of shame and disillusionment, she would gradually readjust her ideas to the facts of life under the instruction of her husband, and if she were fully occupied with household details, would ultimately recover an ideal of wedded happiness. Then, and not till then, would she fully understand why her mother and other wives had wept instead of rejoiced on her wedding-day.

On the other hand, the young husband, with every intention of cherishing her, might find himself in the position of an unintentional brute, and might suffer as great a disappointment as the bride, because of mutual misunderstanding. If he were a man of fine feeling and quick perception, and if the wife were a vigorous and sensible girl, the readjustment might be swift and happy; but if he were just the ordinary thick-skinned, wholesome fellow of the world, the wife merely surrendered, and both emerged into mutual toleration rather than happiness.

When the great adventure of marriage had been undertaken, then, indeed, began the real development of the girl of the past century. Molded and hemmed in by the traditions of what was proper and desirable for girls, she had more or less consciously looked forward to emancipation into a larger life, in which she was to be not only the helpmate of her husband, but a responsible personality. She had been educated to believe that in place of an aggressive part in life, her power lay in her " influence," and with this vague hypnotism she expected to mold the life of her husband and to control her children. In many cases she found herself in the situation of the wife described in the following paragraph:

" A few significant incidents had revealed to her that his good nature covered cold-blooded indifference where all but his own interests were vitally concerned. His apparent pliability hid a dexterity which evaded every recognized principle. In vain she exerted the influence with which he had pretended to invest her. The first effort proved that it never really existed. It was no more in his life than the valuable ornament on his mantel-shelf—a thing to be dusted, preserved, and admired in leisure hours, never set to serious use."

If, on the other hand, the young husband were inspired by happiness and family responsibility to rise above his ordinary level, the young wife's childish ignorance and lack of intelligent sympathy with his aims not infrequently thwarted them.

Misled by the glamor of courtship and the expurgated novels of her girlhood, perhaps also by
her parents' indulgence, the bride naturally supposed that *her* feelings, *her* wishes, would continue to be through marriage, as through the engagement, the determinant of their joint lives.
Her astonishment, anger, and grief, when she
found that she had to deal with a being who had
always had his own way, and had always been
deferred to by womenkind, often became a
tragedy. She made herself and her husband
wretched; while he in turn could not comprehend
why his wife had suddenly become so different
from what his mother was, from the docile
creature a woman should be, from what she had
appeared to be during their courtship.

The period of readjustment in which the husband and wife began to re-form each other's
character might be uncontentious between self-
respecting persons, but it was rarely happy. Out
of it emerged a new ideal of happiness for both,
or an enduring mutual discontent. If children
arrived early the personalities of both parents
were, at least temporarily, subordinated to the
new relation. But the original causes of disillusionment were often merely latent, and gradually
reappeared in the shape of unseemly contests over
the discipline and education of the children, or in
squabbles over expenditure and property. In a

majority of cases that first great schism in their
married life had brought so much pain that both
parties ever after shrank with horror from another clash.   Inevitably the woman, accustomed
to obedience and clinging desperately to her ideal
of a loving husband, gave way first; while the
man, bewildered by the strength of the will he
had met, cautiously avoided invoking it again.
When each had realized the scarifying results of
selfishness toward one they loved, there grew up
a living hypothesis between them: " It is better to
be loving than to be right."   Then, slowly, the
shadowy ghost of their youthful aura of marriage
came back, and, if cherished by both, it might
become a hovering angel of happiness.

Such lives, issuing in mutual readjustment and
soon merged in the development of children,
should have been and were, oftentimes, rich in
domestic satisfaction; but with one phase of them,
we may venture to say, no woman was ever content.   As a child in her father's house, even to
the day of her wedding, she had been by custom
entitled to a living; and, by custom also, as a
wife she had a right to a reasonable provision.
But just when she could afford a new dress, and
how much money for her personal expenses was
to be forthcoming, and when, she did not know.
It was considered unnecessary, indeed, it was
scarcely proper for a wife to have an allowance

—it savored of quarrels and too much wifely independence—for it was assumed that any decent husband would provide for his wife. As a matter of experience, the wheedling or termagant wives of indulgent husbands got more than they should have, in a proper division of the family income, while timid and more self-respecting women had to make suffice whatever a forgetful or selfish husband irregularly doled out; and often wept in secret humiliation before asking for what they were justly entitled to. Although in theory the wife had a right to a reasonable share of the family resources, she was, nevertheless, in the position of asking for it like a child or a charity dependent. That the average American husband was generous did not make the arrangement less unjust, though it might prevent the wife from insisting on a more equitable and self-respecting division.

But if the mother of a family found this financial tradition irksome, the childless wife—if she thought about it at all—was scarcely able to keep her self-respect. While she earned her board and lodging generally, and often the wage of a servant, if she did the whole work of the household, she was at least in a position of relative dignity. But in many cases the married partners took advantage of cheap immigrant service to lift themselves into a higher social stratum. Thus released from the heavier portion of the household cares, without children, without intellectual tastes, without any exacting occupation, she had nothing to do with her leisure but to return to the superficial accomplishments of her girlhood, or to fill the time with social engagements and the pursuit of dress. In short, she made something to do, instead of being compelled to do something necessary to the household and worthy of a human being.

Some wives, under this social régime, became lazy, frivolous, and extravagant; others developed an abnormal devotion to the petty details of dress and housekeeping, or an all but insane love of cleanliness, of order, or of ornament; and all became morally and physically anemic, wreaking on their partners the morbid peevishness of a childish and discontented disposition. Now and then, some stronger woman— with or without the approval of her husband, who could not be expected to know what was the matter—sought in lady-like philanthropy some expression of the pent-up energy within her; and rarely, a wiser man would take her into genuine partnership, replacing the natural tie of children with a useful business interest.

When the initial stages of marriage had settled themselves more or less comfortably, the great adventure of the woman's life resolved itself into a journey along a country road, sometimes green and shady, sometimes dusty and rough, but seldom affording an exciting prospect. Like the farmer, with whose labor the vocation of domesticity has elsewhere been compared, the housewife pursued her unexciting round; or, more like a pet squirrel in a cage—well-fed and cared-for, but debarred by domestic traditions from exploring for herself the interesting world about her. All her knowledge was second-hand, so to speak, filtered through the mind of a partner who told her as much or as little as he thought she could comprehend; and the only other stimuli that were likely to reach her came through the educational experiences of the children or through effeminate publications filled up with household recipes and a little harmless stuff predigested for feminine needs.

The intellectual interests of married women, like those of most persons, are dictated by their experiences in life—a fact upon which modern journalism bases its principal appeal. The racing edition for sporting men; the yellow newspaper for crude people, who live wholly on sensations; the semi-religious, predigested survey of current events for the orthodox; adventure magazines with a few " hells " and " damns " to catch the drummer and the cowboy—or with lurid stories but no swear-words for those who like Western color, but are shocked by the real thing—these, in our era, are some of the thousand kinds for as many people. But before the Civil War there were fewer of any kind, and only one sort deemed suitable for women.

Whatever her taste, the journalistic estimate of woman's needs was adjusted to the kitchen-children-clothing-church routine of the ordinary woman's life. The great body of country and village housewives read the weekly county paper, a missionary or religious journal, and the Bible, regularly but quite unthinkingly. The more sophisticated read a Lady-Book, in which was always to be found a careful mixture of feeble romance, moral essays, cooking recipes, fashions, and designs for needlework. These polite magazines for the promotion of " religion and gentility " had for their aim the expression of " the spirit of progress without compromising true womanliness; " and reached large circulations, owing to an innocuous mixture of platitudes, trivialities, and French fashion plates.

Having had no thorough education in any direction, the ideally domestic woman seldom acquired a taste for abstract or enlightened information. Her idea of the pleasure of reading was to get the practical experience of other housewives on such matters as the making of new variations in crochet patterns and cake, and how to contrive a chair out of old barrel-staves; or, on the other hand, to fill up the lack of the picturesque and dramatic in her life with the emotional adventures of some immaculate heroine of fiction. As the deer comes to the salt-lick; as the laborer, doomed to repetitious drudgery, seeks variety in a drunken spree—so the domestic woman often found in her leisure hours a passive pseudo-excitement in romance. In much the same manner the modern woman of leisure satisfies her natural craving for adventurous interests with emotions induced by the theater and the orchestra. A modern satirist has acutely remarked that, while a man was supposing that his wife's ideal of a husband was a middle-aged, baldheaded man, who was a good provider, his wife was going to the matinée to adore a beautiful young man with dark eyes and a tenor voice.

The only activity outside the home in which married women might take part without violating the proprieties, was the support and promotion of religious work. The finances and the administration of the churches were in the hands of men; but the money for the minister's salary, for a new church carpet, or for foreign missions, was commonly raised by the women through socials, fairs, bees, picnics, suppers—where hot coffee and good pie might be expected to unloose masculine purse-strings. Here the woman of executive ability found a chance for leadership; here house-wives exchanged the gossip of the neighborhood, or the ingenuities and economies by which they stretched their purses. While men were whet-ting their minds on politics, on war or recon-struction, on tariff measures or the panic, and running the churches and the local government, women revolved within the narrow circle of do-mestic and pious detail, and kept silence on larger matters, as behooved the supplementary sex.

The conventional domestic ideal involved, as we have shown in a previous chapter, a girlhood spent in attaining a superficial education which had no direct relation to domesticity or to moth-erhood, and an early womanhood spent chiefly in preening and expectation. With such a prepara-tion it was not surprising if women generally found marriage less romantic and less satisfying as a career than they had been led to anticipate. Instead of an interesting adventure into which they were to be led by the sympathetic and ador-ing hero of their dreams, the wife's rôle was usu-ally that of an understudy for a leading part who never got a chance to take the boards. If, per-chance, she showed dissatisfaction with her lot, she was always assured that motherhood was the only worthy career, to which wifehood and domesticity were merely supplementary—mother-

hood was to be her compensation.   To a consideration of the career afforded by motherhood we
must turn, therefore, if we would understand both
the glory and the inadequacy of the Nineteenth-
Century woman.

CHAPTER III

THE CAREER OF MOTHERHOOD

" There is an African bird, the hornbill, whose habits in some respects are a model. The female builds her nest in a hollow tree, lays her eggs, and broods on them. Then the male feels that he must also contribute some service; so he walls up the hole closely, giving only room for the point of the female's bill to protrude. Until the eggs are hatched, she is thenceforth confined to her nest, and is in the meantime fed assiduously by her mate. . . .

" Nature has kindly provided various types of bird households to suit all varieties of taste. The bright orioles filling the summer boughs with color and with song, are as truly domestic in the freedom of their airy nest as the poor hornbills who ignorantly make their home in a dungeon. And certainly each new generation of orioles . . . are a happier illustration of judicious nurture than are the uncouth little offspring of the hornbills . . . so flabby, and transparent as to resemble a bladder of jelly furnished with head, legs, and rudimentary wings, but with not a sign of a feather."—THOMAS WENTWORTH HIGGINSON.

" It is a fact kept, perhaps, too much in the background, that mothers have a larger self than their maternity, and that when their sons have become taller than themselves, and gone from them . . . there are wide spaces of time which are not filled with praying for their boys, reading old letters, and envying yet blessing those who are attending to their shirt buttons."— GEORGE ELIOT.

" Woman is given to us that she may bear children. Woman is our property, we are not hers, because she produces children for us—we do not yield any to her. She is, therefore, our possession as the fruit tree is that of the gardener."—NAPOLEON.

42

MERELY to be a woman is not a vocation, though formerly many women were obliged by custom to make it serve in lieu of one; but to be a married mother has long been regarded as a quasi-profession which, for the time being, precluded any other. During the earlier part of the Nineteenth Century, while the family still constituted an industrial unit, child-bearing was incidental in the midst of pioneer toil, and not at all the subject of reasoning. As women began to be released from directly productive labor, and here and there ventured into publicity, there grew up in the Press and the Pulpit a habit of lauding the " glory " of motherhood in much the same manner as they dwelt upon the " dignity " of manual labor. Any thoughtful person could see that the conditions of labor were often inhuman and degrading; and no one who could escape from such toil into a cleaner and easier mode of living was prevented from doing so by his belief in its dignity. So, also, the sentimentality of the mid-century was accustomed to play up the emotional and spiritual compensations of motherhood, while ignoring or glozing over its hardships.

There is slight need of writing on the compensatory aspects of motherhood, since healthy, happy mothers in every age have been satisfied with their lot, and have not needed either flattery or a fence to keep them within their sphere. But many mothers—perhaps a majority in the past century—were neither contented nor adequate to their task. That they did not attempt to escape was chiefly due to their conventional limitations. Without discounting in any degree the beauty or the rewards of normal motherhood, it is necessary to point out how far short, in the past, the actual experience often fell of that ideal so constantly preached; and to analyze it from the reasonable standpoint of the career for which it was a substitute. If motherhood were, indeed, a holy vocation, for which women had been set apart, it should be able to bear the tests to which other less sacred occupations were subjected. To comprehend why the conditions of motherhood are still so far from what they should be, it is necessary to draw a plain picture of what they were for the average woman of the past century.

We have seen in the chapter on *Girlhood* that girls were very early imbued with the idea that they did not need to equip themselves for earning a living, nor to acquire more than a limited and superficial education, because they were to be married and, by inference, to be mothers. The Puritan reaction from the sensuality of English society had taken the form of prudery and silence on sex matters, which placed every marriageable girl in an anomalous situation. Marriage and motherhood were constantly referred to in her

hearing as the highest, indeed, the only succcess-
ful, career for woman; yet, nothing in her training had any direct relation to it, and the conventional standard of modesty required her to be
wholly ignorant of its physical aspects. When
she walked up the church aisle in her bridal veil,
she must be as innocent in mind as she was chaste
in body, but at any moment after the marriage
vows were spoken she might know everything.
The conventional attitude is aptly expressed by
Dorothea's Uncle in *Middlemarch,* when he
suggests to the bridegroom that he get her to read
him " light things, Smollett—*Roderick Random,
Humphrey Clinker;* they are a little broad, but
she may read anything, now she's married, you
know."

Just how and when she was to enter upon
motherhood she did not know, but if she permitted herself to think of it at all, she naturally
supposed that she would at least have some choice
as to the convenient season. But since the conventional training of girls prescribed that she
should not think of it at all, the conception of her
first child was almost certainly " an accident,"
neither desired nor predetermined, merely incidental to the period of excitement, fatigue, and
mixed emotion following upon the wedding display and the honeymoon tour. Any sturdy and
vulgar-minded servant maid was in a more

natural and wholesome state of mind upon her marriage than the hyper-modest, carefully protected daughter of the house. The ignorant young wife waited upon her fate more often in fear than in joy, and was, not infrequently, the subject of jest on the matter of her pregnancy before she herself learned what the disturbance of her physical rhythm presaged.

Though she might look forward with joy to having a child of her love, the lifelong habits of exaggerated modesty could not be thrown aside, but were rather intensified by the consciousness of her condition. She tried to conceal it as long as she could by corsets and clothing which were injurious, and when it was no longer possible to hide the fact, she stayed indoors like an invalid, venturing out only after nightfall or in a carriage. Such unhygienic living made her appetite capricious and her temper as well; robbed her muscles —undeveloped enough already—of their proper nutrition and exercise; and made her more and more unfit for the severe physical test of childbirth.

If such a degree of ignorance concerning the facts of sex be thought incredible, one has only to inquire of elderly women still living, or to read the biographies of our grandmothers, to know that their prudish habits were maintained throughout a lifetime. Their code did not permit the mention of approaching confinement even to their female relatives. In the biography of Susan B. Anthony there occurs this paragraph about her mother:

" Lucy Read Anthony was of a very timid and reticent disposition, and painfully modest and shrinking. Before the birth of every child she was overwhelmed with embarrassment and humiliation, secluded herself from the outside world, and would not speak of the expected little one even to her mother. The mother would assist her over-burdened daughter by making the necessary garments, take them to her home, and lay them away carefully in a drawer, but no word of acknowledgment ever passed between them."

And yet Lucy Read Anthony was set down as a very " happy wife and mother," and her husband was an exceptionally kind and generous man.

Before the end of the Nineteenth Century the physical poverty and nervousness of American women had become a matter of serious concern. Medical men were searching for subtle causes, while all the time a perfectly patent group of causes were only vaguely recognized. It was still the fashion to attribute all the weaknesses of women to their inherent nature, rather than to look for their origin in social convention and inactivity. When one realizes how widespread was the ideal of girlish delicacy half a century ago, the wonder is that any wife who had been brought up under the restrictions of that period, survived to bear more than a single child. Perhaps all that saved them was the necessity of caring for the child itself, and sometimes of doing their own housework.

It was the husband's exclusive privilege to initiate the innocent girl whom he married into the mysteries of the sex relation. The only other information regarding motherhood that she received was usually obtained after conception from her mother and the neighbor women. This mother-lore was a mixture of old women's traditions and midwives' quackery handed down from one generation to another, and the prospective mother's sensitive organization was stimulated with the details of miscarriages, premature deliveries, still-births, and all the sensational symptoms within their experience. During the later months of pregnancy she remained altogether indoors, more often than not, waiting from day to day in a state of terror for labor to begin.

The thought that a strange man would attend her at childbirth added to her shrinking, and often caused her to prefer the services of a self-trained midwife, whose ignorance of obstetrical practice and hygiene might leave her a semi-wreck for life. Aside from her own undeveloped physique, the lack of properly trained attendants of her own sex was unquestionably a considerable factor in the preventable miseries from which many a child-bearing woman suffered.

When she was on her feet again, and before she had fully recovered her strength, she was confronted with a new duty, for which she had had no preparation whatever, unless she herself had been an elder daughter in a large family. If she were able to nurse her child, she was fortunate, but if not—as often happened—she entered upon a period of almost sleepless vigilance to keep alive the precious creature who had already cost her so much. For her task of nurse she was as unfitted as she had been unprepared for marriage. In her day there were no specialist treatises on the care and feeding of infants, nor trained nurses at call, to supply her deficiencies and to teach her how to care for her baby. The polite education in music, French, and the rise and fall of European kingdoms, of which she had been so proud, had small application seemingly to the problems of nutrition and bacteriology which must be solved. And no blame could fall on so conscientious and inadequate a mother if, after weeks of exacting care, the poor little life flickered out.

The child-bearing woman of the past century was, indeed, the victim of the traditions of her time, which had predestined her to physical weakness, sexual ignorance, and incompetence in the only career which was open to her. Nor did she alone pay the cost. In every large family there was a miscarriage or an infant death for every two or three children that survived to adult years. The physical exhaustion, the sorrow, and the disruption of the family comfort in such infant losses, cannot be measured in economic terms, but were none the less costly to society.

If the young mother were vigorous enough to endure repeated pregnancies at intervals of fifteen or twenty months, she gradually learned her business and outlived some of her maiden fears and griefs, as all her powers were drawn upon by the demands of a growing family. There is a curious literature of what might be called " tired motherhood " hidden away in old albums and the quaint magazines which constituted family reading from 1840 to 1880. In one of these volumes, printed as late as 1872, there is a series of articles on the " Physical Life of Women," which, in process of giving good advice, affords a picture of the ordinary mother's life.

" She cannot be sick—there is no one to care for her if she is; on the contrary, the whole family feel injured because their comfort is disturbed and their habits of dependence upon ' Mother ' broken in upon. . . . She grows nervous and irritable . . . she has little time for sentiment, but she is shocked sometimes to find how all light and sunshine seem gradually fading out of her life. . . .

" The children! Ah, well, children are a well-spring
of pleasure when the house is wide, the purse long, and
the welcome warm; but how is it when they represent so
many pairs of worn-out shoes, an ever-ascending pile of
unending stockings, continually recurring questions of hats,
and suits, and aprons, and innumerable other articles of
clothing, which not only have to be made, but made over
with every changing season and every addition to the increasing family. . . .

" She is aware that her husband secretly chafes at the
change in her appearance, and is growing indifferent to her
under the combined influence of family responsibility and
the occasional experience of bitterness prompted by her
own soreness of heart. She cannot make him understand
how the bright, sunny-tempered girl whom he married is
dying by inches, leaving a careworn, joyless woman in her
place! And so she goes on her hurried, yet monotonous
way, each day repeating itself, until some morning she is
obliged to take time to die and be buried."

Even when the house was wide, the purse long,
and the welcome warm to each successive child,
many a tired mother must have felt like Samuel
Sewall, the Colonial father, who hoped, when his
fourteenth child was born, that " The Lord would
think that was enough." For, consider the daily
round of the mother of even a moderate family
of five children—the actual physical labor involved in merely feeding and clothing them, and
attending to their toilet. A man who had seen
a woman contractor in a Southwestern city down
in a ditch, showing a laborer how to lay sewer

pipe, remarked thoughtfully that, perhaps, it was not any more disagreeable than the sanitary duties of the mother of a household. Consider the *incessantness* of children—their questions and cryings, their demands and naughtiness, all of which must be patiently and kindly and wisely attended to by the competent mother. The typical father, who spent most of his waking hours outside the house, saw only their pleasant qualities, and seldom experienced to the full the monotony of their importunity and distraction. A delightful mother of my acquaintance was accustomed to invite her friends to visit her only in the evening, because, as she said, " I am only a human being after the children are asleep;" and another healthy mother of three vigorous youngsters used to say that Heaven was to her a place where she could sleep as long as she wished.

Nor must it be forgotten that in the intervals of baby-tending and child-rearing, the typical country house-mother of the past century expected to do the larger part of the housework without the aid of any of the modern conveniences; cooking and dishwashing without running water in the house; washing of clothes without set tubs and washing-powders; ironing of garments—for it would have been slovenly to leave them " rough dry "—without electric and gas devices. Miss Anthony recorded in her *Life and Letters* how

the young married women who were interested
in women's rights, and anti-slavery, and temperance, dropped out of the work as soon as they
were caught in the "matrimonial maelstrom;"
and she remarked in a letter to one of them: "If
you allowed yourself to remain too long snuggled
in the Abrahamic bosom of home, it required
great will power to resurrect your soul."

During the infancy of her children, the mother
had very little life of her own, but, if she were a
happy wife, found her compensation for her personal sacrifices in the satisfaction of the maternal
passion and in the unfolding intelligence of the
children. One by one they left her to go to
school, and began to bring home new ideas; these
furnished excitement and incentive to her vicarious ambition, and throughout their childhood
years provided the chief stimulus of the mother's
life. But by so much as their opportunities were
better than hers had been, they began to outstrip
her intellectually. For beyond the three R's her
education had not only been useless, but it had not
even taught her to think for herself, nor inculcated a taste for serious reading and information.
When the smaller children wanted help in the
solution of some arithmetical problem, or in the
construction of a composition, she found herself
too rusty, if not too ignorant, and covered up her
chagrin with an excuse of busy-ness.

By the time the boys were in trousers, and the girls in long skirts, they had found out that their mother's ideas were not only old-fashioned, but often foolish. In the family discussions on public events they saw that their father had no respect for her opinions, though he might receive them with polite tolerance. The mother's mind, having been for years wholly absorbed in household and maternal details, gradually lost the power to be interested in impersonal topics. Her conversation became inconsequential, and she was, as a rule, quite incapable of concentrating herself for any length of time upon a single idea. The distinguishing mental characteristic of the domestic, especially of the maternal woman, came to be heterogeneity. The necessity every mother was under of giving her mind simultaneously to a great variety of childish and domestic demands, all day long and for years together, produced a habit of mental scrappiness. Having herself been interrupted incessantly, she had no hesitation in breaking in upon any talk or reading with irrelevant questions and comments. If proof were needed, one need only contemplate the intellectual attempts of certain middle-aged clubwomen who are trying to regain, after a life of distracting domestic detail, the power to think intelligently on wider subjects.

In most cases the mother developed the charac-

teristic female virtues essential to family peace—
industry, patience, devotion to physical comfort,
sympathy with petty griefs, discomforts, and ail-
ments, and, above all, unselfishness—to an exaggerated degree, and, in the process, lost sight of
the larger values. The children, therefore, however they might depend upon her affection and
sacrifice, discounted her opinions. The boys were
apt to become unruly before they reached the age
of puberty, and had to be turned over to their
father in the hope that he might instil good behavior, if not respect, by his technically greater
authority. The half-grown girls were likely to
begin to model themselves upon the pattern of
some younger, more attractive woman, less careworn and old-fashioned than their mother.

If, perchance, by the unselfishness and sweetness of her character, she still was able to keep
their confidence, she might remain the confidante
of their troubles and ambitions, though without
the ability to be a trustworthy and intelligent
guide. Like the hen who hatched ducklings, she
saw them swim away, though she could not swim
herself. Some day, when they were married and
had children of their own, they might begin to
appreciate, in the light of their own experiences,
what they owed to their mother; but in proportion as they developed beyond her, they would
also rate her at her true social value, in spite of

all affection. For gratitude grows only in rich soil, and filial piety is apt to flower only in proportion to the quality of parental culture.

If the husband and father were a man who, by virtue of integrity, justice, and gentleness, commanded the willing obedience of his children, he enforced upon them respectful behavior toward their mother, no matter how limited or undeserving she might be. But if, as sometimes happened, the titular head of the family were lazy, incapable, eccentric, or drunken, the competent mother's position became well-nigh intolerable. She must obey her husband—by law of Church and State— and she must continue to bear children to a man whose superior she knew herself to be, but without authority to enforce even nominal respect and obedience upon them. Thus motherhood might become a sort of doom.

On the other hand, according to the standard of the time, there was no woman so petty, so vain, so enfeebled in body or mind, that she might not become the wife of an intelligent and honorable man and, hanging like a dead-weight upon him, become the incompetent mother of puny children. A society which was shocked at a female preacher or painter or doctor, complacently acquiesced in the tradition that any woman was good enough to be a mother, if only she wore a wedding-ring. The convenient theory

handed down from licentious ages, that parenthood was both inevitable and praiseworthy, whatever the qualifications of the progenitors, reduced
some wives to the position of mistresses, without
any of the advantages of that more independent
position.

The teaching of the clergy that all children
came from God, and that the man who begot the
greatest number was a benefactor to the State,
was, in fact, left over from an age when the
survival of a State might depend upon the capacity
of its women to replace those fallen in war. Aside
from the fact that the less intelligent a population is, the more recklessly it will breed, the conditions of rural life in America demanded
abundant child labor. The farmer's daughter
stood on a stool to wash dishes, made patchwork quilts, and acted as a " little mother " to
the younger children; while boys, from the time
they were ten years old, earned their " keep " by
chores and the lighter farm labor.

Children were then an economic asset. Following the English tradition, the prosperous
American farmer of the earlier Nineteenth Century often retired from active labor at fifty or
fifty-five, allowing his wife and his numerous
progeny to support him. By custom the children
who went from home to work turned their wages
over to their parents until they were of age, and

expected nothing more than a " setting-out " when they left home permanently.   In such a society, the more children there were, provided, always, they were vigorous, the richer the parents.

The statistics of the period do not afford any trustworthy information of the death-rate of married women; but, indirectly, the family histories of the time reveal an unusual number of second and even third wives.   There is abundant evidence that the large family of which we read so much was often produced at the cost of the first wife's life.   Even when the mother of a large family outlived puerperal fevers, lacerations, and the exhaustion of rapidly succeeding pregnancies, it was not—as we often assume—to enjoy a vigorous, intelligent old-womanhood, but in a state of premature decrepitude, similar to that of women among primitive races.   In fact, we need only take account of the increasing youthfulness of middle-aged women to infer that many men as well as women have begun to count the cost of parenthood as measured by a rising standard of child quality and child care.

In an economic estimate of motherhood as a vocation, it must be remembered that this " career " became anomalous only when wives ceased to do anything of value, except child-bearing.   So long as married women were producers and manufacturers in their own homes, they needed no other justification in the eyes of their husbands or society, whether they bore many or few children. When, however, they became relatively idle and unproductive, as in the latter part of the last century, the sole claim they could make for accepting a parasitic existence, lay in motherhood. Yet for this their feeble physique and childish mentality had in great measure unfitted them; while, at the same time, children themselves had become less an asset and more of a privilege—or of a burden, from another standpoint—because they must be supported, educated, and launched in life upon a much higher plane.

The confusion involved in the purely sentimental estimate of motherhood was produced by such discordant ideas as the voluntary sacrifice of women to posterity; the dependence of women, whether mothers or not, upon men; and their implied release from economic and social responsibility. Toward the end of the century the cost of such a mixed system became apparent. For the traditions of the home-seeking and home-keeping woman reacted almost as disastrously upon husbands and fathers as upon women. Men were encouraged in reckless paternity—for what else was a woman good for aside from the sex-relation and motherhood! Since home was the woman's sphere, the husband felt himself relieved from all responsibility when he had fulfilled his own notion of being a good provider. He betook himself of an evening to the village store on a plea of business, or to the neighboring town, leaving his wife to the doubtful amusement of gossip and the weekly prayer meeting. He saw no reason for keeping his wife's mind alive by drawing her into the circle of his own broader interests, because he had been brought up to suppose that she had only a puny intellect, and it would be of no use to her anyway. Not until the children were old enough to be interesting in themselves did he take much account of them beyond performing his financial and disciplinary duties. In consequence of this complete division of interests and duties, the fathers and sons, and the mothers and daughters in any town or neighborhood, constituted social cliques separated by a sex-convention analogous to race-prejudice. And each clique had a sort of racial contempt for the ideas of the other, which was a common subject of mutual jests.

Hardly did the busy mother and wife of the Nineteenth Century reach the mid-plateau of her life and begin to rest a little from absorbing family cares, when the second great apprehension of her life would begin to creep upon her. The children grown up, married, and gone away; the finances of the household eased, making hard work and strict economy no longer necessary; she feared to find herself gradually isolated, and of less and less use. She, who had been important to several, was now reduced to petting her grandchildren, seeing that all her husband's tastes were indulged, reviving the semi-ornamental handicrafts of her youth, gossiping over the tea-table with other capable, restless middle-aged ladies as busily idle as herself—striving to pass from wifehood to old age. Coerced by the tradition current among women that she must be physically miserable at the time of the climacteric, and morbidly afraid that her husband would not continue to love her, she wore out the last years of her potential motherhood in teaching herself to be semi-idle, and accustoming herself to be " laid on the shelf." With so little worth while to do, and twenty or thirty years yet to do it in, she descended prematurely upon the tiresome road to her grave.

If she lived out the allotted span of years, they were passed swathed in mourning for those who had gone before; as a widow, perhaps living round in the houses of one child or another, whose more modern habits left her behind; losing through inertia the last ray of the brightness of her maidenhood, and cherishing pitifully the motherhood which had given her life its only profound meaning. To the end the glory of motherhood remained her pride and comfort. Whether her later years proved busy with grandmotherly

cares, or merely wasted away in the futile busy-
ness of old-womanhood, she had, at any rate, fulfilled the appointed destiny of her sex in achiev-
ing marriage and children.   Even if the man had
been a bad husband, and though some of the children turned out poor human specimens, she had,
nevertheless, justified her own existence.

For practical purposes in life the Universe is
no larger than the limits of perception.   The fly
sees no farther than the infinitesimal radius of his
vision, and is at the mercy of the huge thing
beyond it; the dog exists to follow his nose; and
the doves that cross the Mediterranean beat themselves to death against the snares of men.   So it
has been with womankind, whose nature in the
course of evolution has been restricted to the
narrow demands of an inner domestic circle whose
periphery has been constantly expanded by man.

The zoölogists are well aware that in spite of
every care the higher animals will rarely breed
in captivity—yet womankind is expected to do so
successfully.   Not a little of the growing discontent of women with their lot in the past century arose from the unformulated but justifiable
resentments of those elected to be mothers.   In
proportion as they were intelligent they knew
themselves the victims of a sort of social pretense; the solemn talk about the " glory of
motherhood " and the " only worthy sphere "

was by no means always borne out by the facts. Motherhood was, indeed, glorious when joyously and intelligently undertaken; and, as a career, worthy of the best ambition and much sacrifice when the parents were equally yoked to bear the load, and the mother fit for her share of it.   But in many instances the mothers had been led to marry by the deceiving glamor of love, while little more than children themselves in physique and mind, and while wholly ignorant of the serious import of that to which they committed themselves; and in so doing they had been placed absolutely at the mercy of the man who only nominally guaranteed them support.

The mother, even in her best estate, knew herself a sort of charitable dependent; and it is to the credit of men that they were so often more generous than law and social custom.   Yet the logical result of a social arrangement which, in the guise of protection, afforded an opportunity for outrage or neglect, could only be resentment and ultimately protest, on the part of married women.   The startling proposals of the present day, the transition from unalterable wedlock to more and more divorce, the resistance of many women to involuntary motherhood; the entrance of protected women into wage-earning occupations; these and many other symptoms are phases of evolution engendered in part by the

hiatus between the high rank which women believed motherhood should hold, and the realities
of married women's lives in the past generation.

If it be thought that too dark a picture has
been drawn, let it be compared with the educated
and relatively competent motherhood of the present day.   Among younger women there are not a
few—though still too few—who, after a thorough
education, became engaged to men whom they had
known in college or in industry.   Taking their
future task as mothers and wives intelligently and
seriously, they informed themselves on sex-
hygiene and the care of children.   For the marriage ceremony they chose a period of highest
health, declining to make a public display.   During the months of gestation they developed their
muscles in anticipation of childbirth, putting themselves in training as for a race, under the direction of a physician.   Often overcoming their own
hereditary weakness, they have brought lusty,
much-desired children into the world, whose physical and mental development they are capable of
directing.   Such motherhood may well be called
a worthy career, and the joys and glory of it only
bring into darker contrast the childish, unprepared, enfeebled motherhood of the times whose
legacy of miserable children and unhappy homes
has not yet passed away.

CHAPTER IV

DOMESTICITY AS A VOCATION

"Woman's work is a round of endless detail. Little, insignificant, provoking items, that she gets no credit for doing, but fatal discredit for leaving undone. Nobody notices that things are as they should be; but if things are not as they should be, it were better for her that a mill-stone were hanged about her neck. . . . A woman who is satisfied with the small economies, the small interests, the constant contemplation of the small things which a household demands, is a very small sort of woman. . . . A noble discontent, not a peevish complaining, but a universal and spontaneous protest, is a woman's safeguard against the deterioration which such a life threatens; her proof of capacity and her note of preparation for a higher."—GAIL HAMILTON.

"That's what makes women a curse—all life is stunted to their littleness."—From *Felix Holt*, GEORGE ELIOT.

"Any industry, task, or occupation that deforms the hand and hollows the chest, mars the features and destroys the beauty, the health and self-respect of the workers—that makes them indifferent and careless to their personal appearance and cleanliness—is unprofitable, both for the worker and for the community. . . . Any form of woman's work, whether in the home or out of it, that produces similar results will soon come under the ban . . . whether that work be the slavery of the factory or the shop, the drudgery of the household, excessive child-bearing, or the slavish care of more children than can be properly supported and given a civilized chance with the means at her disposal."—WOODS HUTCHINSON.

IN the making of a human being there are three variables—what he was when he came into the

65

world, what he found there, and what he made of it and of himself when he grew up.   Boys and girls, if not precisely alike in the beginning, were probably substantially equal, the advantage of greater size in the one being made up in the other by finer nervous organization and endurance. What each sex found in our American world in the Nineteenth Century was, however, very different; for social tradition ordained a wide differentiation in nurture and habit, which was justified in theory by the sex-specialization of females.   Neither the education nor the duties of girls, in spite of their special function, prepared them in any direct fashion for motherhood; rather, they were consciously designed to fit them to be domestic servers and housekeepers.

There had been a time in history not long past, when the choice of a vocation was confined to certain occupations open to the class in which men happened to be born, but in the new democracy every field was at least nominally open to any man.   Women, meanwhile, whether married or not, whether likely to be mothers or not, were still limited to the group of occupations which could be carried on under the home roof.   At the beginning of the last century these comprised a variety of crafts and manufactures, but in the course of fifty years the sphere of the domestic countrywoman was coming to be limited to a few miscellaneous and belated trades, which were still assigned to women merely because they were performed within the household.

Although it continued to be assumed that the static and limited condition of women was due chiefly to their primary function as mothers and nurses, an analysis of these purely domestic lives will show that a relatively small portion of women's time and energy was spent in actual mothering. Less than half the fifty years of her adult life were so consumed by the average woman; and in all but the largest families the wife actually occupied more hours per day in washing and laundry work than in the care of children. If the capacity to bear children had in fact incapacitated women for other physical exertion to the extent that it was always assumed it did whenever women wished to do anything outside the home, most families would have lacked food, clothing, and comfort for long periods of time.

From six to twelve children were born during twenty years to the average wife, and during those years she did most of the labor of the household, including a good deal of manufacturing now done in factories, with only such help as the older children could give. The life of my own grandmother was typical of that of many another well-to-do farmer's wife between 1825 and

1875, and an almost exact counterpart of that of Lucy Read Anthony, as described by her daughter.

" Lucy Anthony soon became acquainted with the stern realities of life. Her third baby was born when the first was three years and two months old. That summer she boarded eleven factory hands who roomed in her house, and she did all the cooking, washing, and ironing, with no help except that of a thirteen-year-old girl, who went to school, and did chores night and morning. The cooking for a family of sixteen was done on the hearth in front of the fireplace, and in a brick oven at the side. Daniel Anthony was a generous man, loved his wife, and was well able to hire help, but such a thing was not thought of at that time. No matter how heavy the work, the woman of the household was expected to do it, and probably would have been the first to resent the idea that assistance was needed."

Domesticity is here used for convenience to designate all the duties which a married woman of the past century was expected to perform. It consisted first of the physiological functions of wifehood and motherhood; second, of the handicrafts of a civilized household—cooking, sewing, washing, cleaning, and household decoration; and third, the social duties of hospitality and the cultivation of good manners. In the earlier part of the century it involved also the manufacture of nearly all the raw products of the farm into the necessary food, clothing, and bedding for a family of six to twelve persons. The household was then not merely a shelter and a boarding-house, but a miniature factory, to which the men-folk furnished the raw products, and over which the wife presided as the working boss.

The amount of labor, skill, and knowledge necessary to the successful performance of such a variety of duties may be imagined when one remembers that from this family-factory have already been differentiated the separate vocations of nursing, dressmaking, tailoring, knitting, laundering, and baking, every kind of cloth manufacture, and almost all the primary preparation of foods. If a woman really mastered to the point of competence the essentials of most of these handicrafts, she was necessarily strong, intelligent, and skilful. Under such circumstances the vocation of domesticity was an immense and stimulating field of action, and likely, therefore, to produce a high quality of mind and character.

In the attempt to measure the effect of domestic occupations upon women's capacity and character, it is difficult to find any perfect analogy with men's industries. Most of the occupations assigned to men had long ago been specialized into separate trades; while there remained to women, even after a considerable portion of the domestic processes had been transferred to factories, sev-

eral miscellaneous vocations which had no inherent connection except that they were undertaken under a single family roof.   In this respect
domesticity was heterogeneous in much the same
sense that general farming was, and still is.
Agriculture, as practised in America before the
War, comprised several branches, which had no
necessary relation except that all of them required
the use of land.   The raising of grain and hay,
of livestock of the several kinds; the production
of butter, milk, and cheese; the growing and mar-
keting of vegetables and fruit; all required a vast
amount and variety of technique and knowledge,
but the farmer's education, like the housewife's,
consisted in acquiring the traditional methods of
several, if not of all these specialties.   Although
they involved such difficult scientific subjects as the
chemistry of soils, the effects of tillage and
moisture, the laws of heredity and breeding, the
chemistry of milk and its products, the growth
and fertilization of plants; there was no available
fund of information and no opportunity for systematic education on these points.   Each farmer
started with his father's traditional ideas and
methods; if he learned to think for himself, he
varied them, made some experiments on his own
account, and, if he were successful, was imitated
by a few of his neighbors, thus promoting the
progress of science.   If he failed he paid a pen-

alty in a loss of profits and reaped the scorn of the neighborhood.

Housewifery, though as heterogeneous in character and traditional in method as farming, differed from it in several other ways. Though the farmer's work was from " sun to sun," the woman's work was never done. During all the years of child-bearing the mother added to a twelve- or fourteen-hour day of housework the nightly tending of children; and, in case of illness in the family, nursing as well. Toward the latter part of the century, the agitation by workingmen for a shorter day in other occupations reacted to shorten the farmer's day; and, coincidently, the removal of manufactures from the home lessened the amount of labor in the house. It did not, however, perceptibly alter the intermittent character of domestic occupations and, as a rule, it tended to make them less and less educative.

The domestic sphere was gradually being narrowed in much the same way as the shoemaker's. He had once been a highly skilled workman, whose trade demanded a knowledge of a number of skilful processes, from the tanning of leather to the designing of lasts. If he followed his trade into the factory he was reduced to performing a few monotonous operations requiring little intelligence; if he remained outside he became a handy repairer of half-worn footwear. Like the housewife, he was left with only the fragmentary processes of his trade, and those the least interesting, and gradually lost the stimulus to originality and skill which had been in itself an education.

Cooking, which was the most varied of the crafts left in the home, became more and more elaborate as women expended more time and thought upon it. Every housewife tried to vie with her neighbor in concocting some new combination of eggs, milk, sugar, and flour, et cetera; recipes became more complicated and laborious—though the food did not become more nutritious and digestible—until the principal literature of the self-educated woman consisted of cookbooks filled with hundreds of formulæ. Such meager schooling as she received had no relation either to housewifery or motherhood. It was inevitable that when she had mastered the technique of ordinary homekeeping, whatever originality and ambition she might possess would have to be exercised within the limits of her sphere, and would, therefore, develop in the direction of elaboration of living. As we shall see in the chapters on dress, personal adornment and clothes became almost an occupation in themselves, engaging more and more time and attention. Like a squirrel in a cage, she must exercise herself by running around in the wheel contrived for her, instead of roaming freely at large to gather nuts against the winter's need.

Another simple difference between domesticity and farming—the difference between indoor and outdoor life—has produced effects upon women so far-reaching as to be incalculable. The farmer, as general agriculture began to be subdivided into special lines, concentrated his energy and technique on those to which his taste and his land were adapted. He was not shut up in the barn to devote himself solely to milking cows and currying horses and feeding the animals three times a day. Merely from a hygienic standpoint, housekeeping, as it became more narrow and more elaborate, became less healthful. Thousands of steps—patter, patter from one end of the house to the other, upstairs and down cellar; hundreds of mechanical operations—sweeping, dusting, beating of eggs, kneading bread, washing, ironing, and scrubbing; millions of stitches in sewing, mending, knitting, quilting—these and similar petty labors, varied by three meals a day and three piles of dishes to wash, and, mayhap, the care of a baby or two, made up the vocation of domesticity. It was a monotony of heterogeneous drudgery, comparable only to farming, and as much more enervating as four walls and a roof are than the blue sky, the brown furrow, and the live and growing world outside.

A few years ago two college women tested the ordinary household operations by the criteria of hygienic gymnastics.   Beginning with the customary assumption that " gravity is the enemy of woman," they found that all the work of the housewife except scrubbing kept her on her feet excessively, that most of the arm and back movements were in a cramped and strained position; and that she walked from five to eight miles a day in dead, if not altogether bad, air—in short, that housekeeping was hard manual labor.   Though every housewife knew this without scientific demonstration, it has not been sufficiently recognized that housework of the old-fashioned kind lacked fresh air, variety, and exhilaration precisely as factory labor does, and to a much greater degree than farming.

The mental element of joy in the product, which is the highest compensation one can have for any labor, was to a great extent lost in the *repetition* involved in domestic production.   No doubt the woman who made the first chocolate cake or the first pumpkin pie got lots of fun out of it, and so long as she kept her reputation as the superior and original maker, she was stimulated to further skill.   But no woman could keep up her enthusiasm for preparing potatoes three times a day, much less for washing the tri-daily dishes, any more than the ditchdigger could develop his mind and continue to lift with zest so many hundred shovelfuls of dirt during three hundred days in a year.

Work is, undoubtedly, the chief means by which human capacity is increased and moral perceptions lifted to a higher level; but drudgery—that is, the indefinite repetition of operations requiring the minimum of technique and intelligence—deadens the mind and, if pursued in the midst of filth and darkness, brutalizes the worker. In our day it is being recognized that in proportion as drudgery is done under healthful conditions and for the attainment of an interesting and worthy goal, it may become a means of self-development. Professor Lillien J. Martin made more than seventy-five thousand observations, extending over a period of three years, on one subject, in order to determine a certain fact in experimental psychology; in point of repetition it was as wearisome as if she had washed dishes three times a day for a lifetime; but in point of mental interest it had the zest of working in a new field, and for its goal the greatest intellectual joy in life, the making of a scientific discovery.

One further parallel may be drawn between domesticity as a vocation and the occupations of men. At the beginning of the Nineteenth Century the American family was still an industrial unit. All of its members were producers according to their age, sex, and ability, and all pooled their products and shared the results.   Very little ready money was in circulation, and the male head of the family had relatively small chance to rob his dependents while living, although he might distribute his estate very unjustly after he was dead.   When the family gradually ceased to be an industrial unit, the minor children began to control their own earnings as soon as they left home, and the husband sold the products of the farm or the business for money.   But the women of the household, no longer economically important as manufacturers of raw material, were not in a position to sell their services in the public market.   They were still producers, but only secondary producers, so to speak, by so much as a cooked egg is better than a raw one, and a clean sheet than a dirty one; and they were in consequence reduced to a position of quasi-peonage. Just as the serf of medieval times was at the mercy of his master-employer because he could not leave the land for another and better-paid job, so mothers and daughters became dependent upon the goodwill of the master of their household.

Nor did the fact that, unlike the peon, many a woman might receive more than the value of her service, alter her economic dependence.   Greedy, idle, seductive females practised the arts of their kind to wring from industrious men a luxurious living to which they were not entitled; while the majority of hard-working, devoted wives were left without recourse against their particular supporter's notion of what they had earned.

How this situation worked out occasionally is illustrated by the following story, told by a lawyer about an old farmer's wife down on Cape Cod. The farmer died without a will, and his greedy heirs, grudging her the life-use of one-third of the estate, which the law gave her, managed to prove that the farmer had imposed upon her by an illegal ceremony of marriage, and that she, therefore, was not entitled to any of the estate. The Judge, thereupon, advised the old woman to bring in a bill for her services, for if she had not been his wife, the farmer was not entitled to have her do his housework for nothing. Accordingly, she brought in a bill at the current rate of wage for a domestic servant, which the Court allowed, and it took the whole of the estate to pay it. Of course, she had been " supported " all that time, but with the discovery that she was not the man's wife, it was also discovered that her support alone was not a full equivalent for her labor.

The same principle was put in a slightly different way by Higginson, when he wrote:

" A farmer works himself to death in the hay field, and his wife works herself wholly to death in the dairy.

The neighbors come in to sympathize after her demise; and during the few months' interval before his second marriage, they say approvingly: ' He always was a generous man to his folks! He was a good provider!' But where was the room for generosity any more than the member of any other firm is to be called generous, when he keeps the books, receipts the bills, and divides the money?"

The economic disintegration of the Puritan-Colonial family in the last century resulted in taking away from the housewife one of the chief incentives of any labor, *i.e.,* definite money compensation. Marriage, though nominally a partnership, left the second partner in the position of putting in her property and her labor, and then being obliged to trust the first partner to give her as much or as little of the increase as he chose. Stripped of its sentimental aspects, such a bargain was a much greater risk for the woman than for the man, and equally unjust, whether the wife got more or less.

The reaction of an occupation pursued through a lifetime is so tremendous upon the physique and the mental and moral development of men, that its effects are easily recognized everywhere. But in a country where a man is comparatively free to choose or to drift into the occupation to which he is suited, the affinity between a man and his calling would naturally reinforce his stronger

characteristics, and become an element of general
social progress. Men do better that which they
are fitted for, and they are apt to like what they
can do well. Now, the peculiar misfortune of
women has been that, while the original field of
domestic production was rapidly narrowed, social convention, during at least two generations,
prevented them from engaging in any substitute
for it outside the home. Although their primitive sphere was constantly shrinking they were
not yet freed to find another. The theory of
mankind and of the Church was still: all women
must be domestic, whether married or single;
whether by temperament maternal or celibate;
whether adapted to domestic detail or not. The
vocation manacled the woman, the woman could
not choose what she liked, or what she was fitted
to do.

The effect of this social coercion was to
suppress initiative and originality to a degree
beyond imagination. For it was inevitably the
women of most active minds and of largest administrative capacity who found the limitations
of housekeeping most irksome. Suppose every
man in the world had to be a farmer, and could
never break away into law or science or art or
engineering or even literature, without paying a
penalty in social ostracism, and—worst of all—
in the sacrifice of a family and a home; suppose

that he never received any wages directly, but was just " supported," and now and then accepted what his senior partner chose to give. Indeed, we need not suppose, for this was the state of a large class of men in the Middle Ages. But the historian calls them the " dark ages," and explains carefully that under such limitations the development of great men and great ideas was not to be expected. No more was it probable that domesticated women, inheriting an environment and a tradition of smallness, would show, even when the doors of opportunity were opened a little way, a high degree of talent in untried fields. It is only by some such analogy as this that we can realize the effect of housewifery in stunting women of exceptional ability who, conscientiously pinching themselves to fit their sphere, were unhappy or ill-tempered; or, if they had the courage to break through that domestic inclosure, found themselves pariahs, doomed to isolation, if not to failure, in the unfriendly *métier* for which they had no preparation.

When, toward the end of the last century, women first began to organize themselves into clubs for self-culture and social activity, they were ridiculed for their lack of ability to do teamwork. Their critics seemed to have forgotten that there had never been incentive or opportunity for coöperation toward larger ends, except in the sewing-bee and the Ladies' Aid Society. Miss Tarbell has clearly shown that the Civil War was the first occasion in which any large number of women came together outside the home to work for the public good. That excessive devotion to the need of her own family which was the glory of her womanhood prevented her from taking an interest in larger affairs. Just as the lawyer instinctively measured everything by the law, so the specialized domestic woman limited her thinking within the periphery of those matters which it was necessary for a woman to know. She took the personal view, because she had to—her happiness and comfort depended not on town government and trade, not on political theories and international quarrels, but on the will of the person nearest to her. In other words, her vocation was to wait upon and please a small circle of people, and therefore her intuitions in respect to personality were extraordinarily developed.

Many of the minor characteristics set down as peculiarly feminine are, in fact, the product of the universal domestic employment of women in past times; as, for instance, the proficiency in the observation and memory of details. Women remember certain personal details of indoor life for the same reason that the ornithologist sees and remembers the markings of every bird. This same man, however, would probably not remember the pattern of the wallpaper in his bed-chamber, nor be capable of choosing a tasteful necktie; while his equally capable wife could not tell a robin from a peewee, and yet could describe accurately the dress of all her guests at a tea party.

Women are precisely like men in that they follow the line of least resistance, and of greatest apparent self-interest. Since successful domesticity required the mastery of an immense number of petty details inside the house, and the attainment of order, cleanliness, and comfort therein, the mind of the homekeeping woman dwelt incessantly not alone upon these affairs, but also upon the persons whom they concerned. Formerly women could recall the marriage relationship of the whole family connection, and the number of the children; while many a man could not tell how old his wife was, nor whether the first baby was born in the old house or the new one. It is, indeed, no more masculine for men to be oblivious of domestic details than it is feminine to be master of them—it is merely human to be what one has to be in the station to which one was born and reared.

It is a natural corollary to this principle that the purely domestic woman of the end of the nineteenth century should have been quite as " eager in the pursuit of trifles " as the lady of leisure whom Mercy Warren complained of a hundred years earlier. Given a vocation which demanded incessant attention to a thousand small matters, even when the number of those affairs was diminished so as to greatly release the housewife, the average woman would still inevitably pursue trifles until there was both a chance and an incentive to follow larger things. Only a very exceptional girl would make a new path for herself because the cost of any departure from the sanctified conventions of women's lives was so tremendous. It cost a man something to refuse to treat other men to liquor in a country where that was the universal custom, but it did not make him a by-word or prevent him from marrying and having a home. And it is not exaggeration to say that nothing less than this was the penalty for any woman who broke through the appointed sphere and offered opinions on those larger questions relegated to men.

There were thus both negative and positive reasons for woman to become small-minded. On the one hand, the sole occupation of her life consisted of exacting, repetitious, and ephemeral things; on the other, until there was an imperative call to other vocations outside, she could not develop the larger mind and become convinced of the futility of the conventional methods of housekeeping. The more conscientious the housewife was, the more petty she surely became, devoting herself to the elaboration of food, clothes, decoration, and needlework in the effort to be the perfectly correct feminine creature.

Curiously enough, it was not purely domestic women who revolutionized domestic science in the last quarter of the century and relieved it of its terrible drudgery and picayune monotony, but rather *thinking,* educated women who, having escaped into a larger world of scientific, sanitary, and economic progress, looked back and, out of pity, began to rescue their sisters from the bog of household tradition. One woman, Ellen H. Richards, devoting herself to chemistry and hygiene, did more to make the home a livable place than a thousand other conscientious, devoted homekeepers, who remained imprisoned in the woman's sphere of her generation, and that without the sacrifice of any truly feminine quality. The " model domestic woman " is now generally the one whose methods are belated; who cannot keep her servants, and does not yet dream that this is the day of employés; who does her tasks in the old-fashioned way; who still thinks it shiftless to leave any of the laundry unironed; who balks at a patent dishwasher and a fireless cooker; and who has not yet found out that there is a whole library of household science with which she might educate herself and mitigate the endless pettiness of living.

It was inevitable, as soon as women in any numbers undertook work outside the home for wages, that they should begin to compare domesticity disadvantageously with other vocations. The first effect of this was that the American girl would no longer work out as a servant, and, when she married, would have as her social ambition the employment of some immigrant to do the more laborious and tedious things. The next and logical result was that a good many young women declined to keep house even for their husbands, and went to boarding; and that indulgent husbands, who preferred good-temper and dainty, agreeable companionship in a wife, encouraged wives to rid themselves of every form of drudgery. Whenever the wife had earned money before marriage she could not help measuring her wifehood in financial terms—whether she did any household labor or not—for she had been brought up on the theory that because of her potential motherhood she was " entitled to support." At the beginning of the present century not a few such women have become intelligent enough to question the tradition of economic dependence, and cannot keep their self-respect unless they give a full return for what they receive.

The " strictly domestic " woman is a rapidly

vanishing type, eliminated by world-changes in social and industrial conditions, but it will be several generations probably before the effects of domesticity upon the character and mentality of women will disappear. Women of the more belated kind will continue to be petty, devoted to unnecessary details of dress and household affairs, timid, and unoriginal—the sport of hereditary and conventional forces which they do not comprehend. Of necessity, being out of touch both with the old and the new order, they will be discontented and will make the homes of which they are the mistresses as unsatisfactory as themselves. But in proportion as domesticity is remodeled and made tolerable by scientific administration, women, even domestic women, will cease to be petty, gossipy, unthinking servants of the household. There will be as great a revolution in the characteristics of the homemaking woman as there has been in the qualities of the farmer since the spread of agricultural science. It is significant that, as the traditional household labors are modified or vanish altogether from the home, wifehood and motherhood are seen to have no essential connection with sewing, cooking, or laundry-work under the conditions of modern life, and stand out as true vocational functions in themselves.

SECTION II

THE EFFECT UPON WOMEN

CHAPTER V

THE FEMININE TEMPERAMENT

"I would rather have a thorn in my side than an echo."—
RALPH WALDO EMERSON.

> "Mirth and opium, ratafia and tears,
> The daily anodyne and nightly draught
> To kill those foes to fair ones, time and thought."
>   ALEXANDER POPE.

MANNERS and mannerisms, which are the conscious adjustment of their behavior that human beings make to the conventions of society, have a greater significance than is generally attributed to them. The habitual bearing reflects the social stratum from which the person came, modified by the need of making himself acceptable to the particular circle in which he ultimately found himself. Since manner was always a post-natal acquisition, any unforeseen situation or emotion was likely to bring to the surface the unmannerly, primitive human being. A grown man and an adult woman have a code of behavior quite different from each other, which is usually ascribed to the fundamental sex distinction and which, for want of a better term, we may assign to the "temperament" of each.

In a small town in New Mexico I saw playing opposite my window for several weeks a child perhaps six years of age. It was neatly dressed in boy's trousers, but had two long braids of black hair tied with bows of pink ribbon hanging down its back. From the way in which it ran and played, from its tone of voice and manner, it was impossible to know whether it was a boy or girl, and, curiously enough, neither the children with whom it played, nor the neighbors, seemed to know—nor, I might almost add, to care—nor did I ever learn its sex. Yet in a very few years it will undoubtedly learn a behavior befitting the conventions of its sex; that is, it will acquire the mannerisms of masculinity or femininity.

It is well known that a girl brought up among boys becomes " hoydenish," that is to say, boyish in manner; while a boy brought up in a family of women is apt to be " a sissy," or, so to speak, girlish in his ways. It is probable that if they were brought up together from babyhood without having suggested to them that any difference of behavior was necessary, their manners would vary with their innate temperament more than with their sex. In a society where, from infancy, great stress was laid upon sex differences, the tendency to be bold or shrinking, polite or rude, loud-mouthed or soft-spoken, lively or quiet, emotional or judicial, impulsive or restrained, vulgar or refined, became predominant or was rigidly repressed along the lines of social approval or disapproval. Among the few primitive peoples where men and women were approximately equal in status, there was no essential difference in courage, emotionality, and delicacy; but among the majority of races where the one sex has controlled the destiny of the other, the standards both of morals and manners were laid down by men chiefly for their own convenience and pleasure, and continually tended to become exaggerated in the efforts of women to win and to satisfy their masters. It came about that women, particularly of the well-to-do classes, were expected to be excessively timid, gentle, unreasoning, fastidious, vivacious—in two words, charming and docile. Or, in another phrase, the successful woman must be what men approved.

Now, naturally, a member of the ruling class would not like an aggressive subordinate, because she might sometimes cross his will; nor a too-reasoning creature, because she might think otherwise or put him in the wrong; nor a slovenly partner, for she would not make a home pleasant; nor a grumpy one, because she would not be an agreeable companion. In short, civilized man molded woman into the chaste image of what he himself would rather not be, and required her to practise the difficult habits which insured his comfort, pleased his taste, and would not disturb his peace. As a result of a long period of inculcation, in women of successive generations, they have acquired an extreme code of conduct and manners. Having no opportunity and little encouragement to be natural, they suppressed all the masculine, that is to say, the stronger, tendencies of their natures, and became, as idleness and ease permitted, more and more effeminate. The cultivation of abnormal delicacy of feeling, of excessive dependence upon men, and of hyper-weakness, or, to use the current mocking phrase of the past time, " the clinging vine," became the pose of the woman who aspired to be a perfect lady.

Since one of the first results of a democratic régime was to make every citizen try to rise into a higher social stratum, American women of every grade were stimulated to be as ladylike as possible in imitation of the affected manners of the women of greater leisure and resources above them. They seized upon the conventional standard of ladyhood, and affected it to a ludicrous degree. In this way there came to be two conflicting ideals of behavior: the one originally developed in the marriageable type by man for purposes of domesticity; the other adopted by women themselves for the purpose of social elevation.

Of all the habits which woman tried to acquire, vivacity was, perhaps, the most conspicuous—the more so as it was not characteristic either of the primitive or the intellectual type. As civilized woman enlarged her social functions, she added to the tricks of allurement other manners with which to fill up her increasing leisure, and to express vicariously the rising status of the family. In earlier times men offered hospitality and their dependents, of whom the wife was chief, performed the labor which it entailed; but in Nineteenth-Century America one of the principal glories of the housewife was to keep an open house. The English custom of after-dinner coffee, wine, and conversation, and the Continental habit of frequenting a café or a garden for social diversion, had been replaced by the amusements of the Puritanized domestic circle—and, for a certain class of men, by the saloon.

In this new field of mixed society, women took a much larger share of leadership than they had been allowed in the Old World, and talkativeness became a necessary accomplishment for any young woman who wished to marry well. As the " professional entertainer " of private life, she must decorate her person and cultivate a lively, witty, agreeable manner. Whether she had anything to say or not, she must appear to have—she must learn to keep the ball rolling. Unfortunately, her life being largely indoors, there was very little common ground of conversation between a woman and a man. Starting with the instinctive coquetry of the mating female, there was evolved for social purposes a series of devices for exercising her charm and giving young men a good time. The subjects of conversation were necessarily limited to personal relations and social gossip, in both of which there was lacking the element of unexpectedness. It, therefore, became a part of the talk-game for girls to express themselves in veiled meanings, or by teasing, or by pseudo-quarrels, to produce the sensation of novelty. Such a mental paper-chase afforded amusement to the young of both sexes without committing them to serious courtship. Indeed, girls practised it on their fathers and other elderly men, who were entertained thereby as by the antics of a puppy in training.

In order to enhance the bird-like sprightliness which, at this period, was the ideal behavior of a charming girl, somebody invented " silvery laughter." Children laughed naturally, if not always sweetly, as a sign of physical exuberance rather than of wit. Adults outgrew it as they did the animal instinct to maul each other. If belonging to a crude society, they might sometimes guffaw or titter, according to convention, while in more cultivated strata humor met merely with the appreciation of a low chuckle or smile. The girlish habit of constant laughter over trifles that were not at all funny in themselves, was partly, no doubt, an expression of health, but it was con· tinued into womanhood as a means of entertaining and of appearing gay and young. Among men, on the contrary, a youthful appearance was a disadvantage, and the boy, therefore, assumed gravity at the earliest possible age.

The superficial animation, which was merely a curious habit connected with feminine parade, disappeared with the worn-out trousseau. The wife found out very soon after marriage that her girlish tricks did not any longer entertain her husband, and practised them, if at all, on other women. Though no longer keyed up to the maiden tension, she was apt to keep the habit of petty, driveling, scrappy talk about clothes, recipes, babies, and neighborhood trivialities. She had, as a matter of fact, no incentive to discuss or to inform herself upon the larger affairs of the world, having in nobody's eyes any concern with them. If she did offer opinions or ask questions, her men-folk rarely treated them seriously.

The insistent and pervasive character of domestic duty required that women should never forget their household matters, and, if they talked at all, it was inevitably of the things nearest them. It is proverbial that young mothers can seldom be diverted from baby-talk—or talk about the baby—it becomes a sort of obsession. This is, indeed, not so much out of motherly conceit as because the baby itself is so absolutely incessant that it leaves no time for thinking of impersonal matters. The mother, for the first year of a child's life, is much like a patient in a sanatorium, except that her mind is fixed on the infant's symptoms rather than upon her own.

Again, " the typical woman " used to gabble of ephemeral things for the same reason that commercial men will sit smoking and swapping stories in a hotel lobby—it is both amusing and relaxing. But while women, like men, talk not only to amuse others, but to relieve the nervous tension of the day, there was, after all, one striking difference between the domestic woman and the average man in the purpose of their conversation. Having a stake in matters outside the sphere of home, and of general interest, men formed the habit of conversing to get and to give information. Men of superior ability alternated in talking and listening, while the ordinary woman was like a cowboy or a miner, or a countryman whose experience is so limited that he does not willingly listen to accounts of foreign travel or adventure, much less to descriptions of pictures or historic monuments.

The cumulative effect of domesticity has been

to produce scrappy-mindedness in woman. The average housewife's attention hops from one thing to another, never having been concentrated upon a continuous, homogeneous occupation, but rather upon a succession of miscellaneous details, all of which are about equally unimportant, but none of which must be forgotten. Many women, even well-bred ones, constantly interrupt the conversation with irrelevant exclamations. Like children they have slight power of inhibition; they can't wait to be heard, and so two talk at the same time; they spill over, so to speak, and say whatever comes uppermost without discretion or discrimination. Half-grown boys, as well as girls, have these same conversational tendencies, but they usually lose them early because men will not tolerate a talkative, foolish kid, while, in the case of girls, the average man of the Nineteenth Century liked them to be childish chatterers. It is a curious fact that civilized men have always put a premium on foolishness in girls—especially in pretty girls—while they spoke scornfully of it in older women.

In no respect have women been supposed to differ more markedly from men than in the expression of emotion. The feminine type of the past century laughed often and too easily; wept almost as readily with any shock of fear or grief, and not infrequently as a sign of extreme anger.

It is a significant fact, which is generally overlooked, that the women of the Twentieth Century, and particularly those who have made themselves economically independent, no longer behave in this way. Tearfulness, along with talkativeness, has gone out of fashion. The heroines who fainted in the Eighteenth-Century novel, and cried buckets of tears in the fiction of the past generation, now control their emotions almost as well as men—perhaps even better, if one may judge from the copious swear-words which characterize the lively feelings of the typical Western hero. In infants, crying has always been regarded as an evidence that they wanted attention —that they were uncomfortable, or wished to be dandled; and at this age there is certainly no difference between the sexes. Nor throughout childhood—where they have had the same discipline and an equal reason for self-control— did children show any perceptible variation along the line of sex. But by the time the boy and the girl had reached the period of adolescence, girls had usually formed the habit of crying when they were unhappy and displeased; and boys, of fighting, swearing, and smashing things.

In modern systems of education, the power of suggestion is recognized to be as strong as that of authority in molding children. But even in the by-gone period of stricter discipline, suggestion was no less a factor in the formation of character, though not consciously practised. The habits of common decency—brushing the teeth, cleaning the nails, and bathing—as every mother knew—had to be assured not so much by coercion as by appeals to pride and affection. It was suggested to the boy or girl that they could never be grown up till they had learned to button their clothes.

In such matters boys and girls received precisely the same suggestions, but in every habit where the conventional standards for men and women differed, the force of suggestion reinforced girlishness in girls and boyishness in boys. When a boy cried with hurt or fury, he was told he could " never be a man " if he cried. Girls, on the other hand, were expected to cry, out of their feminine temperament, and if, now and then, one did not do so, but raged and smashed things, she was regarded as a tomboy and a scandal to her sex. When little girls wept, they were likely to be petted and comforted; if they kicked and yelled, they were punished and made to understand that to behave like a boy was the most outrageous thing they could do—a sin comparable to lying and stealing. Now if, as is well known, a baby a week old learns that somebody will give it attention if it yells long enough, and takes advantage thereby, it is scarcely possible to exaggerate the effect of the constant emphasis on hysteria as the proper form of emotional explosion for women.

Emotional expression is, in fact, determined far more by race and temperament than by sex. The South European peoples are in this respect more highly developed than the Northern, and the negro than the white race. The so-called "artistic" temperament is merely a display of the characteristics commonly attributed to women and, until recently, male artists were looked upon by other men as essentially effeminate. In so far as the artist has a highly developed nervous organization, he is, indeed, like a finely strung woman, but his effeminacy consists, on the other hand, in an over-stimulation of his emotions, and in the absence of the motives for self-control which usually operate among men.

The artist, too, is the victim of a tradition that singers and painters are inevitably erratic and self-indulgent. The artist is by nature a finely sensitive human organism and, since success depends upon very early specialization in the expression of beauty and feeling, the so-called manly qualities are likely to remain in abeyance or to be suppressed. The feminine and the masculine temperaments are at this moment strikingly typified in two men singers now at the height of their fame. One, born of a southern race, and trained from childhood exclusively in the direction of artistic expression, behaves precisely in the manner of a petted, extravagant, emotional woman. The other, of a northern race, educated in the broad, practical manner of the normal man, and rather late in life devoted to the exclusive culture of his artistic gift, is both a great singer and a controlled and manly human being.

In much the same way, the great preacher and the brilliant orator are effeminate, producing their effects far more by the hypnotism of high emotion than by the ideas which they express. Like actors, they, too, are subject to extreme reaction after the culmination of any emotional effort in which they are often as irresponsible as children. It is particularly suggestive that of all the types of men denominated " effeminate," the actor most nearly resembles the type of woman set up as the ideal in the past century. He, like the woman, makes his place in life chiefly by the cultivation of manner and appearance. He, like her, depends for success upon pleasing rather than being admirable. The " matinée idol " is an extreme example of character—or, rather, perversion of character—by the social necessity of being charming and of trading in assumed emotions.

For this was in truth what the American woman was driven to do in the sphere offered in the past century. With the approach of adolescence and the development of the sex instinct, young people of both sexes began to preen themselves, the boy exaggerating the masculine qualities to attract attention; the girl pretending to be extremely delicate, elusive, and emotional in order to enhance her charms. One of the chief elements of courtship is surprise; and emotional outbursts, whether of laughter, tears, or temper, were one of the readiest means of producing unexpected turns in personal relations. The lover, taken unaware, would succumb to the assault of hysteria just as the girl's father had done in earlier years, and as the husband would do later. Hysteria was, indeed, by virtue of convention and cultivation, as much the weapon of the domestic, feminine type as bluffing, bullying, and epithets were " natural " to men whose traditions did not permit the exhibition of weaker forms of emotional expression. The cultivation of anger from bravado to fisticuffs was one of the insignia of manliness, as tears and weakness were of womanliness, though by nature the boy might be a coward and the girl a fighter.

Since men liked docility in wives, marriageable girls must cultivate the appearance of gentleness, whatever their natural disposition might be. Just as boys in the family might throw their clothes on the floor, expecting mother to pick them up, while girls were trained to put away

their own garments; so boys were rather admired
for getting mad and getting into a fight, while
their sisters, under similar provocation, would be
called "vixens" and meet with severe disapproval. The girl of high temper—which often
indicated superior strength of character—either
became the female bully of the neighborhood, or,
more often, learned to dissemble her disposition
by putting on a "honeyed" manner. One of
the "sweetest" women I have ever known—
and she was typical of many of her sort—one
whose outward manner was invariably defer-
ential, sweet, and considerate toward her neighbors and her family, kept her husband in abject
fear of her displeasure. The temper which this
delicate and gentle appearing creature would un-
leash in private to get what she wanted from a
refined and too-indulgent husband, was incredibly
savage, and was always reinforced with the appeal to tears. She had been a delicate and
only daughter, over-indulged, but, nevertheless,
brought up in the practice of the strictest conventional behavior. She could and did control
herself in every public relation, toward every one
except her immediate family, but, when crossed by
them, she fought like a man, with the only weapons she knew.

The society manner was an extension of the
habits acquired by girls for the purpose of their

sphere, which included entertaining along with
housekeeping and motherhood. Objectively, it
was intended to make the guest have a good time
by putting him at ease, and at the same time pleasing and piquing him with interest; subjectively,
it was the accepted method of displaying the
feminine charm, of giving marriageable girls a
chance to make their market, and of maintaining
the social status of the household. It, therefore,
demanded a careful attention to appearances, the
playing up of all the attractive resources of the
feminine members of the family, and the concealment of whatever might not be creditable. If a
woman thus set out to please everybody, even
within the confines of her own social circle, she
could never say what she thought nor behave as
she felt. Indeed, the more charming she was,
the more insincere she must necessarily be. She
must always be complimentary to her acquaint-
ances, praising their dress, belongings, and performances. The guest who loved music and
sang off the key, must be invited to perform as
cordially as if she were a really pleasing musician;
the man who told wearisome anecdotes must be
met with all the spontaneous laughter due to wit.
The more tactful the woman contrived to be, the
more social success she attained and, *per contra,*
the more insincere she became.

It is evident that slow-witted or straightforward women would have no chance at all in a society where the coin of exchange was mutual and graceful flattery. In the nature of things the quickest-witted women were the most capable of practising concealment of their thoughts, while those of more solid qualities would either not be able to attain the acrobatic grace necessary to social success, or would have an honest distaste for its superficiality. The more intellectual and sincere, and the more reasonable a young woman was, the less likely she was to be socially successful, and she must either be content to be a " blue-stocking," and remain unmarried, or she must conceal her natural common-sense and imitate the feminine characteristics then in vogue.

Thus imitation rather than originality became the keynote of women's lives. In a democratic society composed largely of people born in the working classes, whose social ambitions were chiefly limited to financial ease and the hope of rising into the next higher stratum, there were many kinds of men, but only two sorts of women. The success of a man consisted in material achievement; of a woman in appearing to be what was pleasing to man in order that she might be invited to share his height. Men were making themselves, so to speak, of the genuine stuff— soft or hard, fine or coarse-grained, of pine, oak, or mahogany; while women, of whatever material, must be carefully veneered with a thin and costly layer of unreality—a sort of imitation composite, a spurious femininity.

It is certainly significant that, in proportion as the women of the Nineteenth Century were released from domestic, manual labor, they became more and more extravagantly feminine; and that this phenomenon was a repetition of what had previously marked the behavior of every class of women at leisure throughout the world's history. There is no evidence that our manufacturing grandmothers of the early Nineteenth Century were afflicted with any such degree of effusive, excitable, unreasoning temperament as that which characterized the strictly feminine ideal of their immediate descendants. Among Parisians at the present day, where there is almost no line drawn between the economic sphere of men and women, and where both husband and wife among the masses must work to make a living, there is no marked difference between them in respect to emotional expression. The women of Paris have fought as savagely as men in the revolutions; and French men are notoriously as emotional as the typical American woman, and as unreasoning when carried beyond self-control.

There can be no doubt that the social behavior which is commonly described as " typically feminine " is an over-development of characters not at all uncommon among men, and often lacking in women. When women have been more given to superficial talk and gayety than men, it is because men desired them to be so, and because it was, therefore, to their advantage. If they have been accustomed to use hysteria as their weapon of defense, instead of talking reason or using their fists, it was probably because they had never had either encouragement or opportunity to employ mind or brute force.

With the opening of all occupations to woman, and with nearly equal opportunities for intellectual training, there has been developed in a single generation a large number of American women who are less excitable than a Frenchman, less sentimental than a German, and less emotional than an Italian—in short, almost as reasonable and self-poised as the men of their own class and race.

CHAPTER VI

BEAUTY AND WEAKNESS

"There was no reason why woman should not labor in primitive society. The forces which withdrew her from labor were expressions of later social traditions. Speaking largely, these considerations were the desire of men to preserve the beauty of women, and their desire to withdraw them from association with other men. It is the connection in thought and fact between idle and beautiful women and wealth, indeed, which has frequently led to the keeping of a superfluous number of such women as a sign of wealth."—THOMAS—*Sex and Society.*

"Female selection . . . created a fantastic and extravagant male efflorescence. Male selection . . . produced a female etiolation, diminutive stature, beauty without utility."—LESTER F. WARD.

"The woman who is beautiful and vivacious, and not actually feeble-minded, will be endowed with all graces of mind and soul by three-fourths of all who see her on the street, while the most highly intellectual frump will often be set down as stupid and crabbed, purely on the strength of her appearance.

"In fine, beauty, to a woman of average intelligence and character . . . is her most valuable asset from a worldly standpoint. . . . Beauty is the outward and visible sign of the inward and spiritual grace—health. . . ."—WOODS HUTCHINSON.

THE types of spurious and anemic beauty prevalent in the Nineteenth Century in this country may be accounted for historically by the conflicting ideas inherited, on the one hand from ascetic religion, on the other through the sensual luxury of higher English society. Behind both, permeating and coercing the lives of women even down to the present time, was the idea left over from still older societies, that the bodies of women were owned by the men who espoused them, which carried with it the implication that the chief use of beauty is the satisfaction of sexual greed. One of the foremost modern sociologists tells us that, if we go back far enough, there was a long period of time when women had no need to be beautiful in order to attract their mates; a time, indeed, when males put on a temporary beauty in order that they might be chosen; and that it was not until the power of choice had been transferred from females to males that women in their turn began to cultivate those physical qualities which would most attract men. Even then relatively few women were beautiful in the modern sense, and they only for the short period of extreme youth.

For the ordinary woman, beauty as an aim and asset is quite a modern idea. In the earlier ages of mankind, strength, fertility, and skill in handicraft were the qualities most desired in wives, as in slaves. When King Solomon pictured the ideal domestic woman, he did not dwell upon the color of her eyes and hair, nor upon the symmetry of her form, but described in great detail the things she could *do,* praising her indefatigable industry, and ending with these words:

" Favor is deceitful and beauty is vain; but a woman that feareth the Lord, she shall be praised. Give her of the fruit of her hands and let her own works praise her in the gates."

Beauty in a wife or a slave was a rarity quite out of reach of the common man; a thing of great price, reserved for kings, princes, and the leaders of armies, and to be guarded, like treasure, in harems. The Greek hero, Paris, carried off women from Sidon, not for their beauty, but that they might weave purple cloth for Helen of Troy —a situation typical of the relative positions of the Beauty and the ordinary woman.

There was, in the ancient world, and even quite down to recent times, no economic surplus upon which society could fall back. War and waste, pestilence and the lack of mechanical inventions, made it necessary not only to breed great numbers of human beings, but that men, women, and children—all except a small upper class—should work incessantly. To the ordinary man, who could afford only one wife, strength and fertility were highly important; and though he might prefer the looks of one maid above another, his taste was likely to be overcome by his judgment or nullified by family and financial considerations.

At the beginning of the Christian Era, beauty in women was associated exclusively with luxury and sensuality—a fact which accounts for the antipathy toward them evinced by certain apostolic writers. Among the poverty-stricken masses of the later Roman Empire, severe labor and early marriage destroyed in girls, almost before they were grown, such ephemeral prettiness as they might possess. The ascetic reaction of the early Christian Church, during the Middle Ages, from the frank sensuality of the Roman world, emphasized still further the purely animal aspects of female beauty. With each recurrent wave of social reform in the Christianized world the essential relation between good looks and wickedness was reiterated until it culminated a second time among the Puritans—as it had the first time among the ascetics—in a belief that women, particularly attractive women, were agents of the devil.

Although Puritanism had begun to loosen its hold on the minds of American men at the beginning of the Nineteenth Century, the theory that women were tempters and a menace to every good man, was still generally accepted. The natural instinct of youth to admire and to choose the more attractive maiden was morbidly distorted by the religious teaching of the day into a sinful suggestion, and robbed of all its innocent joy. This unwholesome suppression of the animal side of human nature produced a sort of subterranean vulgarity in the majority of common people, and a revulsion of exaggerated shame in those of greater refinement. The fear of loveliness in women was extended to other forms of beauty in American life—for Puritanism had put a ban, too, upon painting, sculpture, music, and the drama. All were still regarded as frivolous, if not dangerous to morals; and thus our parents and grandparents were almost destitute of any form of artistic pleasure.

But even if there had been the same racial and temperamental sense of beauty as that pervading the French and Italian populace of the same period, the life of a pioneer community was necessarily ugly. The struggle with nature for the crude necessities of living devastated alike whatever beauty of landscape or of human nature there might be, and left scant leisure or desire for the beautiful.

The higher manifestations of beauty, whether in art or in womanhood, are necessarily of slow growth, and are always coincident with a certain degree of material ease. In proportion as the New World became prosperous, the mere abundance of good food, the prevalence of relative peace and plenty throughout a selected population, produced a better grade of human being.

And as the lives of ordinary women became easier, with more comfortable conditions of living and the removal of some of the hardest domestic labor to factories, the young were born with a greater degree of physical symmetry, and were able to keep it through adolescence and even into adult years.

Nevertheless, while the general average of bodily perfection was rising, its higher realization was hindered by the tyranny of religious traditions and the distorted image of what beauty in women consisted in. The entirely inconsistent types of physique which had survived from wholly different classes in the Old World, were still the models for imitation. The " over-sexed cow-mother " of medieval Europe—as Hutchinson calls her—found her analogue in America in the mother of a large family, whose too-frequent pregnancies and incessant industry left her at middle age either an exhausted, wrinkled creature, without a grace of body or mind; or else a shapeless bulk of flesh, more like a breeding animal than a human being. At the antipodes of such a woman was the attenuated fine-lady, modeled upon the type of the Eighteenth Century—as feeble, affected, and under-sexed as the breeding mother was vital. A third type, the French fashion-plate woman, who was, in fact, only slightly modified from the courtesan of Paris—represented a physique in which all the sex characters were emphasized as much as possible by dress and cosmetics, with the conscious purpose of allurement.

These three traditional models of beauty were imitated in turn, and in varying degree, by the American woman of the past century, though all of them were ameliorated somewhat by the prevalence of more wholesome social conditions. The all-mother type was both less wrinkled and less stolid than the old peasant type of Europe, keeping often into middle age and sometimes into old age a certain luscious comeliness. The woman who cultivated delicacy became the sort we still know well, whose " nerves " released her from most of the hardships of life, but who managed, nevertheless, to fulfil all the conventional duties of society and religion. The " stylish " woman of the post-bellum period—whose kind persists in great numbers—patterned her figure and dress as far as she dared upon the French model, but usually drew the line at theatrical cosmetics.

The ideals of art and physique, of beauty and of dress, had a constant reaction upon one another. The Puritan conception of womanhood which dominated this country till quite recently was less patently sexual than that of the older Christian teaching, but, as far as possible, it sup-

pressed romantic love and the beauty-loving instinct.   While the natural conditions in America
were more favorable and were producing a common population of finer physique, orthodox religion was still insisting upon the " vileness " of
humanity, the weakness and ensnaring nature of
women, and the inevitable connection between
vice and every form of art.

The insistence upon the essential sinfulness of
every natural instinct which might have flowered
in art, had a terrible effect upon the minds of
women.   It produced in them a feeling of intimate shame.   The body being vile, all their
functions were shameful and to be concealed.
From suppression to shame; from shame to distortion, were logical steps in the treatment of
their bodies.   The corset, for instance, worn
originally in Europe as a means of emphasizing
sex characters—the bust and the hips—became
the armor of respectability for innocent and over-
modest women.   To be seen without it was not
merely slovenly, it was improper, even vulgarly
suggestive.   As soon as any young girl ap-
proached adolescence, she had to put it on.
Some mothers said, for propriety's sake; and
other mothers, that she might have a good figure
when she grew to womanhood.   That is to say,
she must develop the small waist and the large
hips and bust, like a French fashion-plate, in order

to meet the requirements of Puritan modesty. No better illustration could be found of the conflicting traditions which ignorant women were blindly following.

Without attempting to account for the vagaries of modesty—a subject upon which much has already been written—the effect of a single convention upon the health and beauty of women may be dwelt upon. Throughout the past century, to be obviously two-legged was to be immodest. The Chinese woman—as modest and feminine as any of her sex in the world, perhaps—has had the use of her legs, if not of her feet, for thousands of years, but the American woman has always had to pretend that she had only one. The peasant woman of northern Europe, though burdened with heavy petticoats, might exhibit her body below the knee, but the " free " woman of the new democracy had to conceal, as far as possible, even her ankles.

This convention restricted every activity, and was, unquestionably, one of the factors in the deterioration of the health of American women. For three hundred years western women have ridden on horseback sidewise, with feet enveloped in a voluminous skirt, solely because a French Princess long ago set the fashion to conceal her own deformed spine. Because the roués of a decadent society attached sexual significance to ankles, the American girl walked encased in heavy drapery, which compelled a narrow, uncertain tread. Millions of women lifted their petticoats billions of times in the course of their lives; while housewives scoured their floors, hampered by the uniform of their sex, and endangered their lives whenever they got in or out of a vehicle; all for no other reason than that the particular form of modesty inculcated by Puritan society had tabooed legs in women. The early advocates of Women's Rights were right, if not wise, in associating a bifurcated costume with equality and freedom, but it was equally necessary to the production of true beauty.

Shame and inactivity, thus linked together, produced a strangely distorted and bloodless creature whose only sign of real loveliness was a pretty face. The grace of symmetry and the exhilaration of free motion were denied not only to women of the leisure classes, but to working-women as well, because every woman in America was trying " to be a lady," and the conventions of the Fore-time had so ordained. Even when the Puritan régime declined and women were beginning to be released from the older conventions, they were at the same time presented with a vicious foreign model by the vogue of fashions which had been brought in to promote journalism and manufacture.

Convention has this peculiarity: it is no sooner established than it tends to become exaggerated; probably for the reason pointed out by Darwin, that men like what they are accustomed to, carried to a moderate extreme. In the United States, before the Civil War, the almost total absence of art education in any form—painting, sculpture, and decoration—caused men to be satisfied with the most perverted and crude standards of pseudo-beauty in women. The pinched waist, the flat chest, and protruding abdomen, the bodily outline wholly destroyed by drapery in the wrong places, were merely symptoms of the general crudity of taste displayed in the architecture of the same period. Doric columns reproduced in wood, medieval towers in shingles, and the gingerbread decorations of the planing-mill, represented a riot of untrained, artistic ambition.

This period of base reproduction and violent novelties in art did give, fortunately, an opportunity for the release of varied and less conventional types of beauty among women. Red hair, which for several generations had been considered ugly—all but improper—began to be tolerated and, among people who had acquired some slight culture in foreign art, was even admired. The more permanent aspects of physical loveliness— grace of outline, purity and richness of color— gained some attention. Two extreme types of women—the household drudge who stood for efficiency without beauty, and the doll-woman who represented beauty without utility—began to go out of fashion. For as the new types of men produced by democracy became prosperous and worldly, they wanted something more in a wife than a homely sex-mate and servant; or, than a pretty but half-sick and helpless fool.

There began to emerge among us a conception of human beauty which might have higher reason than sexuality for its existence. The type of beauty developed among the Greeks had lacked, so far as women were concerned, essential elements. While exhibiting symmetry, color, and grace, it had been greatly deficient in expression; that is to say, it was the perfection of the physical female without the capacity for varied emotion and intelligence which is an inseparable part of the modern ideal. The Venus of Melos would probably attract very little attention now as a woman in cultivated society, though she might serve as an artist's model for life study.

Aside from the sensual and ascetic traditions which largely determined the conventional ideas of the earlier part of the past century, another influence of quite a different sort was brought to bear upon the feminine physique. It is not too much to say that science, particularly biological science, has assured the emancipation of woman;

nor that freedom from the limitations and de-
formities of the domestic tradition was impossible
until the facts of evolution had been discovered.
For the perpetuation of the weakness and subjection of women was certain so long as the
Christian scriptures continued to be literally interpreted; around them had been built a wall of
social convention which was all but impregnable.
So long as the doctrine that " the woman is the
glory of the man " dominated the Church and,
therefore, mankind, so long women would continue to be weak because they were dependent;
so long would they mold themselves into what
men wanted them to be, rather than develop their
own capacities.   In less than one century science
undermined the view that the female was necessarily weak, bringing to light a mass of proof
that among many orders of animals and that
among primitive men she was strong, even
stronger than the male.   Physiology and hygiene,
medicine and bacteriology, have uncovered the
hidden sources of the physical weaknesses of
modern women, and have demonstrated that the
greater part of them, perhaps all, are preventable.

At the present day, health and beauty are in
our minds very nearly inseparable, but when we
go back two or three generations we read constantly about the delicacy and ill-health of well-

known society beauties. The very term formerly in polite use—female complaints—stood for the physical poverty of womankind. A perfectly normal function, like menstruation, which rarely gave discomfort to primitive women, or to women of active, outdoor life, had come to be regarded as a periodic sickness. Girls were imbued with the idea that it must inevitably incapacitate them, and this pervasive suggestion, combined with bad physical habits, heavy and constrictive clothing, and inactivity, made it so. The period of gestation, which, among Indian and peasant women, and even among the vigorous farmers' wives of a hundred years ago, caused relatively slight inconvenience, had taken on the aspect of a prolonged, chronic illness.

As the young girl became anemic, and the young wife inactive, for want of vigorous, compulsory outdoor occupation, pregnancy became a serious discomfort, and childbirth a terror. At the very time when the prospective mother should have been developing her abdominal muscles and stimulating her nutrition to the utmost, the conventional prudery of the Nineteenth Century dictated a careful concealment of her condition. Among South European peoples prospective motherhood is a subject for public congratulation, but in America the " sacred duty " and the " only worthy sphere " was a thing to be concealed—a subject of jest and shameful innuendo. This degenerate prudery went so far in the middle of the Nineteenth Century that many girls were married in complete ignorance of their wifely functions, and were, in consequence, the victims of licensed, though unintentional, rape.

It was to be expected that girls, only partially informed about their physical destiny, and observing, as they grew up, the nasty attitude toward the pregnant woman, and her ashamed aspect, would acquire a repulsion for everything connected with motherhood. After overhearing the painful details of the discomforts of pregnancy and of agonizing childbirth, they could not help looking forward to marriage with fear. Such girls would want to marry, but they would be afraid of the consequences. It was not surprising that women began to search for and to take advantage of devices for preventing conception, nor that men who loved their wives should abet them in doing so.

At the time when the sciences were beginning to make their first helpful applications to common life, the health of American women was at a very low point. Pale, undeveloped, over-feminized wives were finding themselves wholly inadequate to the bearing and rearing of even small families, and the suggestive modesties which were demanded of conventionally educated girls prevented them from attaining any high degree of health. Such a state of things might have gone on indefinitely, to the extinction of the native-born American, perhaps, but for the advance of medicine, the gradual spread of hygienic knowledge, and their effects in liberating younger women from the traditions of prudery and inactivity.

But the process of freeing women from the tradition of weakness and bodily shame is a very slow one. Nearly two generations have elapsed since the Bloomer costume was mobbed; and it is only in exceptional places and for special purposes, such as horseback-riding, swimming, and gymnastics, that young women are permitted to reveal their two legs. Even yet the prospective mother must hide herself like a thief or a prostitute till after dark during the latter time of her pregnancy.

The majority of people who lived in the Nineteenth Century did not die of tuberculosis, typhoid fever, cancer, or even in accidents or in war—but in their beds after a period of lingering degeneration. In their last years they reaped the accumulated results of the petty, physiological misdeeds of their earlier life. It is a fact, too little dwelt upon in discussing the physiological limitations of womenkind, that all the minor causes of ill-health have operated with much greater injury upon them than upon men in civ-

ilized life.   A recent writer enumerates a few of
what he calls the commonest physical peccadilloes:

"The respiration of a very little impure air eighteen
times a minute eighteen times a day for twenty years; a few
foods preserved by injurious substances; teeth irregularly
brushed; stuffy sleeping-rooms; living-rooms excessively
upholstered; carpets full of dust; domestic atmosphere at
once motionless, furnace-dried, and kept at high tem-
perature; clothing impervious to sun and air; insufficient
baths; insufficient exercise; late hours; overwork; over-
eating; under-drinking (of water); eating and drinking
together instead of separately; and patent medicines; not
to mention in the case of woman, the strangling of her
vital organs by the stylish harness of society—these are
a few of those so-called 'negligible transgressions.'"

Nearly all of these degenerative influences affected the women of the past generation more
than they do the women of the present; but it
still remains true that, owing to conventionalities
of dress and behavior, to the sedentary character
of their occupations, and their relatively inactive,
indoor lives, they suffer from them far more seriously than men.

It is one of the ironies of social development
that, while ascetic religion has been a most powerful hindrance to women, the stage has become one
of the strongest influences to elevate our ideals
of pure beauty.   At the beginning of the Nineteenth Century the drama was generally regarded

in America as an evil influence, and an actress as a foredoomed prostitute. But in the last hundred years the stage has drawn to itself the highest productions of literary and scenic art, and the acting profession has produced some of the noblest human beings of our time. The vulgarities which appealed to the audiences of the Eighteenth Century are no longer tolerated in the better theaters; even Shakespeare has to be expurgated. While there is still too frequent appeal to the obscene mind in the poorer and cheaper theaters, the level of dramatic art is constantly rising. Dancing, from being an appeal merely to the lascivious imagination, has reached the plane of an art as fine in its tone as Grecian sculpture. The French ballet, with its affected and tortured movements, and its suggestive costume, is being more and more replaced by posture and folk dancing, in which the sensual is subordinated to beauty of line and form, to grace of movement, and to picturesque grouping.

All this has had a perceptible effect on the general standards of modesty, beauty, and taste, and especially among women. In proportion as the stage has become more " respectable," it has been patronized by the religiously minded, conventional middle classes, who have learned from it what a really beautiful human creature may be. The average American at the time of the Centennial, 1876, had seen once, or twice perhaps, a few bronze monuments, possibly a single gallery of poor and very proper paintings, and had probably never seen a nude statue in his life. The cultivation of the eye to enjoy symmetry and untrammeled grace has come chiefly through dramatic art in this country. As the public became accustomed to really beautiful women on the stage, the tightly corseted, flat-chested, thick-hipped figure, encased in mosaic clothing from the ears to the toes, began to look ugly.

The dress of the fashionable woman, too, has been revolutionized by the artistic ideal—a movement in which actresses have set the model and led the way. In the pursuit of novelty and to enhance her own personal charm, each actress has compelled the dressmakers—educated by the French fashion-plate—to devise new and ever more graceful draperies, and more exquisite combinations of color; until now the whole field of Oriental and European art is studied in pursuit of fresh ideas.

The new idea, to be sure, when once offered for admiration on the stage, is quickly snatched up by manufacturers and designers, and usually exaggerated, if not perverted, into some monstrous travesty of style. But at the swift pace of modern changes in fashion, the most extreme, although it is the first to be adopted by persons of crude taste, is also the first to be supplanted by another.   And, owing to the enormous variations produced in any one season in a single fashion, the various grades of taste, from crude to highly refined, will find satisfaction.

But the most conspicuous contribution of the stage to the emancipation of women lies in its liberation of legs and torso.   Good legs are an asset to a chorus girl, and, the city population having become accustomed to seeing them unashamed at the theater, is no longer shocked at a moderate display of ankles on the street.   The corset, worn originally for the distortion of the body to make its sex characters more conspicuous, became conventionalized in this exaggerated style.   The fashion-plate figure admired in the last century was truly hideous—as far from flexibility and grace as the form of the lady of the Civil War period was from that of the Laughing Bacchante. But stage beauties, as a mere matter of business, have demanded innumerable variations, which have stimulated the corsetière to devise models for mitigating the most imperfect figures.   The straight-front corset, an invention for distributing the abdominal flesh, has, in ten years, revolutionized the ideas of every country woman in America, as to what a " good figure " should be. Thousands of women have seen Madame Sara Bernhardt, when long past middle age, play

L'Aiglon, the part of a youth of nineteen; and many more thousands read the interviews in which she explained how she kept her youthful figure by muscular activity and hygienic living. Such examples, and the industrious careers of a large number of actresses at the present day, are having an astonishing reaction upon the physique and dress of young women of the domestic type.

In addition to the correction and cultivation of taste the stage has had an incalculable influence upon the standards of health among women. The actress, the dancer, and the prima donna must have, before all talent, strength to endure the training and the hardships of her profession. However sensual and violent her temper may be, to win success she must deny her appetites and work—work incredibly hard. With the never-ceasing curiosity of the general public regarding the lives of stage people, these facts have become known, and in their dissemination have educated every stage-struck girl as well as many feeble amateurs.

The modification of religious dogma, the discoveries of science and their application to common life, the development of dramatic art, and the practice of physical exercise—these and other less important influences are the first steps toward separating physical beauty from its exclusive association with sensual images. Health and

beauty are becoming legitimate aims for the en-
richment of life, as well as for the elevation of the
race.   Scientific discovery and medical skill are
emancipating women from the enervating complaints once thought inherent in femaleness, but
due in fact to constricting conditions of life, to
over-breeding, and to the contamination of
venereal diseases.   Physical training, the development of the body by systematic activity, which has
only in the last quarter of the century become acceptable, is doing away with the prudery in which
girls were once reared, and preparing them for a
kind of motherhood no longer blindly instinctive,
but adequate and intelligent.   Beauty is no longer
merely " vain," nor favor inevitably deceitful—
and the fruit of her hands shall yet praise her.

CHAPTER VII

THE PURSUIT OF DRESS

"We have plucked up a little spirit and have even signed a sort of feeble declaration of independence against our old enemies, French fashions and perfect uniformity in dress. How well I remember a certain spring season in my childhood, when every woman between the age of fourteen and forty wore a yellow straw bonnet trimmed with green ribbon on the outside and pink on the inside! And that summer, after Napoleon III.'s campaign in Italy, when no respectable person thought of having her bonnet trimmed with any other color than solferino or magenta. . . .

"The study of dress in these days is an approved branch of female education. It has never been wholly neglected, only women have too often pursued it with their eyes shut, and now they mean to keep them open. . . .

"Whether Woman is behind Man in civilization because she pays an attention to dress which she long ago disused, or whether her devotion to it is because Man requires her to be robed in gay attire . . . we are expected in this age to pay more attention to dress than men do, and are justified in doing so— within limits."—From *Social Customs*—FLORENCE HOWE HALL, 1887.

"To get emancipated from Man, or the political sovereignty of men in the State, is a very small matter and a victory quite insignificant compared with the conquest of Fashion."—HORACE BUSHNELL.

THE excessive and universal interest in dress displayed by American women, has been, like many other qualities, denominated " feminine,"

but has been only superficially accounted for.
Whether, as the sociologists suggest, it be
analogous to the gorgeous pelage and plumage
assumed by certain animals in the mating season;
or whether it be associated with caste and class
distinctions in society, one primary factor must
not be overlooked. Before the Nineteenth Century luxury in dress and toilet was quite as characteristic of men of any given rank as of their
womankind. Since the decline of elaborate
clothing among men is historically so recent, the
significant point to be raised is: why has not the
modern woman's interest in personal adornment
declined in the same degree?

In the discussion of dress, as of politics, the
American and the French Revolutions form a
convenient landmark. When the coterie of
Marie Antoinette played at dairying in the cos-
tumes of shepherds and maids, it might be regarded as a mere vagary of idle persons in search
of a new sensation. But when the whole French
nation assumed the dress of plain citizens; and
when the American gentleman laid aside his
peruke and lace ruffles, and went to work in the
costume of the common man, it signified that the
theories of democracy had taken a profound hold
on the human mind. In the United States the absence of a large aristocratic class and the hardy
life of a pioneer population tended to reduce

men's clothing to the simple requirements of utility and cleanliness.   Even for men of wealth and
station, a single " costume de luxe " served every
purpose.   Thus, at the beginning of the Nineteenth Century, dress as an important pursuit in
life was confined to a small class of fine ladies,
while the women of the mercantile and agricultural masses, busied with domestic manufactures,
gave scarcely more attention to fripperies and
changes in style than did their menkind.

In all ages clothing has been one of the first
items of living to be affected by increasing prosperity.   In proportion as the family surplus increased among Americans, it was exhibited in
richer materials and greater variety of clothes—
at first for use on Sundays and gala days alone.
But as the poor, the well-to-do, and the rich were
more clearly distinguished into classes, elegance
in dress became in this country, as elsewhere, the
mark of the least industrious section of society.
And in the latter part of the century, as we shall
see, an occupation in itself for the semi-idle and
protected woman.   The coincidence of great
prosperity, arising in part from universal habits
of industry among all classes of men, with the
gradual release of large numbers of women from
severe household labor by the removal of manufacture from the home to the factory, gave women
money and leisure.   Having slight intellectual im-

pulse toward self-culture, and no conception of philanthropy as a career, such as now engages much of the leisure of protected women, they devoted themselves to the elaboration of their clothes.

The ideals set before the boy and the girl by the parents and the teachers of this period were diametrically opposed: the boy must prepare to *do* something, the girl merely to *be* attractively feminine. One aimed directly at achievement, the other had no definite aim, but was encouraged to concentrate her attention on manners and appearance. Indirectly a premium was put on prettiness and docility in girls, with a covert suggestion that they might find an ultimate reward in marriage. Among young men, marriage was only one, and by no means the first, of several aims in life; while among girls—though not often consciously acknowledged—it was the chief ambition, because, on the one hand, wifehood and motherhood was the accepted and only creditable career, and, on the other, there was no wage-earning occupation, as there is now, offered as an alternative.

Since young women were properly the chosen, and not the choosers of their fate, they necessarily resorted to every indirect method of attracting a partner. Striking and elaborate apparel was the easiest and most conspicuous means of allurement.

This efflorescence—not unlike the mating display among animals—was part of the appropriate behavior during courtship, and to some extent was affected by young men as well as maidens. Grave attention to neckties, the fit of clothing, and the use of hair and shaving cosmetics, was as common a symptom of the wooer as color, grace, and coquetry were of the wooed, but declined even more rapidly when the wooing-game gave place to the marital partnership.

In these displays the young were encouraged by their parents, partly out of affectionate pride, but chiefly, no doubt, as a way of calling attention to their rising standard in life. For in this freer country it was the mark of a good parent to give his children the opportunity and the means of attaining a higher social plane. The sons of sober, industrious people were permitted to splurge into smoking, drinking, horse-flesh, and sports; the daughters were released from the heavier household tasks to spend their time in contriving flirtation, finery, and fancy-work. Long before the destined husband appeared, the bride-to-be was preparing household linen, and accumulating the requisite dozens of hand-made undergarments trimmed with hundreds of yards of crochet, tatting, and embroidery. In all this elaboration there was, fortunately, some opportunity for the development of the artistic sense, and a training in thoroughness of detail, which later found application to the perfection of domestic matters.

Mixed up with the conventional theory of marriage as the suitable outlet for woman's ability, there was also a general opinion that one of her secondary functions should be " to please," not only all marriageable men, but society at large. This involved incessant attention to appearances, to manners, and to lively conversation. Young women, therefore, spent a good deal of their time in pleasing and piquing each other—practising, so to speak, the art by which their future station might be secured, and which would perfect them in the graces expected of leisurely womenkind. The art of setting off the person with beautiful clothes, carefully put on and enhanced with grace of manner, required constant rehearsal, and this, in turn, resulted in competition among women to see who could attain the highest standard.

Women gradually devised, as their occupations came to be less and less directly productive, a round of social functions in which men had little or no part, and in which they found stimulation for their ultra-feminine tastes and trivial duties, to take up the time which, in a previous generation, would have been employed in domestic industries. When marriage provided them—according to the theory—with plenty to do, it was supposed that this harmless and pretty efflorescence of the young female would cease.   As a matter of fact, when the income of the new household was not enough to afford plenty of service, and when children came promptly, it did stop abruptly.   The worn-out trousseau was replaced with few and serviceable garments; the delicate bridal lingerie was often laid away to yellow because it would cost too much labor to launder it; and the young mother, struggling with duties for which she had almost no preparation, was content to dress her babies elaborately, while herself relapsing prematurely into the plainness deemed suitable to motherhood and middle-age.

But when a girl had had urged upon her from babyhood the vital importance of dress; when she had spent not less than ten years of her life in adornment as one of the chief aims of her existence, making a game of it, and enjoying the zest of competition, she did not all at once lose her taste for pretty clothes, even though diverted by motherhood.   If her husband was of the sort who observed such matters, and wished her to please the public as well as himself by her appearance, she might have encouragement to continue after marriage the arts which had filled up her girlish days.   Wherever money is easily made,

as it was in the Nineteenth-Century America,
men are generous with it; but in such a pioneer
society men had not the leisure to cultivate the
habits of luxurious expenditure, and they left to
the woman the function of " vicarious consump-
tion." Her costly and troublesome clothes were
comparable, according to Professor Veblen, to
" the livery of the chief menial of the household."
In default of men's leisure the wife became the
social representative of the family, expressing in
her person, in her entertainments, and her engagements, the rising social status and the degree
of her husband's financial success.

Beyond this, to what degree the lack of absorbing duty and labor on the one hand, and, on
the other, the appetite for amusement, have contributed to the elaboration of dress by married
women, it is not easy to say; but these were unquestionably some of the reasons for prolonging
the excessive absorption of young girls in their
appearance, into the later life of women. The
pursuit of the fashions afforded satisfaction,
moreover, to the desire for variety and novelty;
and here originality and taste found expression.
Thus a variety of economic and social motives
added to the initial impulse of self-adornment in
women a force out of all proportion to its normal value. Under similar circumstances, and
denied so apparently harmless a diversion, men

were accustomed to resort to sports and vice, to gambling, racing, and athletics.

Aside from these two main influences—increasing leisure and great prosperity—another of even greater force was set in motion by the increase of machine-made goods in the latter half of the past century. Until then, rapidly changing fashions had been within the reach of only a small upper class; while all other classes in society continued to wear for generations, almost unaltered, the distinctive dress which marked them off from those above and below them. In the New Democracy, in proportion as the boundaries of class were blurred and obliterated by successful men passing up from a lower to a higher stratum, and taking their womankind with them, the fashion of clothing became more varied, especially among the younger members of the family. And always the women had more time than men to give to these insignia of affluence.

So long, however, as materials and garments continued to be hand-made, the fashions remained, as compared with our day, relatively stable. Too much labor and time was consumed in producing garments for the ordinary person to discard them before they were worn out. The socks, which cost the housewife days of labor in the knitting, besides the expense of yarn, had to be darned and patched and refooted; while in our time they are so cheap that the traveling man and the prospector might almost be trailed by the unwashed pairs he leaves at each stopping-place. The element of irreplaceableness in determining use and value, which now applies to only a few accessories of dress, such as lace, jewels, rare shawls, and the like, once applied to nearly all good clothes. As invention brought about the rapid and comparatively inexpensive production of dress materials, and then of ready-made clothing, the variety of stuffs for clothing increased, and the incentive for women to vary their clothing was immensely augmented.

The manufacturer and the merchant, mean-while, set out to sell an ever-increasing product by coaxing the consumer to throw away the old garment long before it was worn out, and to buy new; and, as if this were not inducement enough, the designer, the tailor, and the dressmaker added a threat in the shape of that Bug-a-boo, Being-out-of-Fashion. Thus Fashion, once the amuse-ment of the highly born and the leisurely, and associated with " reputable futility," became, in the Nineteenth Century, the principal means of stimulating trade. Its subtle tyranny has spread far beyond the original limits of class distinction and occupation: determining the width of mourning-crape and the designs of household furniture; the color of men's hats and the type of auto-cars; the length of hair and the brand of whiskey; the size of trousers and the markings of thoroughbred animals.

Its coercion, now primarily commercial, is felt by men as well as women, though not, perhaps, to the same extent. To be out-of-style marks a man as being unsophisticated or unsuccessful—characters not to be endured except by the day laborer, the artist, and the scholar. Nor do men, as a class, rise superior to this social convention; they merely restrict their changes of clothing to a narrower range of more practicable garments, exercising their taste by proxy, and leave to their wives or a haberdashery expert the determination of what they shall wear. The standardization of men's clothing has reduced them to a certain uniformity of appearance, and has produced a class of clerks whose business it is to act as arbiters of fashion, but it has not done away with the necessity of keeping up with the styles. One has only to recall the punctilious and agonizing care with which modest gentlemen of infrequent social excursions attend to every detail of their evening-dress, to realize that not even they can tolerate with courage the possibility of seeming queer in the eyes of their friends.

Even less can any man endure that his wife or his sister should appear out-of-date, a dowdy or an esthetic freak in dress. When monstrous hats recently came into fashion, the newspapers and mankind generally belabored women with ridicule in order to remove these obscurations at the theater. Yet quite as powerful as the conservatism of women in delaying the reform, was the reluctance of every individual man to let *his* womankind be the first to begin it. The inconsistencies produced in women by the domination of the styles are well-matched by those among men of crude and traditional tastes, who inveigh against the extravagance and vagaries of the other sex, and yet no less openly give their admiration to the most " stylish " women of their acquaintance. Whatever they may say, most men want their own women-folk to be dressed " with the best," and this is, in itself, aside from the stimulus of an ever-changing display, the most potent influence in making older women as well as young girls devote an inordinate attention to self-adornment.

Nothing more aptly illustrates the control which men exercise over the type of women's clothing than the rise and decline of the various dress-reform movements of the Nineteenth Century. Of these the best known and one of the shortest-lived was the street dress misnamed the " Bloomer " costume. Designed for the relief of invalid women from the heavy skirts of the

Civil War period, it was adopted and worn in Washington by a beautiful and cultivated woman whose prestige led to other women—most of them connected with the Woman's Rights movement—adopting it.   It consisted of a short skirt to the boot-tops, at first, with Turkish trousers, afterwards buttoned gaiters, underneath.   It must be granted that it was a sensible and modest, if not perfectly graceful costume.   Yet the violence of men, expressed through the newspapers, and the vulgarities of street mobs, made it impossible for women of the most irreproachable reputations to wear the costume, as the following quotation will show:

" The outcry against it extended from one end of the country to the other; the Press howled in derision, the pulpit hurled its anathemas, and the rabble took up the refrain.   On the streets of the larger cities the women were followed by mobs of men and boys . . . throwing sticks and stones and giving three cheers and a tiger ending in the loudest of groans.   Sometimes these demonstrations became so violent that the women were obliged to seek refuge . . . their husbands and children refused to be seen with them in public, and they were wholly ostracized by other women.

" With the exception of Gerrit Smith, all the prominent men, Garrison, Phillips, Channing, May, were bitterly opposed to the short dress, and tried to dissuade the women from wearing it by every argument in their power.   The costume, however, was adopted as a matter

of principle, and for it they suffered a martyrdom which
would have made burning at the stake seem comfortable.
. . . No pen can describe what these women endured for
the two or three years in which they tried to establish this
principle, through such sacrifice as only a woman can understand." *

When the bifurcated costume was revived in a
modified form toward the end of the Nineteenth
Century by the vogue of the bicycle, it was joy-
fully adopted by a large number of modest but
active young women; and it shortly went out of
use, chiefly because the more conservative men
did not want their feminine companions to be conspicuous.   This illustrates another of the anom-
alies of dress: A woman might make herself very
conspicuous—indeed, was encouraged to do so—
by the novel and bizarre aspect of her dress, so
long as it followed the newest mode from Paris,
but she was always dubbed " strong-minded," or
worse, if she made herself conspicuous by merely
being rational.

In addition to economic motives and the necessity of pleasing men, there are other lesser considerations leading to excessive emphasis on personal adornment.   Whether girls have inher-
ently more artistic impulse than boys, may be
questioned; but there is no doubt that women have
a more cultivated taste in clothing and furnishing

* Harper, *Life and Work of S. B. Anthony*, Vol. I, p. 112.

than men.   It is a difference arising largely from education and incessant attention on the part of women, for the male dressmaker, the male artist, and the curio dealer often have as refined, if not as conventional, a sense of color and design as the woman milliner and the fine lady.   Whatever artistic impulse girls may have had in past times, was expressed within the limits of dress, house decoration, and gardening; and its restriction within these narrow fields served probably to intensify the more fundamental motives, leading them to constantly elaborate and make over their clothes, and to redecorate and refurnish their houses.

The ornamentation of even the most hideously furnished houses of the past century discloses an astonishing amount of crude potential art-sense in the housewife.   The rag carpet, for instance, cleverly woven from the bits of worn clothing, although displaced by ugly patterns of factory-made floor coverings, has now come back again with the revival of art handicrafts.   Fashion, which now encourages originality at any rate in the designers and purveyors of goods, formerly perverted and suppressed it.   If the ability which our grandmothers expended on rag-rugs and woven bedspreads had been turned into channels more free and stimulating, outside as well as inside the house, the artistic capacity and impulse of the modern woman might be much better developed than it is.

Indirectly, the increase in variety of materials stimulated both men and women to desire a greater diversity of clothes. Because men's garments earlier became standarized, the multiformity of materials and modes played within a narrower range; but in women's dress it has, as yet, found no limit. The delicacy and manifold beauty of textiles; the infinite number of patterns; and the constantly changing styles have stimulated the desires of women for varied clothing, just as the ever-widening range of foods in the hotels and restaurants have taught men to demand a larger variety of more elaborately prepared dishes on their home tables. Fragility of texture, too, has been emphasized, until durability has become an essential only of the most expensive articles. That a thing should be showy and stylish was much more desirable than that it should be lasting. When fashions in the accessories of dress, such as collars, ties, bags, gloves, handkerchiefs, stockings, petty jewelry, combs, et cetera, came to be changed at least once or twice a year, the more quickly they grew shabby, the sooner the consumer would be justified in buying new ones. In the case of women, the mere habit of indoor living, which permitted the use of perishable and delicate clothing, in turn reacted to make them want frequent changes; while in the measure that they were at leisure they welcomed dress as an occupation affording an outlet for taste and a variety of interest to break the insipid monotony of their lives.

Briefly, then, the pursuit of dress as a serious matter by a larger number of women than ever before in the history of the world, has been primarily due to a number of political, social, and commercial influences, for which women themselves were not responsible. It was one of the first signs that the " ages of deficit " were ended, and the era of surplus arrived. It was one of the earliest expressions of democratic principles, and, as invention and manufacture have developed, it has become the approved means of promoting trade. And these national forces were acting throughout the Nineteenth Century with constantly increasing strength upon women. The degree of female receptiveness depended upon two things: the amount of leisure, and the extent to which they had imbibed the tradition that a lovely appearance was the quality most to be desired in woman. This beauty-cult is now fast becoming secondary among well-educated women to the cultivation of the mind and the practice of gentle manners. Why, then, do the majority of women still pursue the vagaries of fashion so madly? Because the average woman does not easily outgrow impressions stamped upon her by the traditions of her kind, we must turn for an explanation to the effect of the pursuit of dress upon her personal character.

CHAPTER VIII

CLOTHES AND CHARACTER

"He that is proud of the russling of his silks like a madman laughs at the rattling of his fetters. For, indeed, Clothes ought to be our remembrancers of our lost innocency."—THOMAS FULLER.

"Thy Clothes are all the Soul thou hast."—BEAUMONT and FLETCHER.

EVER since the Civil War the amount of time and expense put upon dress by women in this country has been increasing, until now it has become the chief occupation and the accepted amusement of a very large number of those above the laboring class. It has been generally assumed that this is due to some inherent personal taste on the part of women; but it is a matter of economic history, as we have already seen, that dress as a pursuit has been the result of the development of manufacture and of modern methods of trade promotion rather than of an innate frivolity, to which leisure and idleness have always contributed.

When we visualize the typical jeweler, deft-handed, short-sighted, and stoop-shouldered; or the drygoods clerk, radiating smiles and ladylike manners; or the politician, swollen with self-confidence and over-eating; we do not assume that he could never have been any other sort of man, even though his natural temperament may have dictated his choice of occupation. It is taken for granted in explaining such men that their ambitions in life have been molded by their environment to produce certain types of physique and character. It is a matter of common experience that there are very few human beings so specialized by their hereditary qualities that they could not have been different had they been born in another environment than the one in which we see them. When they are so specialized they are called eccentrics, and sometimes recognized as having genius.

One has only to observe the modifications of character and habits which take place in men who change from one industrial medium to another, requiring very different qualifications, to infer that women of the same breed might show unexpected variations if their environment were as varied and as stimulating. The effect of social surroundings in developing in women an inordinate love of adornment can be best measured, perhaps, by contemplating other and rather unusual types produced by exceptional circumstances. During the past century, wherever a girl, by force of circumstance or natural hatred of physical restraint, refused to submit to the tyranny of dress, she became almost invariably and, it might almost be said, by virtue thereof, a superior human being. The wives of the California pioneers, brought up like other Eastern girls to give the utmost care to their dress, when transplanted to isolated homes on ranches and in mining camps, without servants, and often compelled to do the labor of a large household, while rearing their families, almost always emancipated their bodies from the trammels of long skirts and from corsets. Utility and cleanliness became the sole requisites of their clothing, and thus was released a vast amount of physical and mental energy to be spent in other and worthier directions. They managed complicated households, reared vigorous children, in emergencies guarded water-rights and mining properties with a shotgun; and in their old age were as fearless, as able-bodied, as warm-hearted, and as capable as their partners.

The influence of the Quaker costume and plain traditions in minimizing feminine and developing larger human qualities in women is registered in the Woman's Rights movement, in which the Friends played so large a part between 1840 and 1870. Lucretia Mott, the Quaker preacher, an exquisite, gentle, frail, and yet brilliant woman, was doubtless the most important figure among all the delegates to the World's Convention in

London.   Clothes were the least of all concerns
to her, we may infer, for she wrote of herself:

"My life, in the domestic sphere, has passed much as
that of other wives and mothers in this country.   I have
had six children.   Not accustomed to resigning them to
the care of a nurse, I was much confined to them during
their infancy and childhood.   Being fond of reading, I
omitted much unnecessary stitching and ornamental work
in the sewing for my family, so that I might have time
for this indulgence and for the improvement of the mind.
For novels and light reading I never had much taste.
The 'Ladies' Department' in the periodicals of the day
had no attraction for me."

By dwelling on such exceptional women, it may
be possible to conceive what the effect of ornamentation as a principal aim in life has been upon
the greater number of average young girls
brought up in middle-class homes.   To them dress
involved a constant consideration of money—
how to get it without directly entering the wage-
earning class; how far it might be made to go,
and even how things might be got without it.
Money has rarely been looked at in the large by
women as income or capital, but rather as a succession of petty, irregular sums to be spread over
a thousand necessities and luxuries.   Because the
husband and father was the earning partner he
was inevitably the financial head, paying the larger
household expenses himself, and handing out to

the wife and minor children for their clothing and incidentals such generous or niggardly pin-money as his temperament and means dictated. The effect upon women was similar to that of an irregular wage upon the casual workingman; there was no incentive to thrift, but every inducement to shortsighted and petty extravagance. There was never butter to cover a whole slice of bread, therefore why trouble about butter at all?—why not have a string of imitation pearls?—so women naturally reasoned. Expenditure dribbled along on the hand-to-mouth principle: a girl might need hat, shoes, underwear, all at once, but, as the sum given her at any one time was never enough to cover them all, she naturally bought the hat first, the shoes next, and postponed the underwear, making the best appearance she could. A constantly rising scale of dress accessories often cut off—among poorer girls—garments, and even food, necessary to health.

Such a perversion of judgment in the distribution of income was, and is still, quite characteristic of the average woman. I have known a mother of a family, living on a scale of several thousand a year, in a pretty house, among cultivated people, who set a meager luncheon (when her husband was absent), and never had blankets enough for all the beds, who, nevertheless, " had to have " solid silver and cut glass on her table, and décolleté dinner dresses, in order to feel happy and respectable. There are many others of the same type, who find money to buy pretty clothes and artistic house furnishings, but never to pay adequately for house-services. A woman who lived on a scale twice that of a college professor, who was always beautifully gowned and bejeweled, seriously asked that a university should give her son a scholarship because the standard of living expected of people in their social position did not permit them to send their son through college, nor admit of his working his own way. A lecturer on dress reform, who urged that one conservative tailor-made suit, with the necessary accessories, bought carefully each year, was the most economical way of being well dressed, was continually met by the objection that her hearers could not save up enough ahead to get what they needed all at once.

Even when the woman had a regular allowance her sense of proportion was seldom developed to the point of providing the necessities first, and choosing among a thousand luxuries afterwards. Yet that such lack of judgment is due rather to lack of education in personal finance than to sex may be illustrated by the idiosyncrasies of college boys in the same matters. The college boy usually pays his board bill, because he must eat, and he buys such books as he cannot borrow; but he lets the laundryman and the tailor wait, sometimes indefinitely, wears a sweater and corduroys not merely because he is lazy and they are a sort of collegiate livery, but to economize. He thinks himself justifiably " cute " when he arrives at home in vacation so shabby that his foolish parents insist on presenting him with new clothes without reflecting that he spent in unreported extravagances what should have clothed him properly.

It is evident enough without further illustration that, because women did not earn their money, and received it irregularly in small amounts, they had no occasion to develop a balanced financial sense; but acquired, on the one hand, a wonderful skill in spreading petty amounts thinly over large areas, and, on the other, a perverted judgment of values. If this had produced in them only a petty thrift and foolish expenditure, the remedy would be obvious and easy; but it has, in truth, eaten into character much more deeply. For the love of dress and the necessity of satisfying it by getting it from some man who earned it, made girls from their childhood contrive, deceive, and manœuver. It is a common enough joke that men are better-humored after dinner than before, but among women it is a commonplace quite without any humorous color. Every dependent creature, whether woman or child, peon or dog, as a matter of safety or comfort, learns to read the temper of his master; and in proportion as he is able to play upon it, finds life easier. Wheedling and cunning, the whole battery of feminine weapons from caresses to tears and temper, were inevitably employed upon negligent and selfish men by their dependents; and often to the extent of imposition upon generous men.

Sometimes, when there was no man to supply an income, or the man was too unremunerative, the woman resorted to other means of eking out her purse without appearing to work for a living. The business of the Woman's Exchange was originally devised to give the untrained gentlewoman a chance to market her products without being known. Many a woman, who, in our day, would go into a shop or become a typist, tried to keep herself within the pale of her social class by selling, surreptitiously, embroideries and pastry. While even yet the society girl, whose standard of dress must be kept up as a matter of convention, receives the second-hand dealer quietly at her home, and turns her slightly worn evening dresses into money, which may be spent for those of the latest mode.

If the initial expense in time, money, and thought required in stylish dressing had been all that the pursuit demanded, as it has been generally among men, it might be worth the price, for good appearance has everywhere a recognized value in the world. But it did not end there, as in the case of a man who might purchase a whole outfit and its accessories at one or two stores, and, after a few days, put it on with the assurance that for six months at least he was properly clothed. In our country the ready-made clothing industries have greatly diminished the amount of time and attention necessary to procure the essentials, even of women's clothing, but this is of quite recent date, and has not by any means done away with the minute attention which has to be bestowed on every detail if a woman wishes to attain the recognized standard.

The stylish woman had forever to pursue that will-o'-the-wisp of fashion, " the newest thing," not only in boots, stockings, lingerie, dresses, and hats, but also the latest-uttermost-refinement-of-the-newest-thing in braids, lace, embroidery, beads, passementerie, trimmings, of which there were hundreds of designs rapidly succeeding each other. There were, besides, an infinitude of shades, widths, textile surfaces in an ever-enlarging variety of stuffs; and these had to be combined by herself or the dressmaker, after consultation of several American and French fashion books, in the momentarily approved design. And all this energy was expended without hope of anything more than temporary success, except for those who could make over or replace the garment to meet the next incoming fashion.

The making-over of clothes every year, if not every six months, as the pace of fashion speeded up, came to take the place of many of those spurious handicrafts with which the clever woman of the mid-century had been wont to busy her hands. It became a matter of pride with those of small means to "make something out of nothing," as the complimentary phrase went— to contrive a new and stylish dress out of two old ones; to conceal paucity of material by piecing small bits of cloth together, and decorating the tell-tale seams; to make a jacket of a man's discarded overcoat, lined with the less-worn portions of an old silk petticoat. As the rule of Fashion spread to carpets, curtains, bedding, and furniture, the inexorable principle of multiplying designs to stimulate buying, invaded this field as well; and the devoted housewife, according to her means and her ingenuity, conscientiously set herself the duty of keeping her house as well as herself and children "in the Fashion." In all this she exercised her brain as much as her manufacturing grandmother had done before her, but with infinitely less of real value to show for it.

Perhaps all the more because the result did not command satisfactory appreciation from her men-folk, whose crude tastes and practical turn of mind did not readily grasp the desperate need of women to be in the fashion, she required the approval of other womankind.   So much struggle and economy must be worthy of recognition; and if, unhappily, her men friends did not notice and praise the triumphs of her ingenious—and often wasted—skill, she turned to other women to secure their proper appraisal.   It is no doubt true that women competing in the dress contest are often jealous of each other, but it is far more significant that they have devised a code of manners with which to satisfy each other's hunger for appreciation.   Each agrees to admire, or, at any rate, to appear to admire, the other's dress. When two women meet, it is customary, after the conventional greeting, for one to say: " How pretty your new hat is! "   And for the other to reply: " I'm so glad you like it—I saw the new shape at Smith's Emporium, and I trimmed it with the velvet off my last winter's hat."   When this topic has been canvassed to the satisfaction of the wearer of the hat, she in turn will compliment her friend's taste and ingenuity by praising something she is wearing.   In such wise have women expended their perverted abilities and kindliness, spurred on by the race of commercial fashion, and lacking an education in larger things.

Dress, moreover, came to take the place of healthful exercise and recreation. The lazy afternoon parade through the shopping streets, to see the newest fashions displayed four times a year at the change of seasons, became a weekly excursion as the varieties of materials and style increased. And in our day many women of small means know scarcely any other way of spending their leisure except to drag a fretful child past the shop windows every weekday afternoon; and then to go home and try to copy the most violent combinations of color and the most striking designs in slazy, cheap imitations.

It is a trite old saying that a man with a champagne taste and a beer income is sure of trouble. In women a similar desire for display, gratified at the cost of the earning power of which they themselves have no direct experience, is equally disastrous in producing effeminacy and discontent. The capacity for detail developed through a thousand generations of domestic necessity has been turned into a few narrow channels, the chief of which has at last come to be the pursuit of dress. Their age-long economy has become shortsighted pinching in some, and equally ill-judged extravagance in others. And the constant chase after fashions which no amount of money would enable them to really come up with has produced a state of chronic dissatisfaction with themselves, their lot, and with the men who supply their in-come.   Petty-mindedness has at last become the distinguishing characteristic of the average woman.   The marvelous thrift which enables her to dress stylishly on a small sum; the originality with which she contrives and imitates ever-new prettinesses; the ingenuity with which she makes a good show on small resources—all these valuable but perverted qualities would, if applied to the larger problems of common life, clean up the cities, find a home for every normal child, and reform our haphazard domestic economy; and would produce that sureness of aim, that sense of being a useful cog in the world's machinery, with-out which no human being can be happy.

One has only to listen to the conversation of women among themselves to realize that clothes are sure to come to the top.   From the latest sensation in the newspapers or the last play, the talk drifts quickly around to the newest departure in fashions proposed by the *Ladies' Scrap-Bag,* the pretty knitted capes for babies depicted in the last number of the *Perambulator,* or the wonder-ful bargains in petticoats to be had at Rosen-berg's.   They skip from topic to topic without apparent logic, each new subject being suggested by the speaker's latest interest in dress.   Since the experience of the domestic woman was necessarily limited to a certain round of topics—clothes, cooking, servants, and children—her conversation had rarely any continuity, because her life had none. It consisted rather of hopping from one unrelated fact to another without that impulse of a ball lightly tossed back and forth by which an intelligent conversation is developed. When opportunity offered, her talk degenerated into that bog of narrowness and ill-breeding, a monologue of her personal grievances.

The female mind, thus fed on details of ephemeral importance, had no reason for larger intellectual interests; and constant occupation with the attainment of the correct accessories of her costume left little leisure for reading. Such books as she found time for would naturally be of the emasculated sort, whose heroines were the beautiful and perfectly dressed kind she strove to be; to whom impossible, but perfectly moral, adventures happened, until they culminated in a blissful engagement. For a quarter of a century at least, the Sunday-school novel and magazines of the type of Godey's *Lady's Book* supplied the mental pabulum of the majority of American women. The magazines inculcated the pursuit of dress as a most important duty of woman, as part of the ideal of gentility and religion set before the perfect lady.

And if it be thought that women no longer feed on this anemic literary diet, one has only to examine any one of the strictly feminine journals to learn how pervasive it still is. Many of them prófit by, if they are not published in, the interest of trade and manufactures for women, and it is highly important to them that the love of dress should be intensified. From one of them, which may be matched by many others published in 1910, I quote the following passage:

" Indeed, all women in this enlightened age study the subject of dress in a way so thorough that it would have been considered irreligious a century ago. Now, it is as well understood and accepted as any other duty, for being well-dressed, which means suitably dressed, imparts the serenity and poise which make for happiness; and the woman who is happy and well-poised makes everybody around her better and more serene."

This harping on the " duty " of being well-dressed, which is, in plain English, an invitation to throw away the old and buy new, whether the woman can afford it or not, is the stock in trade of the Fashion writers:

" Since hats first came into fashion woman has found them an inexhaustible source of interest. The quest for becomingness is always fascinating, and though we do not always find it, it is every woman's duty to make the most of herself. . . .

" It has become wellnigh impossible to create anything sensational in the way of a hat. Extreme size and over-abundance of trimming have ceased to surprise."

In the same magazine I find another appeal to the feminine conscience:

"There never was a time when Dame Fashion's hair-dresser made it so possible for every woman to look her best as now. No matter what her features, she can make them appear to the best advantage by adopting the most becoming style of hair-dressing. . . . It is a common fault of women that they fail to realize the importance of making the most of their crowning glory—the hair."

In an article on the mistakes of women in dressing, the matter is put on a higher plane:

"The study of clothes is considered to be a good deal of a frivolous subject, unworthy of thought or consideration by serious people; and yet to attain the good taste which results thereby, and which means true simplicity and good art in clothes, requires the same effort and thought which are necessary to reach a high standard in any other art worthy of the name."

The elderly woman is then encouraged not to let herself be left behind by the statement that "fashion no longer relegates the woman past the youthful years to circumscribed styles . . . as worn but a short time ago;" and the crafty expert in female psychology then gives a page of charming heads of middle-aged women with lovely complexions, regular features, and not a wrinkle, encased in the smartest of hats—not in

bonnets.   The plain elderly woman is still further
tolled along by such phrases as " these have more
dignity," or " have an indefinable sense of fitness," until, by the time the sheet is finished, a
thousand women are convinced not only that they
must have a new hat, but that this particular new
style will make them young and beautiful.

In order to focus the feminine mind on the
spring fashions—and incidentally to sell their
wares—another journal has a clever article on
the Paris dressmakers, in which we are led to see
the poetry of design, in this wise :

" For there is something in the atmosphere of Paris
. . . that seems to create a desire for lovely things and
to furnish dressmakers with an incentive and an inspiration for their work. . . . Perhaps it is because Paris has
always been a sort of playground for rich men and lovely
women, exquisites with whom pleasure is a life study,
dress a fine art, beauty a religion.

" If the dressmakers do not create their styles out of
thin air they at least have a wizardry of touch that makes
the dross of the commonplace turn into pure gold in their
hands. . . . Manufacture is rather a sordid term, perhaps, to apply to the turning out of masterpieces that
will surprise and delight the expectant public at the coming openings."

After a résumé of the dominating characteristics of the styles, this subtle promoter of novelty

soothes us into the delusion that, after all, we are not compelled to adopt any one of the new ideas:

" Further than that no one, not even the dressmakers themselves, can say what will be worn, for the decision on a new style or a change in an old style rests with the public.   Ultimately by continually harping on one string the dressmakers may lure the populace into dancing the tune they pipe, but they cannot force it.   They can only lead and suggest, and make their suggestions so attractive that the public, like a spoiled child, drops its old toy and reaches out its hand to grasp the new."

Since the days of the forties, when French fashion-plates were successfully introduced, this sort of literature has been served up to make women buy new, and always more fantastic, clothing.   It requires no great acumen to conclude that it would inevitably lead to extravagance. Having no responsibility for earning their own money— though indirectly they might, nevertheless, earn it—and very little experience in handling it, except in small amounts, they did not reckon its value in the large.   And having been encouraged to concentrate their energies on appearance, they came to have a highly cultivated taste—nay, more than taste, appetite—for pretty clothes which, like an appetite for drink or games of chance, must be satisfied.   Yet it, like many another social habit, could never be satisfied.   It might also be said that the more time and money they had to give to dress, the more discontented they were sure to be. If the father or husband could not meet this rising demand, they pitied themselves for his lack of success; if he set a limit of expenditure, they regarded him as a selfish brute. Now and then they degenerated into dishonest schemers, running up large bills for which their menkind were responsible; cheating the dressmaker and the milliner; sending back garments as unsatisfactory after wearing them; practising the deceits of the adventuress in the guise of a respectable woman of society.

Yet, in justice to womankind, it must be granted that the dress-mania produced very few of these types, as compared with hundreds of conscientious, economical women, who, misled by the conventions of their social station, took out of themselves, rather than out of men's pockets, the wherewithal to achieve the proper clothes of a lady. These dear, fussy, dutiful creatures sacrificed their health, their love of nature, their taste for art, for literature, even their companionableness, to the Juggernaut of women—Suitability. Moreover, because men were conspicuously the producing class, and women for the most part obviously the consumers, extravagance came to be regarded as a female propensity; while, as a matter of fact, it was no more truly characteristic of one than of the other. What men spent in cigars and tobacco, in heavy eating and drinking, in club life and dues, and in careless, unconsidered sums, women balanced by their equally wasteful but careful spreading of small sums upon the elaboration of dress.

One of the last and most demoralizing aspects of fashion-promotion has been the infliction upon children of the over-developed taste for tawdry ornament. The women's magazines cater to the mother's pride by providing embroidery patterns to be worked upon little boys' blouses; suggestions of how to cut over little girls' dresses to keep pace with the newest idea. While the laundry bills mount ever higher, the fashionable little girl is rigged out in more fragile and impracticable and unwholesome clothing. It is as if the mother were still a child herself, playing with a live doll which, though it cannot be broken, may still be distorted into her own foolish image.

As a result of the combined influence of economic forces and social traditions, centering in dress, women have acquired a set of habits of expenditure and thinking which lead to discontent and waste of time in the trivialities of taste, in the pursuit of petty economies, and in the discussion of dress detail. These are, however, the least of the evil effects of the dress-cult: in many women they degenerate into exploitation of men, dishonesty toward tradespeople, and the vulgarities of conspicuous display. It may almost be asserted that competence, good humor, and intelligence in women are now in inverse proportion to the amount of time they spend on the fashion of their clothes. A woman of influence and a " real lady " in the Twentieth Century is known, more often than not, by the fact that she is not dressed conspicuously in the latest fashion. She may be known even more by the fact that her children are dressed in the simplest and most child-like manner.

CHAPTER IX

THE VIRTUES OF SUBSERVIENCE

"The virtues of the man and woman are the same."—
ANTISTHENES.

"I am ignorant of any one quality that is admirable in woman which is not equally so in man. I do not except even modesty and gentleness of nature; nor do I know one vice or folly which is not equally detestable in both."—DEAN SWIFT.

"Virtue consists not in refusal, but in selection."—LESTER F. WARD.

THE old-fashioned word, virtue, is now familiar to us chiefly in certain phrases from the Hebrew Scriptures. The translators of King James used it in the original Latin sense as denoting the qualities of a man—strength, courage, capacity—as may be seen in the tenth chapter of Proverbs, where Solomon is describing the ideal mistress of a household. She whose price was "above rubies" appears to have been valued most for incessant and varied industry, and for her administrative ability; at any rate, nothing is there said about her personal appearance, nor her bodily habits. Words, even Biblical words, however, have a way of changing color according to the lights of those who use them. In the mouths of the Puritans of the past century the vigorous word virtue had all but lost its strong tint of manliness. It had come to signify, rather, the qualities of the chaste and docile female, who was the ideal Christian housewife in that society; and these qualities were carefully inculcated by a process of domestication.

In their development under domestication there is an interesting analogy between human-kind and animals. The bull is still a thick-necked, violent, undisciplined creature, of slight use, except to propagate his kind; while his mate, the cow —which is not merely maternal, but also specialized along an important line of production —has developed the qualities of domestication to a high degree. She bears her young and gives up her milk meekly at the will of a master, losing the characteristics of the wild bovine under the discipline of unremitting fertility. In the United States, the male horse, unless deprived of the organs of sex, is isolated almost like a wild beast; in French cities he is made useful as a draft animal only by excluding mares entirely from the environs, and consigning them to the rural districts. Thus, in modern life, the sexual qualities of male animals often make them nuisances.

The point of significance of all this in the present discussion is, that the female domestic animal and the unsexed steer and gelding have been compelled, under the hand of man, to suppress the more aggressive traits native to them, and to put on the milder qualities of domestication.   In much the same way the human female, under the double discipline of maternity and hard work, originally acquired the passive qualities of endurance, at the same time suppressing the ruder and more pugnacious virtues. This change took place, it may be supposed, just in proportion as her relation to the economic and political arrangements of society became indirect.   As soon as wives and daughters ceased to be direct producers and accepted support and protection for as much or as little personal service as they chose to give, they put on, of necessity, the qualities which their supporters demanded or admired.

Mastery—or control, as we politely call it now —was the natural ambition of men not fully civilized; but, in a brutal, competitive world, they found it difficult to achieve over other men and contrary circumstances.   All the more, therefore, they desired mastery in their households—it was easier to begin at home. The head of a family who spent his days even in mere commercial contest with other men, would naturally expect subservience in his wife and children, just as he did in his employés; nor would he be likely to tolerate in them original opinions and independent action.

Womenkind have generally had to please the Head of the Family if they wished to be comfortable and happy. Herbert Spencer remarks that the gentler type of women survived among primitive peoples, because they had to practise obedience or be knocked on the head; and that the sympathetic female was at a premium, because she could adjust herself to the moods of her lord. It is certain that even in quite modern times men have unconsciously preferred girls whose inexperience and apparent docility gave promise that at home, at least, the man's will would prevail. It not infrequently happened that the lover was deceived by the yielding temper of his betrothed, which, like the mating plumage of the male bird, had been assumed instinctively merely for the season.

The virtues of subordination in women, as in the laboring classes, are even yet found in tolerably exact measure as these classes are industrially dependent. Our grandmothers of the early Nineteenth Century were first-hand producers and, inevitably, partners with their husbands. Within the sphere of domesticity at least, they ruled with a degree of independence. The social history of their time dwells upon their courage and prudence, their loyalty and industry, but scarcely mentions docility and obedience, although these were required of them by the code of society and religion.   But by the middle of the century the emphasis upon the qualities desirable in women had perceptibly shifted from the positive virtues of relative independence to the more negative qualities of subservience.

The discipline of dependence and maternity was further reinforced by the approving emphasis of society upon those qualities which men preferred in their subordinates. Women were taught by the clergy that " the men of the nation are what their mothers make them," and that they should not desire any power beyond the domestic circle.

" Of this realm Woman is Queen; it takes its cue and hue from her. If she is in the best sense womanly—if she is true and tender, loving and heroic, patient and self-devoted, she consciously and unconsciously organizes and puts in operation a set of influences that do more to mold the destiny of the nation than any man."

This kind of flattering half-truth was constantly urged as the reason why women should obey their husbands, and not venture outside their appointed sphere.   The curious theological argument by which women justified it and convinced themselves that they were, therefore, morally superior to men, is rehearsed at length in the *Woman's Record* of 1872.

" For this cause ought the woman to have power on her head because of the Angels. (I Cor. xiv, 10; also Tim. ii.). . . . Angels are witnesses that the woman is ' the glory of the man '. . . . This glory she would forfeit, should she attempt to usurp authority over him. And while the wife is commanded to reverence and obey her husband, is he not the superior? In the estimation of the world he is, because he holds the highest place in the family; but the tenure of his office proves her superior moral endowments. The wife must reverence and obey her husband because ' he is the saviour of the body ' (see Ephes. v, 22-23) ; that is, the worker, the provider, the law-giver. God placed man in this office . . . and the wife should unhesitatingly submit to this law. . . . God, by commanding husbands to love their wives, has set his seal to this doctrine—that women are holier than men. The world also bears witness . . . for of all the sinful deeds done on earth, nine-tenths are committed by man. . . . The Church bears witness to this truth—more than three-fourths of the professed followers of Christ are women."

The ingenious feminine author of this logic, Mrs. Sarah J. Hale, not being wholly ignorant of the discontent of modern womenkind, clinched her argument with the following:

" Does any wife say that her husband is not worthy of this honor? Then render it to the office with which God

has invested the head of the family; but use your privilege of motherhood to train your sons so that they may
be worthy of this reverence and obedience from their wives.
Thus through your suffering the world may be made
better."

It is one of the humorous commonplaces of
morals that men most admire the virtues they
themselves possess, and minimize the value of
those they find it difficult to practise.   From time
immemorial men have cultivated the qualities acquired by predominance, leaving to women and
servants the less spectacular virtues of self-sacrifice, patience, obedience, humility, sweetness of
temper, and sympathy, which were needed to
make the home atmosphere soothing.   While
men found it convenient to inculcate the gentler
attributes, women, *per contra,* found it safe and
praiseworthy to exercise them.   In truth, a triple
premium was offered for the virtues of obedience,
self-sacrifice, and patience—husbands demanded
them, the Church insisted upon them, and any
female who neglected to acquire them—who exhibited self-will, who scorned the deceits of af-
fectation and loved truth, who was intellectually
and physically brave—was almost sure to find herself outside the pale of marriage; or, if within it,
a misfit.   In any orthodox society she was regarded both as immodest and superfluous, a sport
as it were, from the true feminine type.

The cultivation of these virtues produced, however, some corresponding feminine deficiencies. The more women practised obedience, the less occasion they had to reason, for to reason is often to differ from authority. Like the soldiers at Balaklava:

> "Theirs not to make reply,
> Theirs not to reason why,
> Theirs but to do and die."

The " smart " woman, who could not help reasoning, while still under the necessity to obey, developed a sort of compensatory shrewdness. The " managing " wife was formerly a very common type; the woman of strong character, who nominally deferred to her husband in everything, yet achieved her own will by subtly persuading him that he was having his own way. Her powers of indirection—if not of deceit—thus became highly developed, while he was pacified with a swollen and often unmerited self-importance. The children, too, as they grew to discretion, sometimes joined in making the master comfortable, while at the same time outwitting him. But a clever woman in so anomalous a position was not altogether a dependable creature. She was likely to acquire vexatious tricks—refusing to be bridled now and then, and biting in the stall. Like the domesticated driving-horse, if she ever took the bit in her teeth and ran away, she could scarcely be trusted afterwards for family use.

In the past century, nevertheless, by far the larger number of women were well broken; and, in proportion as they were, they lost the power of thinking and deciding for themselves in any matter outside the household affairs for which they were responsible. Such women not only followed the lead of their husbands, but asked advice of the neighbors in every detail of life. If a child took the scarlet fever, the doctor might be called, but his orders were supplemented by the contradictory suggestions of the neighbor-women whom the mother consulted. She had, in fact, " no mind of her own," and submitted herself to every wind of doctrine, while thinking herself conscientious in doing so. Such a woman acquired a habitual state of indecision—choosing a dress pattern one day, and, after exhibiting it to a critical friend or two, returning to change it for another, which " she didn't know whether she liked or not;" and which, when made up, she would regard with discontent.

The model wife, when left a widow, transferred her submission to an older son or, in default of male relatives, to the attorney in charge of her estate, blindly accepting his *dicta* as to where she should live, how much she should spend, and what was " proper " for her, regardless of her own comfort or her technical rights. After half a lifetime, perhaps, of loyal industry and maternal sacrifice she was " bossed about " by people who naturally regarded her as childish and incapable. In the practice of deference and submission she had often lost, also, not only the capacity to judge and decide for herself, but the belief that she ought to do so. It was as if the helpless people of a State should constantly exercise the *referendum* without the power to initiate measures or to recall those who fail to fulfil them. And, withal, she was apt to fall into a morbid state of suspiciousness toward those who attempted to guide her. Her second childhood thus began at middle age, or as soon as her husband's hand was removed.

There is no more dangerous virtue than self-sacrifice, for it cultivates complacency in those who consciously practise it, and is apt to produce selfishness in those who accept its benefits. Exceptional men have practised it in all the Christian ages for the purpose of attaining merit, while upon women it was enforced both by inevitable maternity and by their social dependence. If the quality of self-sacrifice in women and servitors had been as productive of antagonism and discomfort as moral courage, for instance, or just-mindedness, it may be doubted whether it would have been so disproportionately lauded by man-

kind. Or, if women themselves had found unselfishness as difficult and odious as these upset-
ting attributes, it seems probable that they
would not have claimed it for their characteristic
virtue.

There is no virtue for which women have been
more indiscriminately praised than patience. Of
that blind acceptance of duty which is necessary
to get the monotonous and unpleasant tasks of
the world done, they have certainly the larger
share as compared with men. It was a necessary qualification for child-rearing and domestic
success—as it has been in the laboring peasant and
the donkey on the treadmill. The mother who
gave her whole time to the nurture of children
and to household cares, would have become im-
becile had she not been able to adjust her mind
patiently and cheerfully to a succession of petty
demands and services. She acquired, perforce,
an instinctive endurance like that of the draft animal which has never learned to balk and does not
know that it can run away.   The woman who did
not learn patience met with the disapproval of the
world of men and women alike; and she who ran
away faced social ostracism, if she were not cast
into outer darkness.

But of that considered, reasoning patience with
which the scientist and the inventor pursue far-off
and inspiring mysteries through years of labori-

ous experiment and failure, the ordinary woman developed very little. Because the issues of her life were small, innumerable, and rapidly succeeding each other, she had no time to consider them in perspective, or to do aught but attend to each faithfully as it arose. Her capacity for sustained effort was, therefore, determined by things closely related to her. Great numbers of men in the business world subordinate desire and comfort to the attainment of far-off ambitions; but women, like children, want to see immediate results.

But from the standpoint of the Nineteenth Century, self-devotion and uncomplainingness were, after all, subsidiary endowments in women as compared with physical purity. It might almost seem from the emphasis laid upon The Feminine Virtue, that our fathers must have misread one of their favorite Scripture passages:

"Though I bestow all my goods to feed the poor, and
        though I give my body to be burned,
    And have not chastity,
            It profiteth me nothing."

Under a tradition which had arisen when women were property, and with the injunctions of religion, this one quality became the specific and exclusively feminine attribute. Virtue had come to mean, not strength, courage, capacity, but chastity —the female *sine qua non*. A woman might be violent in temper, cruel in speech, selfish, idle, a devourer of the substance of industrious and generous men, yet if she were technically " pure " she kept her place in the Church and in her social circle. But if, like Mary Wollstonecraft or George Eliot, she gave herself openly, though there might be extenuation, and though she might have every other feminine virtue and some masculine ones besides, the pure women and the unchaste men of her world would have no place for her. Not even the high quality of courage and honesty with which she accepted her anomalous position, could save her from being classed with the parasitic mistress who gave bodily service in return for luxury. As for the few who, tormented by the natural human hunger for joy and adventure, broke away from home ties altogether, there was seldom even a modicum of pity. Yet, however futile their quest, they were at any rate, themselves not hypocrites—and surely every human being may have a choice of the kind of evil that is most tolerable.

For us, in an age more generous and discriminating toward human frailties, it is difficult to understand how so cruel a standard could have come about; yet it goes back to the primitive conditions of society, in which women were quasi-slaves and chattels. Professor Thomas has very acutely remarked:

" The morality of man is peculiarly a morality of prowess and contract, while woman's morality is to a greater degree a morality of bodily habits, both because child-bearing, which is a large factor in determining sexual morality, is more closely connected with her person, and in consequence also of male jealousy. . . . In the course of history woman developed an excessive and scrupulous concern for the propriety of her behavior, especially in connection with her bodily habits; and this in turn became fixed and particularized by fashion, with the result that not only her physical life became circumscribed, but her attention and mental interest became limited largely to safeguarding and enhancing her person." *

Darwin, in the *Descent of Man,* says that habit was a more effective factor than selection in the development of human morality. It has already been shown, in the chapter on the Conventions of Girlhood, that a prudish degree of modesty was enforced upon girls literally from the cradle; and that the vaguely evasive phrases of teachers and clergymen about purity, coincident with a complete " conspiracy of silence " as to physiological facts, produced an abnormal state of mind toward the whole subject. Although clergymen were, as a class, more refined and gentle than average men, they were not the less inclined to insist upon men's standards of propriety for their female parishioners. In each community they stood for conservatism—for the " superior past," for the

---

* Thomas, *Sex and Society,* pp. 219-220.

gospel of the Fathers as then interpreted—and, naturally, resisted any attempt to ameliorate the Puritan code of morality. Indeed, to men so high and narrow, *propriety was morality.* Humility, obedience, charity, Godliness, and, above all, propriety of behavior and chastity—these were the virtues indispensable to Christian women.

As to the attitude of women themselves, Miss Ida Tarbell has correctly described it:

"They got from the Church the reason for things as they found them—the reason for their submission to masculine authority—the explanation for their place in society, their program of activities . . . and, as a rule, they took the teachings quite literally and devoutly."

But, aside from the emphasis laid upon bodily purity by parents and moral teachers, the two great economic influences from which that insistence had originally come, dress and slavery, were operating in the Nineteenth Century, and still persist in some degree at the present day. The sociologists tell us that so long as the habit of nakedness was general, no such theory of modesty existed; but that so soon as humankind for any reason began to cover the body, nakedness became conspicuous, and, thus, clothing reinforced the suggestiveness of sex characters. It is a pertinent fact that in proportion as clothing became elaborate and dress a pursuit in itself, ideas of propriety became more inflexible and perverted. Among civilized peoples décolleté dress has no longer any relation to climatic conditions, but is coincident with a luxury-loving society; and the conspicuous outlining of the figure, which was once solely practised by the slave and the professionally unchaste class, has been adopted by the modest female of modern times.

In primitive and semi-civilized societies women were marketable commodities rather than human beings. Immodesty—that is, any behavior calculated to attract the attention of strange men—might cause the human chattel to be stolen, and the female who was unchaste, whether by accident or choice, was regarded as damaged goods. The phenomenon of jealousy even yet goes back obscurely to the fact that not even an unmarried woman owned her own person; while the appeal to the " unwritten law "—still sometimes made to escape the penalty of murders of passion—is based on the convention that the possession of the body is the asset of an owner, not the gift of a partner.

The idea so prevalent in the Nineteenth Century, that chastity in a female constituted her chief qualification to the respect of mankind, produced some curious and even humorous perversions. Modesty—the behavior becoming to the

chaste female—became an end in itself. It is related of M'a'am Betty, the dame-tutor of Lydia
Child, " a spinster of supernatural shyness," that
the chief calamity of her life was that Dr. Brooks
once saw her drinking water from the spout of a
tea-kettle. Yet this same proper lady, we are
told, was not only shockingly untidy, but chewed
tobacco! A similar distortion of ideas is illustrated by the persistence in some churches of
the convention that women must not be uncovered; the woman who should take off her hat
would be regarded as an " immodest female."

It has come to be a fact that *conspicuosity,*
which is everywhere and in all ages the professional qualification of the unchaste, may now
be safely practised by any nice woman, so long as
it is achieved in accordance with the current
fashion. On the other hand, the adventurous
woman, who is a sort of composite produced by
idleness and ennui, by love of excitement and of
luxury, plays on the passions of men while re-
taining the control of her own person. She begins, at least, by drawing a clear line between her
own technical virtue and the wickedness of those
who sell themselves frankly into bodily service.

Both the inflexibility and the inconsistency of
the conventions involved in the requirements of
technical chastity in the past century are best illustrated, perhaps, by the laws relating to the

age of consent in young girls. Even as late as 1885, by the laws of many states, young girls were made capable of consenting to their own ruin at ten years of age, and in Delaware at the age of seven. Even yet there are two states which set the technical age of seduction at twelve and one at ten years of age. Yet girls in tutelage might not make wills, contracts, or deeds, under eighteen to twenty years of age. They were never willingly permitted to know anything about the physiology of their own bodies or the processes of reproduction—they must obey their parents—but they might be seduced with impunity during and even before the age of puberty. And when their childish bodies had been devoured by men, the virtuously conventional society of the Nineteenth Century made outcasts and harlots of them. In truth, there is no cruelty more terrible than that of ignorantly good people.

In the feministic literature of two generations ago certain words denoting moral qualities of the highest status are conspicuously lacking. Females were repeatedly adjured to be humble and patient, but courage was not urged upon them; they were besought to be tender and devoted, but just-mindedness was not included among their cardinal virtues. Charity, in both its senses, was inculcated, but of honor it was assumed that women could have slight need. The differentiation of morals was seemingly as complete as the social habits of the two sexes. For courage might have implied conscientious independence on the part of wives and daughters; which did not, of course, appeal to heads of families any more than it does now to political bosses. Justice is a far-off word, even in the mouths of men, and was certainly too high for the feeble minds of our foremothers. Such justice as there was, was precious; to be handed over in homeopathic doses by the heads of families, whose moral standards were practical rather than ideal. And as for honor, whether moral or commercial, men were, theoretically at least, still the protectors of women, and therefore entitled to its exclusive exercise.

Thus, in brief, it had come about in the Nineteenth Century that women had a monopoly of the passive virtues of subservience, and, for lack of exercise, the more positive and fundamental moral attributes were in abeyance. Their one essential and superlative virtue, chastity, overshadowed all and led to the neglect of others more spiritual and not less important. The more "typically feminine" a woman was, the more she was destined not merely to subordination, but to become the prey of shrewd and selfish persons. Her humble and narrow principles, evolved in devotion to home, husband, and children, gave her no leverage upon a wicked world; and she must piously shut her eyes to the unchastity of any man who offered himself as father to her unborn children. Lacking initiative, courage, and the normal egotism, when she was blindly driven into competitive industry she beat about among the underbrush, bruising her tender inexperience, and unable to follow or to mark out her own trail.

SECTION III

SOME EXCEPTIONS

CHAPTER X

THE ELECT AMONG WOMEN

"The Gospel is the most tremendous engine of democracy ever forged. It is destined to break in pieces all castes, privileges, and oppressions. Perhaps the last caste to be destroyed will be that of sex."—HELEN B. MONTGOMERY.

"The power of educated womanhood in the world is simply the power of skilled service. . . . The world is full of need and every opportunity is a duty. Preparation for these duties is education, whatever form it may take and whatever service may result. The trained, which means the educated in mind and hand, win influence and power simply because they know how."—ISABELLA THOBURN.

"There is nothing in the Universe that I fear, save that I shall not know all my duty or shall fail to perform it."—MARY LYON, 1849.

THE forces which were transforming and destroying the established traditions of women's lives in the last century produced very different effects upon them, according to their individual temperaments and breeding, and the degree of social restriction to which they were subjected. While some exploded in an indignant demand for their rights, others, scarcely less discontented, but lacking initiative and courage, set conventional-

ity aside with more discretion. By far the
larger number, however, unconscious of the impulse that moved them, instinctively responded
to it while still endeavoring to remain within
their appointed sphere. They accepted as ordained and necessary their indirect relation to
the world outside the home, and adapted as best
they might their fledgling spirits to the shell in
which they found themselves. They were assured that woman's power lay in her " influence."
If the lives of their men-folk showed small im-
press of their prayers and innocent admonitions, they, nevertheless, believed themselves appointed agents of morality and trusted to an in-
scrutable Providence to make that influence
effective.

A few—whom we have called the Elect—felt
a call from God which transcended any that
women had ever known. To those who believed
that their social responsibility lay in domestic
sacrifice and consecration, the religious awakening of the early Nineteenth Century brought a
special opportunity for the exercise of womanly
devotion—a way not in any wise inconsistent
with the strictest canons of female duty, yet
leading out into a foreign world, where pro-
founder consecration was required. The terri-
fying, yet fascinating, tales of the heathen in
kingdoms on the other side of the globe lent a

glamor to the work of foreign missions. Their strange unchristian customs woke, in hearts filled with religious fervor, the primal instinct of the born adventurer. And not alone among men; for among women missionaries there have been some with as great a desire as a Stanley or a Peary for the unknown and the picturesque.

Men who dedicated themselves to foreign missionary work were expected, as part of their preparation, to choose for wives women of exceptional piety and bodily vigor, not only as a safeguard against evil, but to double their own efficiency by establishing among lost souls a model Christian household. Now and then these quite human apostles took with them some exemplary but feeble young girl, who shortly laid down her life in a strange country for a cause that she did not comprehend; but, for the most part, they chose prayerfully some young woman whose local reputation for piety and competence marked her out as suitable for missionary labors. Many a romantic girl, filled with religious enthusiasm, and after the slightest acquaintance with a young clergyman, married the Cause rather than the Man.

Whether congenially mated or not, there was scant time for uxorious sentiment in the exactions of the arduous life to which they went. The hardships of their physical existence, and

the ever-pressing miseries of the needy creatures
to whom they had dedicated their service, over-
topped their merely personal griefs. Into many
such families child after child was born, to fade
away prematurely in an enervating climate; and
such children as survived were of necessity sent
to America to grow up among strangers. Both
parents found their reward in the glory of the
greater sacrifice; and the sons might well dedicate
their easier tasks, as did the son of Adoniram
Judson:

"To the children of the missionaries, the involuntary
inheritors of their parents' sufferings and rewards."

On first thought it might seem that no woman
would be farther from sharing the discontents
which were moving her sex in America to
struggle against their social bonds, than the missionary wife. There was certainly nothing novel
in the consecration of wives to their husbands
and children, since it had been the accepted duty
of woman throughout the ages. But little as she
might sympathize with woman's rights, it was
the peculiar distinction of the missionary wife to
dedicate herself, not like plain women to her
family, but to the Cause of Christ, counting it all
glory to share the perils of the pioneers who carried Christianity wherever men lay in darkness.

" Judson in his prison, Moffat with the savages in South Africa, Chalmers in the wilderness of New Guinea, Hunt and Calvert in blood-stained Fiji, Patson in the New Hebrides, all these and thousands more had some woman who stood shoulder to shoulder to them, sharing weariness, danger, loneliness, sickness, death."

It is written that of twelve missionaries sent to Sierra Leone in 1823, ten of whom were husbands and wives, six died that year, and four more in eighteen months; of the women none survived, and three were buried in the first year, with their babes beside them. However unaware of it, these women were as much fulfilling their inevitable share in the emancipation of their sex as those who suffered ostracism for demanding equal rights.

No more inspiring illustration of the unpremeditated manner in which such women took a new place in the world can be given, perhaps, than the lives of Ann Hasseltine, Sarah H. Boardman, and Emily Chubbock, each of whom successively became the wife of Adoniram Judson, the first missionary to Burmah. Of the first it has been said that her record and her sufferings have no parallel in missionary annals. A well-born and well-educated New England girl, she was fascinated as much, it may be, by the mission as by the personality of the young theological student; and her life was looked upon by them both as even more a partnership in apostleship than an obedience to wifely duty. During the fourteen years of her marriage, while she carried domestic cares and bore children for whom there was no hope of survival, she performed also prodigies of missionary labor. When, during the war between England and Burmah, Dr. Judson was thrown into the death prison, she was left quite unprotected. With an infant in her arms, she daily visited and comforted the prisoners, and her diplomacy and moving appeals to the government prepared the way for the ultimate release of all the English captives. Even when she went home with health undermined by fever, hardships, and grief, she spent her furlough in rousing interest in missions, finding time to write and translate extensively in the difficult Burmese language. One is not surprised to learn that when her body at last gave way from sheer exhaustion, she was "glad to go" to a world which promised rest. She had sacrificed her children as ungrudgingly as Abraham; she had laid down her life as deliberately as John Huss; for she had given herself body and soul, not to Adoniram Judson, but to the work of the Lord in whom she believed.

Sarah Boardman, the second wife, gave herself with just as clear a vision when she married Dr. Judson, for she was then the widow of a missionary who had died in the field. And again the union was a partnership in the promotion of the missions rather than for the attainment of any mere domestic comfort. After ten years she too gave her life gladly on the altar of missionary teaching. Yet this ruthless man of God had no hesitation, apparently, in inducing a delicate literary woman a few years afterward to return to the Orient with him. Though he died prematurely, and she was able to return to her native land with his children, she, too, paid the penalty in an early death, though not until she had written the biography of the first Mrs. Judson.

Estimated by the unchristian mind, the lives of these women might appear to have been sacrificed to the visionary egotism of a religious fanatic. But the utter absence of any petty feminine exactions toward their husband, and the evident admiration which each displayed, not only for his mission, but for her own predecessor, leaves no doubt that these martyrs to a cause counted it a privilege so to die for a great idea. Many a sister at home made almost as great sacrifices of her personal desires and comfort to some merely human man, who accepted it as due to himself and quite inevitable in the life of a proper domestic woman. The wives of Adoniram Judson had at least the compensation of giving their lives to something larger than themselves; and of breathing freely in a world from which all the pettier feminine coercions had dropped away.

Their pitiful and more profound experiences served other women, too, by affording inspiration to those who, not elected to special work, pursued the commonplace round of living. Comfortable women, in whom the horrors of jails and asylums in their own towns had not roused an active sense of social responsibility, felt their imaginations kindle at the recital of heathen barbarities and missionary sacrifice.

" Though they had little to give, the egg money, the butter money, the rag money, was theirs to squander in missions if they chose. Hundreds of female cent societies . . . mite societies, female praying societies, sewing and Dorcas societies, sprang up in support of missions."

They begged from door to door; they devised leaflets, wrote missionary stories and poems, and published news from the foreign field; and by such inconspicuous coöperation gained enlargement of their own lives. At the same time they became imbued with the thought that some women might be elected to a wider destiny, not less feminine and moral, but larger than their own.

Thus the members of churches were being

prepared for the proposal that single women should be educated to go out as teachers and medical missionaries. Yet it was thirty years before this proposal was acted upon, so deep-rooted was the tradition still that an unmarried woman could properly do nothing in the world alone. Even after its practical adoption, the missionary spinster was often regarded as a sort of social roustabout to the men in the field. It is related of Bishop Thoburn that, convinced that it was impossible for men to reach the Hindu household, he sent for his sister, Isabella, to come out to India for this work. Miss Thoburn, who had had a large experience in teaching and nursing, objected to her brother's assumption that she had come out merely to be his clerk and assistant, and the Bishop was compelled to reconsider the situation. He wrote thus frankly of his conversion to a broader view:

" I accepted the fact that a Christian woman sent out to the field was a Christian missionary, and that her time was as precious, her work as important, and her rights as sacred as those of the more conventional missionaries of the other sex. The old-time notion that a woman in her best estate is only a helper, and should only be recognized as an assistant, is based on a very shallow fallacy."

Yet even so just a man as this could not wholly divest his mind of the tradition that woman was made for man, for he adds:

" She is a helper in the marriage relation, but in God's wide vineyard there are many departments of labor in which she can successfully maintain the position of an independent worker."

The increasing demand of the foreign mission work for women trained in nursing and medicine, reacted helpfully upon the struggle then in progress at home for the admission of women to the medical profession. While the Philadelphia Medical Society was excommunicating some of its members for lecturing in a woman's medical college, the experience of men in the evangelization of the heathen had forced upon them and their boards of management the conviction that " the heathen woman drowned all ideas; " and that " the citadel of heathendom was in the home, which could only be taken by the assault of women." This imperative need created a demand for trained women. As Helen Montgomery puts it, in her *Western Women in Eastern Lands:*

" Whether there were to be women physicians in America was a matter of interest; but in Asia it was a matter of life and death. The women of half the world were shut out from medical assistance unless they could receive it at the hands of women."

Here was a field of high professional labor which men had perforce to yield to women.

While the clergy at home were still preaching that medicine was outside the sphere of woman; and the medical profession itself, with greater vehemence and less excuse, was denying them opportunities for study and practice, a few young women began to prepare themselves for this service. Clara Swain, the first fully-equipped medical woman to be sent to India in 1869, suffered to the full all the hindrances set by prejudice in the path of the unusual woman. Upon her fell the combined resistance of men physicians, of the conservatives in the churches, and of a society still permeated with the conventional views of feminine limitations.

While more than a thousand women, married and single, were suffering moral and social exile in foreign lands for the succor of lost souls, the sisters at home were also caught on the swell of a humanitarian wave that was destined to carry a great body of pious, domestic women far outside the limits of orthodox femininity. Temperance reform, already a generation old, had languished while men and women alike were absorbed in the exigencies of war. But the experience of that struggle had given women occasion for the development of their powers of organization; and when it was past they no longer desired to return to that exclusive sphere from which they had been wrenched by a national emergency.

Most of the temperance leaders were as far as possible from supposing that they were allied with the emancipation of their sex. They had little sympathy with woman's rights, and no intention of adopting its direct and startling methods. Although there was scarcely a state in which drunkenness was then recognized as cause for divorce, the temperance women were shocked by the proposition of Elizabeth Cady Stanton to adopt a resolution that no woman should remain in the relation of wife with a confirmed drunkard. They, nevertheless, justified their own unprecedented campaigns on the orthodox ground of their peculiar mission for the moral uplift of mankind. The Woman's Crusade, which spread in 1874 from Ohio over all the Northern States with a kind of pentecostal power, has been sympathetically described by Frances E. Willard:

" That women should thus dare, after they had so long endured, was a wonder. . . . Woman-like, they took their knitting, their zephyr-work, or their embroidery, and simply swarmed into the drink-shops, seated themselves, and watched the proceedings. Usually they came in a long procession from their rendezvous at some church, where they had held morning prayer-meeting, entered the saloon with kind faces, and the sweet songs of church and home upon their lips, while some Madonna-like leader

. . . took her stand beside the bar, and gently asked if she might read God's word and offer prayer.

"Women gave of their best during the two months of that wonderful uprising. All other engagements were laid aside; elegant women of society walked beside quiet women of the home, school, and shop in the strange processions that soon lined the chief streets, not only of nearly every town and village in the state that was its birthplace, but of leading cities there and elsewhere; and voices trained in Paris and Berlin sang ' Rock of Ages, cleft for me,' in the malodorous air of liquor-rooms and beer-halls.

"Thousands of men signed the pledge . . . others slunk out of sight, and a few cursed the women openly; . . . soon the saloonkeepers surrendered in large numbers . . . the liquor traffic was temporarily driven out of two hundred and fifty towns to which the Crusade extended. . . . In Cincinnati the women . . . were arrested and locked up in jail, in Cleveland dogs were set upon the Crusaders, while in several places they were smoked out or had the hose turned upon them. Men say there was a spirit in the air such as they never knew before; a sense of God and human brotherhood."

This extraordinary outburst on the part of the mothers of the country, a class that had hitherto been untouched by the political and social reforms proposed by the woman's rights group, culminated in the organization of the Woman's Christian Temperance Union, which spread throughout every state in the Union, and ultimately to foreign countries. In 1890 it was publishing 130,000 pages of temperance literature, and a journal of its own; it had established a temperance hospital, and a lecture bureau, built a woman's temple, and was extending its work to schools, restaurants, lodging-houses for the friendless, and many other forms of philanthropy. With the extent and variety of its work we are not here particularly concerned; the significance of this movement for our present purpose lies in its unconscious expression of precisely the same expanding spirit as that displayed by such widely separated groups as the suffragists, the missionaries, and the literary amateurs.

Men had concentrated their temperance agitation chiefly upon legislative reforms, and promoted it by exhortation. But women, in their characteristic manner of inexperience, attacked it from forty different sides, all of which grew naturally out of their feminine conception of the disasters wrought upon the family life by the use of intoxicants. Their methods were perfectly direct and simple. Total abstinence and prohibition were the uncompromising words around which they rallied. They pledged and converted the drunkard, and they made the saloon odious and often ridiculous. They harassed politicians and legislators with petitions, until public men dared not refuse directly the measures they demanded for fear of having their devious records on the drink question, and on the social evil, exposed. Like the *enfant terrible* in the family, these devoted women said everything right out—innocently setting an example to their imitators, the modern muck-rakers.

Nor did they limit themselves to direct attack upon institutions and legislation. Since they were " to carry the home into the world," they must needs devise means for the protection of their children from the three curses: " the curse of narcotic poisons, alcohol, and nicotine; the curse of gambling; the curse of the social sin, deadlier than all." The preventive measures which they undertook, and especially the so-called scientific temperance instruction which they succeeded in introducing into the public curriculum, afford a striking illustration of both the strength and the weakness of the organization. Peculiarly ignorant as women have generally been on physiological matters, they adopted statements as to the effects of alcohol on the human system which suited their personal bias; and by their pertinacity managed to get them officially accepted by school authorities.

They had previously commanded the approval, if not the coöperation, of the general public, and even of the drinking class, in their campaign against drunkenness, the treating habit, and the saloon. But when they filled schoolbooks with dogmatic statements, unjustifiably exaggerated, if not untrue, concerning a scientific question about which the scientists themselves disagreed, they exposed their cause to easy attack. The mistake then made—not because they were women, but because they were ignorant—checked the sympathy and undermined the confidence of many intelligent men and women whose support they could ill afford to lose.

Aside from important concrete results in social reform with which the Woman's Christian Temperance Union should be credited, their contribution to the feminist movement was also considerable. Thousands of housemothers had learned to work in small groups together, and even aggressively, for the public welfare outside the church and the home. Having no experience in parliamentary tactics, they developed remarkably flexible methods of their own. By ignoring theological disputations, as women generally do, they were able to avoid sectarianism and sectionalism. The organization is, in fact, one of the few instances in which women have not been in the least imitative, for they neither asked nor took the advice of men. By the very spontaneity and originality of their measures, these women of a purely domestic type emancipated themselves into a world of larger ideas. Beginning with a disavowal of connection with the militant section of femininity, they ended with a motto as unequivocal as that of the suffragists:

" Woman will bless and brighten every place she enters, and she will enter every place."

The woman's temperance movement — " of women, by women, for humanity "—exhibits in a peculiar degree the unpremeditated and instinctive character of the impulses which drove even mothers, a specialized and isolated class, to break the conventions of their time and to express themselves in larger ways than domesticity.

A third class of homekeeping women—the Ladies Bountiful—illustrates the tendency of their conservative kind to adjust the traditional feminine limitations with some form of religio-humanitarian service outside the home. In so far as they were merely using their advantages of wealth and birth in the service of the poor, they were following the traditions of religion from the time of the early Christian church. Among this class of domestic philanthropists, Mrs. Sarah Platt Doremus, though inconspicuous in her own day, was, perhaps, the most typical. Born of a family noted for its piety, wealth, and charitableness, she was early married to a man of similar social station, and became the mother of nine children. Her private benefactions were countless; and, in addition, she founded several charitable institutions, extended perpetual hospitality to impecunious missionaries of every sect, and was constantly serving on boards and committees. We are assured that, in spite of these incessant and varied activities, " nothing was ever allowed to interfere with her home life." Although she attained a place among famous women by her benevolence, her biographer is at great pains to describe in detail her feminine charm and housewifely accomplishments:

" All her labors for suffering humanity were so unostentatiously performed that much was not known until after her death. No outside duty was undertaken until the claims of her household were minutely discharged. From her youth she was a notable housewife, and her delicacies for the sick were among the crowning achievements of her education. She was skilled in all the accomplishments of the day, and her paintings and embroideries were preserved as evidences of her versatile talents. To the last day of her life she was to be seen making dainty fabrics with the dexterity and rapidity of the young.

" Her beauty was retained to old age, and her clear, cameo-cut features, her delicate complexion, with its soft color, and deep blue eyes, gave her a passport to all hearts.

" Her power to organize undertakings, broad and far-reaching, was only equaled by her execution of the minutest details . . . especially with a delicacy of health which might have precluded all service. The secret of her success in every department of work was her entire consecration to the Lord's service."

It is certainly not surprising that, in her case, as in that of almost every married woman in the first half of the Nineteenth Century, all this was accomplished with the accompaniment, if not the result, of ill-health. It is, in truth, incredible that any woman should have borne nine children, performed every conventional feminine duty, practised the most exacting accomplishments, exercised unlimited hospitality, and still have had time left in which to be chairman of committees and founder of half a dozen societies, and as many more institutions. Beside such a record, the activities of the modern clubwoman and charity worker seem inconsiderable.

Mrs. Doremus was, indeed, one of a type soon to pass away, for she represented the very limit to which the domestic woman of exceptional ability could go without breaking through the appointed sphere. When women began to reform charitable institutions, besieging legislators on behalf of the neglected insane and town poor, and invading prisons to expose their horrors, they were regarded as going quite beyond the conventions of almsgiving. To understand the repugnance which their aggressive ideas aroused, we must see them with men's eyes, in perspective with the social conditions of the period. Men might themselves attempt to reform a society in which they had always been leaders and dictators, and they could accept without injury to their pride the proposals of other men; but when women presumed to criticise and, moreover, to overturn by public agitation, that which had been established and called good, the proceeding was held to be almost as outrageous as the demand for equal rights.

When Dorothea Dix, a school-teacher of exceptional culture, visited, in 1843, every almshouse and jail in Massachusetts, and appealed to the Legislature for the reform of their horrible conditions, she was doing as unfeminine a thing as Susan B. Anthony, when she attempted to vote in the face of threatened arrest.

"She then went from state to state, in a time when traveling was difficult and tedious, ignoring fatigue and a system actually saturated with malaria, until she saw twenty asylums in twenty states under proper management. In less than four years she traveled ten thousand miles, visited eighteen penitentiaries, three hundred county jails and houses of correction, and more than five hundred almshouses, besides hospitals and houses of refuge. No place was too horrible, no spectacle too sickening, to damp her enthusiasm or to hold back this delicate and refined woman from her self-appointed task."

From America she went to foreign countries to revolutionize there the methods of charitable institutions; and rounded out her long life of social service with work in the hospitals during the Civil War. Because we now venerate such women as Miss Dix it is the more difficult to realize the criticism which their rare and unprecedented behavior created. She definitely smashed the theory that a single woman had no duty outside the home, accomplishing, in spite of opposition and limited physical strength, tasks of which men might be proud.

Long before the War, there had been other women liberated here and there to social service through their characteristic feminine sympathies. While some were laying down their lives to help heathen women and children, others found their election at home in teaching negroes. Before the suffragists were mobbed and hooted in the streets of Eastern towns, Prudence Crandall was arrested, imprisoned, convicted, boycotted, and inhumanly persecuted in a town in Connecticut, for carrying on a school for colored girls. While Clara Barton was giving herself to the work of the Sanitary Commission, and conceiving the great idea which was to make the Red Cross a symbol of worldwide humanity, Josephine Griffing was devoting herself and her property to the relief of the thousands of homeless negroes that were pouring into the City of Washington. When the War was over, it was her plan for the Freedmen's Bureau that was adopted by the Government. From Margaret Gaffney, the uneducated daughter of an Irish immigrant, who, childless and widowed, founded orphan asylums in New Orleans with the profits of her dairy and bakery, to Josephine Shaw Lowell, the well-born and well-educated young girl bereft of her husband by the Civil contest, who gave her whole life to the charities of New York State, and left an indelible mark on the philanthropies of her generation—women of every class felt the breath of a spirit which compelled them to do strange, new things in spite of their domestic traditions.

In all that dignifies human nature, they surpassed their sex. Some carried themselves against criticism with the courage of the well-born among *canaille;* some with the inspired fanaticism of religion; breaking through the prejudices of a complacent society in the service of unpopular causes, defying ostracism, ignoring weakness of body and physical hardships, sacrificing the thing dearest to woman—her reputation for womanliness—in devotion to the larger human need. By their deeds and their social martyrdom they justified their commission as "moral agents." As the numbers of such philanthropic women increased toward the end of the century, it might almost seem that here was their destined field of work outside the home. Certainly they contributed to humanitarian enterprises a quality of devotion and sacrifice not often seen before; blindly imposing upon them the standards of the pious, domestic circle with a singlemindedness born of ignorance and consecration.

While thousands of Christian women were dedicating themselves to foreign missions, carrying on temperance crusades and entering innumerable fields of philanthropy—thus more or less unconsciously enlarging their sphere—one woman alone was destined to leave an ineffaceable mark on the Christian religion. The life of Mary Baker Eddy covered more than three-quarters of the Nineteenth Century; and at her death, in 1910, she was acknowledged, even by those who were not followers of her faith, to be the most remarkable woman of her time. Only the briefest résumé of her career is required to show that that opinion was well founded.

Mary Baker was born in 1821, of plain New England parents, and brought up in the stern religious beliefs of that period. She was always a delicate child, but she seems to have been somewhat better educated than most girls of her time. She married, and bore one child, and was not unlike other women, except, perhaps, in being less strong and less happily situated. At forty years of age she seemed a confirmed invalid. At forty-six—an age when most women have finished all the constructive work of their lives—

she passed through mental experiences which led to the foundation of the system now known as Christian Science. Yet another decade of life was passed in " finding herself," and in teaching and writing. Her best-known book, *Science and Health, with Key to the Scriptures,* was not published till 1875, but has now gone through some hundreds of editions of one thousand copies each. The First Church of Christ, Scientist, was not organized till 1879; yet, at the time of her death, there were nearly one thousand churches of this sect, which claims a million adherents throughout the world. " No other faith . . . as far as human annals go, has risen and extended so rapidly, so quietly, so persistently."

It has been truthfully said that Mrs. Eddy built up a career " out of nothing that is physical, no great fortune, no industrial invention, no inherited opportunity." Her achievements were based, rather, upon a recognition of " God as Divine Principle, and the consequent allness of good and unreality of evil." Although neither of these ideas—the non-reality of matter and the influence of mind over matter—was new, she gave them new vitality by interpreting both the Hebrew and the Christian Scriptures in their light. The doctrines of Christian Science, like those of older sects, were dependent upon a literal acceptance of the Bible; but Mrs. Eddy transferred the emphasis from the passages of wrath and painful prohibition to those of faith and cheerful assurance.

Christian Science was one, and perhaps the most conspicuous, of the reactions against Puritanism on the one hand; and, on the other, against materialism and the negations of physical science. In both aspects it met the spiritual needs of men as well as of women, and therefore reacted upon other Christian denominations to humanize and revivify the Gospel message. Aside from this effect, it was also destined to alter the attitude of Christian thinking toward women. Repeatedly in the preceding chapters of this book, it has been pointed out how an excessively masculine interpretation of the Scriptures and the conservatism of the clergy together reinforced primitive social habits to keep women in subordination. But Mrs. Eddy interpreted the Scriptures wholly without reference to sex. Nor does *Science and Health* contain any peculiar earmarks of feminine authorship—not even in the chapter on Marriage—unless it be in the emphasis upon the reciprocal and equal duties of husband and wife.

Mrs. Eddy's chief contribution to humane religion lay probably in the negation of fear. For many generations the teachers of Christianity had been dwelling upon the wrath of God, the terrors of Satanic evil, and the punishments of hell; to the neglect of those large and tender mercies which Jesus himself had chiefly preached. Suffering was believed to be necessary, inevitable, sent by God for the chastening of the wicked human soul; poverty and sickness were irremediable and " Providential." To all this the doctrine of Christian Science was flatly opposed. One of its basic propositions was declared to be true, whether read forward or backward: " Life, God, omnipotent good, deny death, evil, sin, disease—Disease, sin, evil, death, deny good omnipotent, God, Life."

Such a doctrine of cheerfulness came as a revelation of divine goodness to overburdened, neurasthenic, fearful, hyper-sensitive people; and whatever may be thought of the system of therapeutics taught by Mrs. Eddy, the insistence upon a humaner interpretation of the Scriptures has been an incalculable benefit to mankind.

In her own personality, Mary Baker Eddy illustrated in a high degree the very qualities in which the average woman of the past century was lacking: her indomitable will, her serene assurance and belief in her own message; her genius for large organization, and her power to hold the allegiance of men and women alike, were absolutely " unfeminine," judged by the standards of her time. Her career was, indeed, a

signal example of the sexlessness of great gifts.
In no respect was she more exceptional than in
the courage with which she endured ridicule and
opposition:

" For more than half a century, the most powerful
oppositions and antagonisms beat around her. For years
. . . she was the target for ridicule, abuse, slander, and
calumny. Conventional religion and organized medicine
vied with each other in attacking her theory, ridiculing her
position, and impugning her motives. Foes arose within
her own household. . . . This persistent, tireless, and
many-sided opposition would have crushed any one not
sustained by invincible living faith."

It is not the province of a non-adherent, nor
the purpose of this sketch, to estimate the
ultimate religious significance of Mrs. Eddy's
teachings; but, from a purely worldly standpoint,
she rises unchallenged—an exception to all
criteria of feminine capacity. Even if the cult of
Christian Science should ultimately decline, as
many others have done, the sheer indomitable
dignity and power of the woman herself will remain to suggest what may be possible to any
woman. While all the other sects were clinging
to masculine interpretations, a woman of limited
training, under the handicap of physical weakness, and quite without appeal to any personal
charm, founded a new, prosperous, and humane
denomination; and this not among the ignorant,

but among a highly intelligent class of people. While tradition was still reiterating the necessary inferiority of the female sex, women like Mrs. Eddy and Dorothea Dix, and many another whose name is scarcely remembered now, were attacking men's problems with a grasp of intellect, a fertility of resource, and an indomitable force of will such as go to make a great statesman or a great commander. But if they had done no more than prepare the world to follow the social leadership of Jane Addams; or even if they had been no more than moving illustrations of the need under which all women labored for lack of opportunity and training, they would have served their kind and time. By so much as they rose above their weakness and their limitations, finding courage for rare deeds, they helped to liberate all other women from paralyzing conventions.

CHAPTER XI

THE PHANTOM OF THE LEARNED LADY

"Women are free to adorn their persons, but if they seek to cultivate their minds, it is treason against the prerogative of man."—SARAH JOSEPHINE HALE, 1868.

"Let the woman learn in silence with all subjection. But I suffer not a woman to teach, nor to usurp authority over the man, but to be in silence. For Adam was first formed, then Eve. And Adam was not deceived, but the woman being deceived was in the transgression."—*Epistle of Paul to Timothy.*

NOTHING is more unaccountable in the attitude of Nineteenth-Century society toward women than its unreasoning fear of the effect of freedom and education upon their natures. As the diffusion of knowledge had been resisted in preceding centuries lest it should corrupt the common man and undermine the accepted forms of dogma, so in our own country there was set up a sort of straw-woman—the learned female—an unsexed, monstrous perversion of the traditional model of femininity. Women's rights and anti-slavery in the United States were, indeed, merely later phases of those class and race struggles which had agitated civilized Europe. One historian illustrates the modern apprehension by the tale of Saint Avila, who was said to have gained renown by a marvel of self-control. Once when frying fish in a convent she was seized with religious ecstasy, but she did not drop the gridiron, nor let the fish burn. At the beginning of the last century most men, even men of intelligence and generosity, were convinced that an educated woman would drop her gridiron.

In 1819, when Emma Willard petitioned the New York Legislature to endow institutions for girls equal to those already established for boys, her greatest fear was that " the phantom of the college-learned lady would rise up to destroy every good resolution in her favor." Some men thought women so inferior to men mentally as to be quite incapable of reasoning; others, though granting a degree of capacity, were sure that higher thinking was wholly incompatible with the domestic and family duties for which God and Nature had designed them. These two theories —really inconsistent with each other—which were traceable partly to a military society, in which women and non-combatants had always been held in contempt; and partly to the degeneracy and sentimentalism of Eighteenth-Century England, had become the ruling traditions of the American Colonies. Not until the political and social revolutions of the end of that period had definitely broken the ties between the old and new society were they likely to be questioned. Education is necessarily an art of peace, and not until the American states had entered upon an era of nationalism was there leisure for its promotion.

Aside from the prevalent tradition of women's inferiority, other social influences delayed the provision of educational privileges for girls. Learning had always been associated with the idea of aristocracy, and was certainly not to be offered to women while still denied to ordinary men. In the Colonies the chief motive for the education of a select class of men had been to provide a learned ministry capable of interpreting the Scriptures. Both the Pauline and the Puritan interpretation taught the subjection of women, and the current secular philosophy of the time corroborated it. Rousseau's dictum— " She is to know but little and the little she knows is to be pleasing to man "—was as acceptable to free-thinkers as the theory that her subordination was " ordained by God " would naturally be to an always conservative clergy.

The safety of a democratic nation must lie in diffusion of intelligence—but this commonplace of our day was not at once recognized by the states as an inevitable consequence of their ideal phrase, " Life, Liberty, and the Pursuit of Happiness." Even when the movement for public schools began to gather headway, English traditions still pervaded them to the exclusion of girls; and when, here and there, it was realized that girls required something more than desultory home training, their schooling was often fearfully and grudgingly granted. Throughout the century, as grammar and high schools, academies and seminaries, semi-colleges and full-grown colleges, and at last true universities were founded, the sharing of such opportunities by girls and women was steadily resisted. Even when that resistance was gradually broken down, girls were often prevented from making use of them by the general opinion which still prevailed, that women did not need for domestic purposes an education as thorough or as extensive as that of men. When girls, in process of time, came to be taught at all, it was not simultaneously with boys, but during vacations, before and after the regular hours of sessions, by inferior and overworked teachers, and with a limited range of studies. Although constantly gaining opportunities for higher study, they were yet, at the very end of the so-called " woman's century," weighted with limiting conditions.

While the active resistance to the equal admission of girls to educational privileges was made by the men who controlled taxation, endowments, and school equipment, it must be acknowledged that a far more subtle and effective check lay in the tradition current among women themselves, that intellectual attainments in their sex were both improper and unattractive. The same elusive and belated convention, which still prevents the general adoption by women of bifurcated garments, prevented them earlier from taking advantage of the higher education. Women who had themselves attained a degree of culture were often doubtful of its usefulness to their sex generally. The accomplished Mrs. Barbauld thought young ladies ought only to have " such a general tincture of knowledge as to make them agreeable companions to a man of sense, and ought to gain these accomplishments in a more quiet and unobserved manner, from intercourse and conversation at home, with father, brother, or friend." If women at this time ever consciously reasoned out their situation, the logic must have run something like this: It is the business of women to please and to serve men— men do not like women to know as much as themselves, nor does a servant need education. Since learning adds nothing to our attractiveness, let us not appear intellectual, even though we may have inadvertently acquired a little knowledge.

The legacy of advice left by Dr. John Gregory to his daughters in 1774, was still quite appropriate in the middle of the following century:

"Be even cautious in displaying your good sense. But if you happen to have any learning, keep it a profound secret, especially from men, who generally look with a jealous and malignant eye on a woman of great parts and a cultivated understanding."

In an old *Ladies' Magazine* of the ante-bellum type, advice of precisely the same tenor is given:

"She ought to present herself as a being made to please, to love, and to seek support; a being inferior to man and near to Angels."

It was, indeed, almost as improper a century ago for a lady publicly to display an intellectual interest as it would now be for her to attend a prize-fight or drink at the hotel bar. Until after 1830 women were not expected to attend any public lecture except those of a religious character, nor to avail themselves of public collections of books and pictures. The shy and eager-minded Hannah Adams, "who learned Greek and Latin from some theological students boarding in her father's house, and who had written books," was the first woman to scandalize Boston by making use of the Public Library.

Without rehearsing in detail the formal steps

in the growth of education for girls, it is amusing
to recall what was considered desirable for a
young woman to know before the days of public
schools and seminaries. One of the most cultivated women of her time, Abigail Adams, the
wife of the President, said in her old age:

"The only chance for much intellectual improvement
in the female sex was to be found in the families of the
educated class, and in occasional intercourse with the
learned of the day. Whatever of useful instruction was
received in the practical conduct of life came from
maternal lips; and what of farther mental development,
depended more upon the eagerness with which the casual
teachings of daily conversation were treasured up, than
upon any labor expended purposely to promote it. Female education in the best families went no further than
writing and arithmetic, and in some few and rare instances, music and dancing."

A quarter of a century later girls were still
not generally admitted to the public schools, and
the education thought necessary for them consisted of reading, writing, spelling, the first rule
of arithmetic—addition—good manners, needlework, and knitting. To this the best educated
girls added no more than music, grammar and
rhetoric, and geography. Even fifty years later
Thomas Wentworth Higginson complained:

"When you hear of a young lady as 'splendidly educated' it commonly turns out that she speaks several

languages admirably, and plays on the piano well, or sketches well. It is not needful for such an indorsement that she should have the slightest knowledge of mathematics, of logic, of rhetoric, of metaphysics, of political economy, of physiology, of any branch of natural science, or of any language or literature or history except those of modern Europe."

The progress of education for girls was further checked by the deference which local communities paid to the opinions of the ministers of their churches. They continually emphasized the idea that the mission of women in the world was exclusively moral, not intellectual, and that the possession and pursuit of worldly knowledge was incompatible with the higher womanly destiny. Their line of reasoning was carefully presented in the preface to the *Woman's Record,* a biographical compilation published soon after the close of the Civil War. The author, after disclaiming all sympathy with the woman's rights movement, assures her readers that the book is not designed to assert any intellectual equality with man, but to demonstrate her distinctively moral mission by means of historical examples:

" I believe and I trust I shall make it apparent, that woman is God's appointed agent of morality, the teacher and the inspirer of those sentiments and feelings which are termed the virtues of humanity; and that the progress of these virtues and the permanent improvement of our race, depend upon the manner in which her mission is treated by man. . . . Man by the fall was rendered incapable of cultivating by his own unassisted efforts, any good propensity or quality of his nature. Left to himself his love becomes lust; patriotism, policy; and religion, idolatry. He is naturally selfish in his affections . . . but woman was not thus cast down. To her was confided, by the Creator's express declaration, the mission of disinterested affection; her ' desire ' was to be to her husband— not to herself. . . . Truly she was made ' for man ' . . . she was not made to gratify his sensual desires, but to refine his human affections, and to elevate his moral feelings . . . and her soul was to help him where he was deficient —namely, in his spiritual nature."

This " covert glory of the womanly nature," as the Reverend Horace Bushnell called it, was to be the compensation of women for mental inferiority and for the denial of freedom and opportunity.

But in this, as in many other instances in history, while the most plausible arguments were being invented to prevent the admission of another class to an equal opportunity, social and economic forces were steadily undermining the accepted tradition. As the public-school system expanded under the impetus of national prosperity, the demand for teachers could not be supplied from the ranks of pioneer young men, who saw a thousand better openings. The religious awakening, which found expression in foreign and home missionary enterprises, could not be carried on without the aid of the missionary wife, who must add, to housewifely and motherly cares, the duties of teacher, nurse, and exemplar to heathen women and children. Even temperance leaders were compelled to call in the assistance of female organizers and financiers. Then suddenly it was perceived that the demand for women of some education in social work outside the home was increasing faster than their educational opportunities. And at the same time it began to be realized that, even for a purely moral career, women needed something more by way of training than ethical platitudes deduced from distorted Scripture lessons.

The demand for better educated teachers found response in the establishment of Normal schools and in the general admission of girls to high schools, to Oberlin Collegiate Institute, and to the small denominational schools—called colleges—founded chiefly by the highly democratic sect of the Methodists. While the pioneers of the Middle West were thus preparing the way for the acceptance of co-education in the state colleges which arose after the Civil War, Emma Willard and Mary Lyon were struggling to provide girls with an education approaching that open to boys, but free from the dangers of defeminization. The Troy Female Seminary laid especial emphasis on "domestic instructions" adapted to the softer sex; and it was pointed out that women, if given a proper training, could teach children better and cheaper than men, thus releasing them to pursue "the thousand occupations from which women are necessarily debarred." Mt. Holyoke Seminary, more than any other school, expressed the passion for knowledge and for the conversion of the souls of mankind of which its founder, Mary Lyon, was possessed. When the General Association of Congregational Ministers of Massachusetts refused to indorse her plan for the higher education of girls, her clerical friends advised her to see in the rejection "The hand of the Lord;" but Mary Lyon replied:

"I may be fifty years in advance of the age, but the work is of God and must surely go on."

In all the increasing provisions for the education of girls there was as yet no hint of courses identical with those offered to young men. The studies required of girls, though sometimes nominally equal, were neither so severe nor so respected as the classical trilogy. Even in co-educational institutions, "female" courses and "ladies'" courses were substituted for the straight classical requirements, and often measured by inferior standards. The War, in this as in every phase of national life, made an abrupt cleavage in the lives of women. They came across it with minds broadened by nursing experience, and by the economic necessity they were under of replacing men in industry. Whereas all forms of culture had hitherto been emasculated to fit women, they now began to demand for themselves truly equal opportunities. With the foundation of the state colleges under the Morrill Act of 1862, and of the separate woman's colleges, there was definitely precipitated a struggle to make the standards of women's education not only equal to but identical with those of men's institutions. At the same time, and interwoven with it, arose a conflict of social ideals between co-education and segregate instruction, in which the phantom of the intellectual woman returned to terrorize anew the believers in strict feminine tradition. The sarcasm and hostility endured by Mary Lyon and the ridicule suffered by Mrs. Willard and other pioneers in the seminary movement, were as nothing when compared with the scorn and violence aroused by the attempt of women to prove themselves equal to men in the field of classic learning.

When the first few generations of college women, in spite of many limitations, had demonstrated their ability to reach a higher average standard than their competitors, there was still to be overcome the Giant Dreadful of Physical Incapacity. That strange old book, Clarke's *Sex in Education*, which proves conclusively that a woman is by virtue of her feminine functions a semi-invalid one week out of every month, and that she must, therefore, be unfitted for motherhood by the strain of systematic mental training, had a wide approval in the third quarter of the century. Dr. Clarke dwelt at length on the existence of a great number of " weak, neuralgic, dyspeptic, hysterical, menorrhagic, dysmenorrheic " girls and women, assuming that the chief cause of these conditions was their education by the same methods as boys. He declared that the identical education of the two sexes was " a crime before God and humanity, that physiology protests against and experience weeps over . . . it emasculates boys, stunts girls, makes semi-eunuchs of one sex and agenes of the other." After devoting a whole chapter to the clinical details of seven cases of educated women who had come under his treatment for female diseases, he concludes:

" Physiology declares that the solution of it will only be possible when the education of girls is made appropriate to their organization. A German girl yoked with a donkey and dragging a cart, is an exhibition of monstrous muscular and aborted brain development. An American

girl, yoked with a dictionary, and laboring with the cata-
menia, is an exhibition of monstrous brain and aborted
ovarian development."

At the height of this controversy, it was customary for the college woman to be spoken of as
" hemaphrodite in mind," and " divested of her
sex," and to predict that she would lose not only
her feminine attractions, but become incapable of
performing her essential functions. All these
predictions were quite *a priori,* and founded on
fears rather than facts; for of the eight colleges
in the Eastern States which at this time admitted
women, only one had been open as long as four
years, and of the separate institutions of collegiate rank, Vassar alone had been in existence
as much as seven years. But the belief in the
physical inability of girls to endure a regimen of
regular, hard study, was so general that it compelled the promoters of their education to disarm
it by special measures. Wellesley College announced at its opening in 1875 that it was not
hard study, but violation of law, which injured
young women, and that it would offer opportunities, equal to those of the best colleges for
young men, " but with due regard to health."

Just as the word " female " had been superseded by the less suggestive term " woman," so
the old ideal of physical delicacy as an essential

and desirable feminine characteristic now began to be set aside. A systematic effort began to be made to develop women into beings robust enough for whatever family and social functions they might undertake. But even when it came to be evident, in the latter part of the century, that college girls were, on the whole, healthier than other girls of the same social station, the ghost of that same unsexed lady that had haunted us for a hundred years rose again. It was mournfully prophesied that such learned and vigorous creatures would not marry, and if, perchance, they did, they would not bear children. But even this later Shade had to vanish when, after a full generation, it was discovered that many such women had been marrying just like ordinary folk, and had produced, if anything, rather a larger proportion of healthy children than other women of their class.

There are always in any society a large number who prefer to trust what has been good rather than attempt what might be better. To such people co-education was a veritable bogie-woman of the most hideous sort. Though it had long been adopted from motives of economy and social convenience in the Middle and Western States, the discussion was continued by Eastern educators, who feared it might seriously endanger that fragile veneer of womanhood, the habits of femininity. When it could no longer be asserted that co-education involved more scandals than segregation; or—what was then regarded as almost equally scandalous—more marriages; when co-educated girls could not easily be distinguished from graduates of the separate colleges by any stigmata; yet again a feeble old Spook came back to whisper tormentingly, that schools and colleges were being " feminized," and young men deprived of their birthright, unhampered masculinity, by the presence of so many females. The century which began with a complete " masculinization " of education ended in shrill and ineffectual protests on the part of a small class of left-over males, because their monopoly of opportunity and opinion had been broken.

During all this period every pioneer woman who attempted to enlarge her intellectual horizon or to prepare herself for a profession was met with ridicule and hostility. When reluctantly admitted to partake of the crumbs which fell from scholarly tables, she knew herself unwelcome, and was constantly reminded that her sex must forever prevent her from full participation in the feast. It should not surprise any one that her attitude was, more often than not, antagonistic to men. Like other self-made beings she often understood, but would not acknowledge, the crudity of her half-trained powers; and inevitably she bore about her the marks of the hardships through which she had come. Where one pioneer survives with scars, a hundred fall by the way, and the hardier survivor, however strengthened by the experience, is likely to be an exceptional, if not an eccentric, person.

Among these early women graduates, a few came out arrogant and aggressive, with a chip on the shoulder and a conviction that sex ranged against sex was the only way for women to win an equal chance. Some who had not the fighting temper carried, nevertheless, a deep sense of injury toward men who thought themselves entitled to the best, and would not admit women willingly to share it. Others starved their womanly natures in the devotion to learning, vowing themselves to a sort of conventualism in the Cause of Woman and narrowing their outlook to purely feminine experiences. Those who married sometimes dropped back into the accepted and limited conventions of femininity, and wore an apologetic air for their collegiate temerities; or, finding no solution for their anomalous position between the old and the new, agreed with the *alumna* who said:

"To be intellectual is all right—to be domestic is all right—but to try to be both is hell!"

But by far the larger number came out wholesome and unperverted by opposition, and took their place as leaders of succeeding generations. Though not less womanly than their ancestors of the domestic régime, they walked with a more serious air, feeling themselves consecrated by their own exceptional privilege to the help of their sex. As the number of *alumnæ* increased and opposition declined, their sense of responsibility broadened to include the young, the weak, the limited, and every class who, like themselves, needed the equal chance. That feminization, whose impalpable shade still hovers near, has come to mean, in its large aspect, the brooding of the maternal instinct over all mankind.

It will be remembered that Emma Willard, in her petition to the New York Legislature in behalf of state endowments for girls' schools, urged that, among the sciences proper to the sex, " domestic instructions " should be considered important; and suggested that housewifery might be reduced to a system as well as other arts. Though many girls' seminaries, and even some of the women's colleges, at their foundation required a certain amount of domestic labor from their students, it was rather to economize, and to disarm prejudice, than for its educational value. It gives a humorous aspect to the controversy between the segregate and the co-educational factions for the strictly feminine party to be obliged to grant that the co-educational institutions, which were opposed because they might defeminize young women, provided the first and best equipment for training in the subjects related to housekeeping and the family. The tardiness of the women's colleges to offer courses having a direct application to the domestic occupations is to be explained partly by the prevalence of the tradition that only the classical training was real education. Only very recently, for instance, have the sciences been accepted as equal in disciplinary and cultural value to Greek and Latin. The difficulty with which the applied sciences of Agriculture and Engineering were introduced into the curriculum alongside of the classical courses, warned women not to try to climb up by any such disputed way.

What women had come to want was The Best, and The Best was symbolized by the classics as taught at Harvard and Yale. To this standard, therefore, every woman's college must come before its degree would be accepted. With its students prepared in inferior schools, with limited resources, and hampered by the timidity of its patrons, it was all that such a college could do to teach the traditional requirements. It could not afford to jeopardize its reputation by any experiments in coördinating its work with the future lives of its students.

The classics were, in truth, as well adapted to the average girl as to the ordinary boy, so far as training and culture were concerned, and were scarcely less related to the practical needs of life. It was not until the exclusive domination of the curriculum for gentlemen was supplanted by an elective system broad enough to meet the cultural and vocational needs of all classes, that the idea of a modified curriculum for women could be safely entertained.

Although this is essentially a man's world— since women have not yet had time to contribute the full fruits of their freedom and belated opportunity—yet every woman who reads the history of their slow emancipation must acknowledge that the slowness was due as much to the apathy of women themselves as to the reluctance of men to endanger their traditional ideal of female purity and competence by bringing it in contact with their own strength and coarseness. Nor should the modern woman fail to pay her debt of appreciation to the few truly liberal-minded men who primarily made that progress possible. But for the vision of Joseph Emerson of Byfield, Massachusetts, Mary Lyon would perhaps not have set out on her mission of found-

ing a school where girls could be adequately prepared to save the world. When Sophia Smith—
who had herself been refused admission to the
public schools of her native town—inherited a
fortune, her timid desire to do something for the
education of girls might not have ended in the
foundation of Smith College but for the encouragement of her pastor, Dr. John M. Green. Co-
education—a method offensive to Old and New
England alike—owed its prevalence in the West
to the democratic spirit of the Methodists, and
to the personal sacrifice and foresight of individual men.

All along the road, women have been led and
encouraged by the exceptional man. That they
have not even yet attained a truly equal opportunity for self-development is as much due to
outworn traditions of their own cultivation as
to the fact that men who wish to be just are still
in the minority. It is, indeed, a curious world
where mankind dreams always of perfection, yet
is afraid of the processes necessary to attain it;
and it is still haunted by many phantoms like that
of the Learned Lady who was to defeminize herself by the human exercise of systematic thinking. A strange world, indeed, where the light
from which all such shadows flee is regarded
with terror. Women have at last, however, arrived at a stage where they may at any rate

grapple directly with the reality of their own conventionalized natures.

The results of women's education were regarded by many, at the end of the century, as disappointing. It was said that the trained woman was imitative rather than original; superficial, as might have been expected, and lacking in concentration of effort—in short, the critics were astonished that women had not succeeded in attaining in three-quarters of a century what only the exceptional man had achieved in all the ages of his own making. Without in the least discrediting the remarkable achievements of individual women, or overlooking the altogether higher level which women in the mass have reached, it must be granted that the depth and breadth of their ideas has been limited by the narrowness of their experience. Professor Thomas very justly points out that women's attainments have been to men's so far, as those of an amateur to a professional, because of their intellectual sequestration.

Yet the scholars who have been most friendly to women's mental advancement have not comprehended, apparently, that the petty traditions of feminine duty have, after all, been the chief hindrance to women's intellectual growth. The male scholar of the past century did not darn, cook, nurse his sister's children through the measles; make his own clothes in scanty vacations; play the church organ, teach a Sunday-school class, or take his mother's place when she fell ill. Nor was the lack of money any serious difficulty to the clever young man. While many a young girl was doing the work of a common servant in order to earn the sixty dollars necessary to pay her way through Mount Holyoke, Harvard College was offering not less than twenty-five thousand dollars a year in cash premiums for study; and, as in the Chinese family, mothers and sisters at home pledged themselves for the support of the brilliant boy, who was to be of the "literati" and reflect honor on the household.

At the beginning of the Twentieth Century it was perfectly apparent that not until women ceased to be the pensioners of men; not until they could command their own money and limit their duties in the household; not until endowments and scholarships for their use were as abundant and as generously provided as for men, could any considerable body of women attain an unquestioned intellectual status. Nor could their attainments be justly appraised until the phantom of the learned woman had vanished. So long as men were reluctant to let their womenkind take their chances in education, as they have to do in matrimony; so long as they wavered between the fear that young men will be inoculated with the *bacillus femininus,* and the theory that women themselves will become immune to it, women distrusted their own powers, and the legitimacy of their commission. They have yet to learn to be themselves, and to follow the inner vision wherever it may lead.

CHAPTER XII

WOMEN INSURGENTS

" In times like these every soul should do the work of a full-grown man. When I pass the gate of the Celestials and good Peter asks me where I wish to sit, I will say: ' Anywhere so that I am neither a negro nor a woman. Confer on me, Great Angel, the glory of white manhood, so that henceforth I may feel unlimited freedom.' "—*Letter* of Elizabeth Cady Stanton to Susan B. Anthony.

" It was not because the three-penny tax on tea was so exorbitant that our Revolutionary fathers fought and died, but to establish the principle that such taxation was unjust. It is the same with this woman's revolution; though every law were as just to woman as to man, the principle that one class may usurp the power to legislate for another is unjust."—*Letter* of Susan B. Anthony to her brother.

" Whatever is morally right for a man to do, is morally right for a woman to do. I recognize no rights but human rights."—Angelina Grimké Weld.

DOUBTLESS nothing more surprised the orthodoxy and the social conventions of American society in the earlier half of the Nineteenth Century than the way in which a few hundred women broke loose, so to speak; coming out from the domesticated masses to demand all sorts of unprecedented rights, to champion unpopular causes, to enter activities where their labors rather than their voices had hitherto been acceptable. And yet the modern student of history sees in this ebullition simply the logical consequences of the political and intellectual ferment of the later Eighteenth Century, which left as its principal residuum the doctrine of equal rights and opportunities for all classes of men.

When once the doctrine had been implanted it was inevitable that reasoning minds should soon begin to ask: Why not for women, too? Acute and just-thinking men could not but see the inconsistencies involved in a career like that of Mercy Warren, whose satirical poems and dramas were of as great service to the revolutionary cause as that contributed by many a fighting man; but whose status remained that of an inferior and childish being:

"Noble and understanding as this lady of '76 was in fact, and recognized by the men of her day to be, in theory she was anything but that. She was a person of inferior mind, unable to master the strong meat of education, unfit to be trusted with the guardianship of her property or her children, lest both suffer, not to be allowed free speech in public lest her tongue run away with her and disorder and loose doctrines be encouraged, not to be allowed to mix in the gatherings or deliberations of men lest her household, her manners, and public morals suffer. The greatest men of New England are on record on these points, and the Church and the Law upheld them." *

* Tarbell, *American Magazine,* vol. 69, p. 14.

The appreciation of human rights engendered by the struggle for independence was quickened by the teachings and social experiments of Robert Owen, and by the socialistic propaganda of the early forties. In the wake of the extraordinary prosperity following the panic of 1837, and as a result of all these economic and humanitarian theorizings, two movements arose which were destined to precipitate a concrete feminine protest. Temperance and the abolition of slavery were calculated by their very nature to appeal to the highly developed sympathies of womenkind; and, as moral issues, might naturally have been deemed suitable to their sphere in life. The instinctive interest of women was not in social or religious theory; rather, there were many like Lucretia Mott, the Quaker preacher, who wrote of herself:

" The highest evidence of a sound faith being the practical life of a Christian, I have felt a far greater interest in the moral movements of our age than in any theological discussion."

Inspired, therefore, by the humaner aspects of religion, women organized temperance meetings, raising the money and doing the largest part of the work, only to be excluded not merely from the rostrum, but even from the debates on the floor. The spectacle of Antoinette Brown, the ac-

credited delegate of two societies to a temperance convention in New York, standing for an
hour and a half, while the men delegates
wrangled and fought over her right to speak, and
the clergymen cried, " Shame on such women! "
is incredible in our day.   One must enter into it
from the standpoint of a woman to comprehend
the effect of such injustices and insults repeated
again and again upon women whose only offense
was that they wished to share in a philanthropic
movement.

The denial of free speech, based on Paul's in-
junction that women should keep silence in the
churches, was, in fact, the exciting cause of the
first and most extreme phase of the woman's
rights movement.   The women delegates who
accompanied William Lloyd Garrison and Wendell Phillips to the National Anti-Slavery Convention in London in 1840, were refused seats
and the right of taking any active part in the
meeting.   Eight   years   afterward   the   first
woman's rights convention met, at which the
most extreme anti-man resolutions ever produced in the history of the movement were
adopted.   Wholly untrained in the underlying
historical causes of their situation, and accustomed to dealing with the concrete in domestic
life, they made a violent attack on mankind in
the tone of slaves denouncing their masters.

" The history of mankind is a history of repeated injuries and usurpations on the part of man towards woman, having in direct object the establishment of an absolute tyranny over her.

" He has never permitted her to exercise her inalienable right to the elective franchise.

" He has compelled her to submit to laws in the formation of which she has had no voice.

" He has withheld from her rights which are given to the most ignorant and degraded men.

" He has made her, if married, in the eye of the law civilly dead.

" He has taken from her all right in property, even in the wages she earns.

" He has so framed the laws of divorce, as to what shall be the proper causes, and, in the case of separation, to whom the guardianship of the children shall be given, as to be wholly regardless of the happiness of woman.

" After depriving her of all rights as a married woman, if single and the owner of property, he has taxed her to support a government which recognizes her only when her property can be made profitable to it.

" He has denied her the facilities for obtaining a thorough education, all colleges being closed against her.

" He has created a false public sentiment by giving to the world a different code of morals for men and women, by which moral delinquencies which exclude women from society are not only tolerated, but deemed of little account in man.

" He has usurped the prerogative of Jehovah himself, claiming it as his right to assign for her a sphere of action, when that belongs to her conscience and her God.

" He has endeavored, in every way that he could, to destroy her confidence in her own powers, to lessen her self-respect, and to make her willing to lead a dependent and abject life."

One of the most characteristic human tendencies is for the aggrieved of any class not to stop with the mere enumeration of their grievances, but to place the blame for their condition upon those in power. The historian, however, having divested any protest of this inevitable and bitter tone, must determine whether the wrongs alleged did in truth exist. If they did, the violence of expression is explained, if not always fully justified. The grievances for the first time categorically stated by women in 1848 were not exaggerated, although the blame for their existence could not justly be laid upon men then living; for even now, after the lapse of more than half a century, four of the dozen complaints still stand, and others have been only partially remedied.

It is not surprising, therefore, that a class so limited in education and social experience, and awakened all at once to the injustices of their position, should allow their indignation to get away with reason and prudence, nor that their tactics should be amusingly feminine. Perhaps they were not the less effective on that account. For thirty years after this declaration, Mrs. Stanton and Miss Anthony were partners in agitation—" pertinacious incendiaries " their contemporaries called them—having no compunction in harassing the most dignified bodies of men. Mrs. Stanton confessed:

"Whenever we saw an annual convention of men, quietly meeting year after year, filled with brotherly love, we bethought ourselves how we could throw a bombshell into their midst, in the form of a resolution to open the doors to the sisters outside. . . . In this way, we assailed in turn, the temperance, educational, and church conventions, agricultural fairs, and halls of legislation."

Yet, if the picture of these insistent methods brings now a smile, it brings, too, contradictory feelings of pity and respect—pity that educated men should have been the most narrow-minded of all; and respect for feminine conviction and courage which led women to risk, in behalf of their sex, all that they had been taught was most lovely and respectable.

The denial of an active and recognized share in the temperance and educational reforms of the time was by no means the most serious of the grievances of thoughtful women. The married woman was still under the status of the Common Law, which gave her no control of her children, no matter what her husband's treatment of her or of them might be; and which made her almost wholly dependent on her father, her husband, or her son in affairs of property. Lockwood states

correctly the position in which women found
themselves:

" Till the late forties the Common Law provisions respecting the property rights of married women obtained
in every state except Louisiana. These provisions wrested
from women all property rights. If an unmarried woman
through gift or inheritance came into possession of property, real or personal, she forfeited all claim to it and all
right to its management and control when she married.
It then at once became the property of her husband, and
if he died, leaving no children, it passed to his nearest
kin, leaving the widow with but a dower in real estate
and a small share in the personal property."

Owen, in *The Free Inquirer,* put in less dispassionate terms the bitterness which women
themselves no doubt felt:

" She can inherit nothing, receive nothing, earn nothing,
which her husband cannot at any time legally wrest from
her. All her rights are swallowed up in his. She loses,
as it were, her legal existence. She may be—thanks to
occasional and gratuitous generosity she sometimes is—
kindly and even rationally treated; but she has no right to
demand—I will not say kindness—but even the most
common justice and humanity. A man may not beat his
wife too unmercifully, nor is he allowed to kill her. Short
of this he can scarcely transgress the law, so far as she is
concerned."

It is a truism of history to say that, to whatever degree there is unchecked power over help-

less or inferior persons, there will be a corresponding degree of abuse. Susan Anthony protected and concealed a married woman, who ran away from an abusive and unfaithful husband—a man of conspicuous station—in order to keep her child. Miss Anthony was persecuted by her friends and the anti-slavery people because she would not reveal the fugitive's hiding-place, but she declared:

"As I ignore all law to help the slave so will I ignore it to protect an enslaved woman."

The wife was able to earn her living in secret for some years, but her husband finally drew the income from her books, and stole the daughter from her. Such cases were by no means uncommon at this period. One of my very earliest recollections is a picture of a wretched and determined woman with a baby under her shawl, who had taken refuge after nightfall behind our kitchen stove, begging my father to help her run away from a drunken husband, because there was no safety for the child, nor help to be invoked from the law. The little Elizabeth Cady saw many frantic women appealing to her father for legal protection, and when she was told that it was "The Law" encased in the yellow volumes on the shelves which prevented him from help-

ing them, she began to cut the " woman laws "
out of his law books.

Alice Stone Blackwell has expressed dis-
passionately the attitude of thinking women with
regard to the legal view of women's services and
their property rights which was current in America at the time the woman movement began:

> " Most men are better than the law, and few hus-
> bands use the extreme and tyrannical power which the
> law gives them; but there the law is, ready for any bad
> husband to take advantage of it. . . . This does not show
> any special depravity on the part of men. If women
> alone had made the laws no doubt the laws would have
> been just as one-sided . . . only it would have been the
> other way round. No doubt it would have taken a long
> and arduous man's rights movement to bring about the
> needed improvements, and . . . we may be sure that the
> women would not have so far altered the old laws as to
> make them glaringly unjust to women."

It required ten years of incessant attack in the
state of New York to get a modification of the law
giving the man sole control of the children; and
when the women agitators, diverted by the Civil
War, rested from their vigilance for one session,
the Legislature quietly put the law back on the
statute books in almost its original form—and
the women had to begin all over again. And at
the time of this writing only thirteen states give
to women the joint guardianship of their children.

It is necessary constantly to remind ourselves of such facts as these if we would comprehend the bitterness with which the woman's rights movement began. Nor must we forget that marriage and motherhood was the only career held open to women or deemed creditable to them; that from the Pulpit and the Press their potential motherhood was urged as the unalterable reason for their protection and support by mankind. Such inconsistency between doctrine and deed on the part of men, though disguised under the veil of religion and domestic purity, was too evident to be missed even by the untrained female intellect. Many a domestic woman, without the courage or capacity of the exceptional leaders of the woman's rights movement, had as great a sense of injustice which she dared not express. Very few men, even, have the courage to quarrel with their bread and butter, or to disrupt their family peace for the sake of a principle; how much less, then, should women accustomed to ages of subordination be expected to do so, although it might ultimately bring them greater freedom and happiness?

Besides the growing sense of human rights in the air about them, and the social injustices of which they were becoming keenly sensible, another kind of limitation began to chafe women who had to support themselves outside the home.

The widespread movement for common-school education, for better private schools, and, finally, for people's universities, created a sudden demand for teachers. Then, as now, men could make more money and have more exciting careers in other occupations than teaching. Moreover, when the male population was reduced and families were impoverished by the Civil War, the number of women who must earn wages was greatly increased, and, for the educated woman, teaching was the easiest and least unwomanly path to self-support.

They found themselves compelled to accept from one-half to one-third as much as men for their work in the same positions. Miss Anthony, for instance, taught twelve years before she undertook her life-work as a reformer, during most of which she received eight dollars a month in positions where men had been paid from twenty to thirty dollars. At a state teachers' convention, held in Rochester in 1853, there were five hundred teachers present, two-thirds of them women. All of them had paid their fee, but not one of them was allowed to speak or vote—except Miss Anthony, who, by her pertinacity, won a grudging permission from the male minority to make one short speech. At this time, in Rochester, New York, a woman principal received two hundred and fifty dollars a year in positions where men received six hundred and fifty dollars; while in the state at large there were eleven thousand teachers, four-fifths of whom were women, yet the women received only one-third of the total salary fund.

No sooner did women begin to teach in considerable numbers than they discovered the superficial and inadequate character of their book education, which they had to remedy as best they might by night study and scanty courses in schools invariably inferior to those provided for young men. In this respect girls of good birth who did not attempt to earn their living were scarcely better off than their poorer sisters. Elizabeth Cady went two years to a boarding-school, which was then considered the best in the country, but she records those years as "the dreariest in her life." Lucy Stone's parents expected her to stay at home and work on the farm, while her brothers went to college; but she refused to do so, borrowed the money to go to Oberlin—the only college of good rank open to her—and there discovered her remarkable gift for public speaking. Of Lydia Maria Child it is recorded:

"She combined the authorship of more than thirty books and pamphlets with a singular devotion both to public and private philanthropies, and with almost too exacting a faithfulness to the humblest domestic duties."

Yet, although she had a superior mind as compared with that of her brother, Convers Francis, who became one of the most advanced thinkers of the Unitarian body, she had

"a very unequal share of opportunities, having, in fact, only such preparation as she could get in attending the public schools and one year in a private seminary."

Girls who, by their ambition and innate capacity, could not help rising above the feminine standards of the day, were pitied rather than encouraged to utilize their powers. The father of Frances Gage, when she was helping him to make barrels, used to be sorry for himself rather than for her, because she was not a boy. After the premature death of her brother at Union College, the little Elizabeth Cady studied very hard and won a Greek prize, with which she hoped to surprise her father and comfort him somewhat for the loss of his brilliant son. But when she brought the trophy to him, he only bemoaned the fact that she was not a boy. And, although in later years she read law so as to entertain intelligently her father's legal guests, when she joined the woman's rights movement he brought all his authority to bear, and told his married daughter, who was to prove herself as able as he, that he would rather "see her under the sod" than engaged in such an agitation.

When once the exceptional woman had mustered courage for the hardships of getting an education, or had jeopardized her social standing by joining in some of the current reforms, her resentment toward narrow-minded men was doubtless intensified by their refusal to acknowledge her capacity, or to recognize ungrudgingly the value of her service. The experience of Antoinette Blackwell was certainly calculated to make a beautiful and talented woman into an iconoclast. Having partly worked her way through Oberlin College, and taught for several years, she returned there to study theology, and at the end of her course was refused a license to preach solely because she was a woman. Theology was, indeed, a scandalous field of labor for women from the standpoint of church conservatism, but in fields of social service far less unusual, and in which the feminine gifts were certainly useful, women workers found just as little appreciation.

The story of Frances Gage is an example of the tardy and inadequate recognition of services as valuable and far more exceptional than those of many fighting men during the Civil War. Although poor and in the midst of bearing and rearing eight children, she yet found time to read and write and speak of slavery, temperance, and woman's rights; she suffered the loss of property because of her abolition principles; and when, by reason of her husband's illness and business failure, she had to support the family as assistant editor of an agricultural paper, the War destroyed the paper. She sent four sons to the army, and she and a daughter went to the South to give their unpaid services to the soldiers. So terrible were the conditions there that she came back, to travel through the North and speak merely for her expenses, in order to rouse the public to remedy them. When over fifty years of age, she was still serving as unsalaried agent of the Sanitary Commission; and, finally, after the War, she still had ability enough to earn for herself a home for her old age. In this woman was combined the practical business ability of a man, with the largest motherly and humane instincts, and yet her life has been given slight notice, except in woman's rights publications.

How deeply this lack of appreciation of the sacrifices, the hardships, and the labors of the women of the country incident to the great war has cut, may be known from a single paragraph in the *Autobiography* of Susan B. Anthony.

" There can never be an adequate portrayal of the service rendered by women of this country during the Civil War, but none will deny that, according to their opportunities, they were as faithful and self-sacrificing as the men. . . . Yet not one of these ever received the slightest official recognition from the government. In the cases of Miss Carroll, Dr. Blackwell, and Mrs. Griffing, the honors and the profits were all absorbed by men. Neither Clara Barton nor Dorothea Dix ever asked for a pension. All of these women at the close of the war asked for the right of suffrage. . . .

"What words can express her humiliation when, at the close of this long conflict, the government which she had served so faithfully held her unworthy of a voice in its councils, while it recognized as the political superiors of all the noble women of the nation the negro men just emerged from slavery, and not only totally illiterate, but also densely ignorant of every public question."

Here was in truth a cause for humiliation even to those women who had taken no part in the woman's rights movement, and one which has had its share in converting the conservative women of our day to the necessity for self-assertion. For the suffrage, extended to the negro as a measure of protection, has inevitably been given to foreigners of every race and class, until there is presented the curious situation of a government, founded for the expression of democratic ideas, all of whose ignorant citizens may vote, and nearly half of whose educated and property-owning members are shut out from representation or share in public issues.

It was customary for a generation after the War to give as an unanswerable reason why women should not be given the vote, that they

could not fight for their country. Although this
is not so often heard in modern times, it was
none the less untenable even when it was in vogue.
The figures of the Provost Marshal's Bureau
during the War showed the physical condition of
more than a million men. Two hundred and
fifty-seven out of every thousand were declared
unfit for military service, and their unfitness was
in inverse proportion to their social and political
importance, as shown below:

Unfit:	Unskilled laborers	348	out of each 1000
	Tanners	216	" " " "
	Ironworkers	187	" " " "
	Lawyers	544	" " " "
	Journalists	740	" " " "
	Clergymen	954	" " " "

In a time when these facts were familiar it was
no doubt galling to women to know that of the
divines, the editors, and the lawyers who filled
Congress, nearly all of whom were opponents of
women's rights, the majority could not themselves be defenders of their country.

Since the orthodox churches were the chief dis-
seminators of the traditional views of woman's
sphere, it was inevitable that exceptional women
should take refuge in the societies representing
newer and less conventional forms of religious
and social dogma. The Society of Friends put

no hindrance in the way of women becoming preachers, and recognized their capacity as human beings, regardless of sex. Lucretia Mott, with a family of little children about her, felt the call of the Spirit, and, in spite of delicate health and many cares, became one of the rarest as well as one of the keenest of the early women in public life. It may be that the strong heart of Susan B. Anthony would have failed but for the wise and wholly sympathetic backing of her fine old Quaker father. The incorrigibly honest, sensitive, hungry-minded Anna Dickinson might, perhaps, have been stunted to the stature of a mere Ishmaelite instead of becoming a great political speaker, had she not been born in a gentle and earnest community of Friends.

In all the Utopian and socialistic colonies characteristic of this period of our history there were women drawn from their home churches by the larger and more prophetic atmosphere to be breathed there. Frances Wright took refuge in New Harmony with the followers of Owen. The Unitarian societies received accessions both from the less liberal Friends and from the Trinitarian bodies, of women as well as men, who could no longer endure the narrow and inhuman bonds which they set. Such colonies as New Harmony and Brook Farm, though founded from motives far removed in the beginning from those which were precipitating the woman question, inevitably promoted the development of exceptional women whose careers were in themselves a contradiction of the accepted views as to feminine capacity. Then, as now, whenever a thinking man came to know such a woman, he ever afterwards had an enlarged idea of what women might become under the stimulus of broadened opportunities.

Although a few of the most striking of the early come-outers from domestic womenkind were made so by some thwarting personal experience, by far the larger number were normal women driven into publicity by the necessity of self-support, or by their attachment to some benevolent cause or social reform. The husbands of some failed in business; others were widows obliged to earn a living for their children, or daughters helping their parents. In such cases they were of necessity blindly doing men's work, because they could not earn enough in the purely domestic avocations. This unpremeditated escape from domesticity was often made imperative by the change from an agricultural to an industrial régime in the communities about them, and by the exigencies of war. Just as on the Continent of Europe women have for ages been replacing in the fields of production the men drawn from them for military purposes, so many women in the United States, during and after the War, replaced the men in the field, the office, and the factory.

A modern novelist makes one of his characters says:

"There have been thousands of Queens. Only a few have been great. Do you know why those few were great? Because there was no King to meddle; they had to be queens, and so they became immortal."

In our day it is so common to see women who have been released from the domestic routine by loss of family, or childlessness, or failure to marry, making themselves efficient in the same fields as men, that it requires an effort to realize the strength of character on the one hand, or the social compulsion on the other, which was necessary half a century ago to make a woman break through the conventions.

If they had but known it, these women, who formulated the Declaration of Sentiments in 1848, touched only lightly the basic question which underlay all the struggles of the women of the Nineteenth Century, when they declared:

"He has usurped the prerogative of Jehovah himself, claiming it as his right to assign for her a sphere of action, when that belongs to her conscience and her God."

Beneath the demand for specific rights and the protest against definite injustice, lay something

more fundamental which conditioned them all:
should women be allowed to judge for themselves what was right and wrong, and to act accordingly? Were they at last grown-up human
beings, or still only in tutelage to men? Without
being aware of it, these first come-outers were
arming themselves against the oldest traditions
of society—the authority of the Church over the
human mind, and the authority of man over
woman. Dimly, and as yet by instinct, rather
than reason, the first exceptional women knew
that their case was analogous to that of the slave
—for he, too, was caught in the meshes of a
tradition pegged fast at every point to the Christian Scriptures. The doctrine of plenary inspiration and the practice of literal interpretation
still gave to every man an unanswerable rebuttal
for every argument in behalf of female freedom.

In much of the literature of the woman movement it is assumed that the women insurgents of
the last century set out to emancipate their kind
in a temper of sheer eccentricity and belligerency
—but nothing could be further from the truth.
They were rather like the patriots of the American Revolution: for a long, long time conscious
of injustice, but unwilling to precipitate a
struggle; then, when the fight was suddenly im-
minent, a few went into it as into a joyous contest, but by far the larger number went re-

luctantly, at the call of duty, and shrinking from the necessity of making themselves odd and conspicuous. Not one of the women who are now recorded as the leaders of the movement began as a deliberate promoter of female rights; all were literally driven into the fight by the arrogant complacency of reformers who were perfectly sure that God had ordained them a chosen sex for the guidance and control of the weaker vessels.

Looking upon the pitiful beginnings of the woman movement, it seems as if the Spirit of Justice, wearily hovering for centuries about the world, at last breathed upon the altar fires of homekeeping women, and kindled them into flame, until they were obliged to join in some of the moral issues of their time, though it might lead to social martyrdom. Of all the moral questions bruited in the thirties and forties, slavery was the most odious; but women who began to work most modestly for educational and temperance reforms found themselves driven by their very femininity to take part in it. Inasmuch as by their potential motherhood they were sensitized to finer human issues, they could not escape being caught up by the wave of humanitarianism which was engulfing the Western World.

From whatever little islet of homekeeping

traditions they came, no sooner did they set out for a larger continent than they began to find themselves tossed about on a stormy sea, and, in the minds of their conservative friends, regarded as wholly lost. In an old book called *Eminent Women of the Age,* the tone of which is extremely conservative, I find the following paragraph:

"The women who devoted themselves to the antislavery cause in the early days, endured the double odium of being abolitionists and 'women out of their sphere.' . . . The Press and the Pulpit exhausted the English language to find adjectives to express their detestation of so horrible a revelation as 'a woman out of her sphere.' A clerical appeal was issued and sent to all the clergymen of New England calling on them to denounce in their pulpits this unwomanly and unchristian proceeding."

But when once they had faced and accepted ostracism as the price of a share in social service, it was natural, if not altogether wise, that they should lend themselves to every other kind of reform. They could not be satisfied to pursue single-mindedly one chosen and greater cause— they must give their support to every small and ill-advised one as well; bringing upon themselves and upon higher issues the cumulative odium and ridicule of them all. For three-quarters of a century the fundamental human question, whether woman was made " for man," or whether she was an adult being with an "inalienable right" to judge and act for herself, has been obscured, distorted, and delayed by the opprobrium attached to contemporary social reforms. From infidelity and free-love, with which the Owenites were charged, to the subversion of society by abolition; from the derision heaped upon the "water-cure" and transcendentalism, to the Bloomer costume, every form of public ridicule has been associated with the reforms demanded by and for women.

Miss Anthony was one of the first to see clearly that, so far as the solution of the woman question was concerned, this policy was a mistake. After reluctantly adopting the Bloomer costume, she abandoned it, and wrote in explanation to a friend:

"I found it a physical comfort but a mental crucifixion. It was an intellectual slavery; one could never get rid of thinking about herself, and the important thing is to forget self. The attention of my audience was fixed upon my clothes instead of my words. *I learned the lesson that to be successful a person must attempt but one reform.* By urging two, both are injured, as the average mind can grasp and assimilate but one idea at a time."

In our time the phrase "woman's rights" is almost exclusively used to refer to woman suffrage; but when the Declaration of Sentiments

was made in 1848, the denial of suffrage was
only one, and by no means the most important,
of the twelve grievances enumerated. To-day it
remains the most important of those not yet
remedied, the others being already partially accomplished and fallen back to the normal position of a few among many desirable reforms for
the public welfare. The extremely slow progress of opinion with regard to suffrage has been
due partly to the discredit shed upon it by its
connection with anti-slavery; but still more to
the decline of enthusiasm with respect to manhood suffrage, which was originally looked upon
as the democratic panacea for all political and
social ills.

The disappointing results of manhood suffrage,
attributed in part to the addition of the illiterate
negro and the unassimilated foreigner, has led
to a reaction against the extension of suffrage as
a means of social reform. The apathy of
women themselves and the conservatism of intelligent men with regard to woman suffrage may
be assigned in great measure to the general feeling that, since manhood suffrage has not
reformed the world, the calling in of women,
presumably less intelligent, would produce even
worse conditions.

As so often happens in the development of any
truth, the aspects deemed most important in the

beginning are gradually subordinated to broader ones. The emphasis upon freedom from the moral domination of men, made by the first female insurgents, is now transferred to a readjustment of the marriage relations and the question of economic responsibility. Because the tradition of feminine docility and tutelage is still in possession of a majority of men's minds, the woman who breaks through it anywhere pays a penalty. Not so terrible, not so far-reaching as the first fugitives paid for their venture outside their sphere, but a very real one, nevertheless.

Miss Tarbell, in her *History of the American Woman,* has summed up the debt which the world owes to the militant type of womanhood:

" She was then, and always has been, a tragic figure, this woman in the front of the woman's movement—driven by a great unrest, sacrificing old ideals to attain new, losing herself in a frantic and frequently blind struggle, often putting back her cause by the sad illustration she was of the price that must be paid to attain a result. . . . But there is no home in the land which has not a better chance for happiness, no child which does not come into a better heritage, no woman who is not less narrow, no man who is not less bigoted, because of the impetus their struggle and sacrifice gave to the emancipation of the sex."

To the first martyrs among women we owe above all the fact that, however mistaken in a particular cause or method, a woman may now judge for herself; that she may now begin to remake her own sphere, upheld and encouraged by men of larger minds, and of sympathies which are at last human, not simply masculine.

CHAPTER XIII

LITERARY AMATEURS

"Even the most serious-minded women of the present day stand, in any work they undertake, in precisely the same relation to men that the amateur stands to the professional in games. They may be desperately interested and may work to the limit of endurance at times; but, like the amateur, they got into the game late, and have not had a lifetime of practice, or they do not have the advantage of that pace gained only by competing incessantly with players of the first rank."—THOMAS— *Sex and Society.*

"The chances are that, being a woman, young,
And pure, with such a pair of large, calm eyes,
You write as well . . . and ill . . . upon the whole,
As other women. If as well, what then?
If even a little better . . . still what then?

.   .   .   .

                                        . . Women as you are,
Mere women, personal and passionate,
You give us doating mothers, and perfect wives,
Sublime Madonnas and enduring saints!
We get no Christ from you—and verily
We shall not get a Poet, in my mind.   .   .   •

You never can be satisfied with praise
Which men give women when they judge a book
Not as mere work, but as mere women's work,
Expressing the comparative respect
Which means the absolute scorn. 'Oh, excellent!
What grace! What facile turns! What fluent sweeps!
What delicate discernment . . . almost thought!
The book does honour to the sex, we hold.

Among our female authors we make room
For this fair writer, and congratulate
The country that produces in these times
Such women, competent to . . . spell.' "
—ELIZABETH BARRETT BROWNING.

THE process of making any new tradition is curiously hesitating and erratic. The new idea, at first proposed in some extreme form, draws to its support a few strong-minded people who become martyrs for its sake; and is then likely to be taken up by the freakish or the zealously unwise, and to become odious to the conventional majority. Between the proponents of the theory and the conservatives, however, there will always be a third group who, while lacking the courage of complete conversion, will, nevertheless, have a sneaking sympathy with the venture. Such as these will decline to identify themselves with the movement so long as it is unpopular, but they cannot avoid furthering it unconsciously by indirect expressions of their own sympathies.

Many of the early women writers of the Nineteenth Century belong to this intermediate class. While the radicals embraced woman's rights and anti-slavery with uncalculating fervor, and were getting themselves mobbed by the populace, reproved by the clergy, and ridiculed by the press, many a clever woman of the more timid and domesticated type was encouraged to break through the domestic traditions by the demand for

popular reading matter, which had opportunely
opened a new avocation to women. It does not
appear that they entered it because they were
especially gifted, but rather because writing was
a ladylike occupation, which could be pursued
in the seclusion of the home, under the protection
of a *nom de plume,* and in the midst of domestic
duties. While a few, bolder or more talented,
tried to compete with men in the well-worn paths
of literature, the most of those who, by virtue
of personal inclination or of bread-and-butter
necessity, began to write, merely followed the line
of least resistance. Although they and their ad-
mirers abjured the taint of strong-mindedness,
they were really in some wise driven by the same
human and unfeminine impulse as their militant
sisters. They, too, in varying degree, were
" sports " from the traditional feminine type, and
their less extravagant departure from it makes
their characteristics and achievements all the
more significant.

Among men the first national impulse toward
expression took the form of oratory, but among
conventionalized women writing was the easier
outlet, and the one least disapproved of by society. Out of six hundred women born after
1800, and listed in the biographical dictionaries
of the last quarter of the Nineteenth Century,
more than half entered the life of the larger

world outside the home through " literature " in
its varied forms—through cookbooks, nursery
tales, journalistic letters, poetry, fiction, or history. Then, as now, a " facile " pen and a little
" inspiration " were thought to be sufficient equipment with which to undertake this graceful and
ladylike profession; and the amount of copy
turned out by such women as Mrs. Sigourney and
Mrs. Child was exceeded by few of their masculine contemporaries.

As might have been expected, they almost invariably began with subjects distinctively feminine, partly because it was familiar ground, but
chiefly, no doubt, because it would not be deemed
" unwomanly " by their critics; or, as Higginson
caustically put it: " Any career you choose so you
begin it from the kitchen." Lydia Child, who
afterward wrote an anti-slavery argument, which
has become a classic, began with a cookery book,
The Frugal Housewife, which went to thirty-
three editions; and followed it up with *A Biography of Good Wives* and *The Family Nurse.*
In all of these she was highly popular; and might,
perhaps, have been equally so with her romance
of ancient Greece, *Philothea,* but for her fatal
espousal of the anti-slavery cause, and her defense of John Brown. Her " Letters from New
York " to the Boston *Courier* show a profound
insight into the social and political problems of

the time, and have a rarely " masculine " direct-
ness and grasp. There was scarcely a field of
writing—except science—to which she did not
contribute; and in all of them—housewifery, history, biography, religion, reform, journalistic
correspondence, novels, and verse—she made
a more than creditable showing.

But in Mrs. Child's performance, as in those
of most of the thinking women of her time, we
see both that diffusion of abilities characteristic
of the amateur and that tendency to subordinate
artistic talent to a philanthropic cause which, even
in our day, are conspicuous traits of intellectual
women. Higginson said of her:

" She is one of those prominent instances in our literature, of persons born for the pursuits of the pure intellect
whose intellects were yet balanced by their hearts, and both
absorbed in the great moral agitation of the age. . . . In
a community of artists, she would have belonged to that
class, for she had that instinct in her soul. But she was
placed where there was as yet no exacting literary standard; she wrote better than most of her contemporaries,
and well enough for the public. She did not, therefore,
win that intellectual immortality which only the very best
writers command and which few Americans have attained."

The career of Lydia Sigourney, the versifier,
illustrates even more vividly the facility of those
early women writers as well as the way in which

the domestic-feminine tradition pervaded and perverted all their work. One of her earlier biographers devoted ten out of his fifteen tedious pages to a laudation of her womanly character, ending with this paragraph:

"Yet even with the temptations which her literary tastes might be supposed to offer, she could never justly be reproached for neglecting any home duty . . . we find her at the head of her household, which at times was large, shrinking from no burden of self-denial needed in her work—living to see her two stepdaughters educated and settled in life, and the brother, at the age of forty-five, consigned to a consumptive's grave; to educate her own daughter and son, and then, just on the verge of a promising manhood, to follow him, too, to his grave; to give her own only daughter away in acceptable marriage; and then to settle herself down, joyful and trustful yet, in her own home . . . until her own change should come."

Having thus forestalled the criticism likely to be brought against this harmless literary creature he grudgingly and fearfully adds:

"But, doubtless, it will be as a literary woman that she will be most widely known. And no estimate of her career which leaves out of account the character and value of her writings can do justice to her memory."

Then, at last, we learn why she should have a place among the "Eminent Women of the Age": she had published *fifty-seven volumes* of prose

and verse; of newspaper and magazine articles
nearly as much more; and for several years had
averaged seventeen hundred letters per year,
amounting to more than all her published work;
while all this time she was also visiting reform
schools, orphanages, and deaf-and-dumb asylums,
attending to church duties, raising a family of
children, and performing every required feminine task. In truth, the modern woman, when
she thinks herself busy, may well humble herself
before such a combination of orthodox womanliness, diluted talents, and prodigious industry.

If it was natural for the women writers of
America to enter romance and poetry *via* the
kitchen and nursery, it was not less inevitable for
them to experiment in the field of journalism.
Progressive newspapers and periodicals, if not
as sensational then as now, were just as eager
to get something novel. The chatty, effusive,
clever copy produced by women of quick but
superficial and untrained minds was immediately
recognized as having a popular value; while the
nom de plume under which they usually wrote
protected them from the direct criticism suffered
by women more conspicuously out of their
sphere.

Mrs. Parton, although three times married,
wrote a series of " Fern Leaves," which sold into
the second hundred thousand; and punctually fur-

nished the New York *Ledger* with a weekly letter for fourteen years. For fear " her practical
and democratic genius " should mislead a world
suspicious of women who did clever things, we
are told that she sacrificed the latter years of
her life to a little granddaughter, and that
" whatever masks of manly independence, pride,
or mocking mischief Fanny Fern may put on, she
is, at the core of her nature, pure womanly."

Mrs. Lippincott, likewise, wrote " Leaves "
under the name of " Grace Greenwood," and in
the forties was regarded as the most copious
and brilliant lady correspondent of the day. But
the manner in which she is supposed to have done
it assures us that she, too, was all feminine:

"As plain Sara Clarke, she had helped her mother
through the morning work, sweeping, dusting, watering
flowers, feeding chickens, sitting down for a few moments
to read two stanzas to that white-haired father of hers.
. . . In the heat of midday she seeks her chamber, gazes
for a few moments with the look of a lover upon the
glorious landscape, then dashes off a column for *The Home
Journal* or *The National Press.*"

Mary H. Dodge, better known as " Gail Hamilton," although apparently as feminine in nature
as the others, made for herself a somewhat
unique position as a satirist. Her fluent and
vitriolic, but, on the whole, just satires on society,

dress, housekeeping, men, and manners, had the quality, rather rare among the earlier advocates of women's rights, of presenting the masculine as well as the feminine side, and on that account, perhaps, produced an effect quite out of proportion to their literary value.

Two other women—Lydia Child, who has already been mentioned, and Margaret Fuller—stand on a far more dignified plane, and their writings constitute a part of the history of American letters in the transcendental epoch.   Margaret Fuller—because of her now acknowledged genius, her conspicuous position as the editor of the *Dial,* her keen, prophetic estimates of her literary contemporaries, and her tragically premature fate—exhibits more than any other the limitations under which any woman of talent had to struggle, in the first half of the Nineteenth Century.

Although brought up in the most cultivated city in America, among men whose literary ideals have dominated our literature for two generations, she had no systematic advantage of the higher learning, but educated herself while performing the petty duties of her father's household.   Just as she was about to undertake writing seriously, her father died, leaving her the practical head of a family of six, and with very small means.   Foreign languages being the most salable of her accomplishments, she began to teach, and at the same time to translate and to publish foreign masterpieces. Then followed the establishment of her " Conversations," the brief editorial work on the *Dial,* and a variety of other literary products—travels, romance, and criticism. According to Professor Bates, her literary significance does not chiefly depend upon her actual writings, which were creditable and suggestive rather than symmetrical, but rather upon her " inspirational personality," which counted for more than her best paragraphs.

" She was not an artist born, and her education, though pursued at high pressure, had been solitary and partial. It is no part of Lowell's greatness to-day that he showered with sneering witticisms the ' Miranda ' of his *Fable for Critics,* and Hawthorne's harsh detractions have redounded to his discredit rather than to hers; but it is permanently to the praise of Emerson, Higginson, and James Freeman Clarke, that, beyond plain face and repellent bearing, they discerned what the English poet Landor was to hail as ' a glorious soul.' "

Margaret Fuller's estimates of men and literature have been justified for the most part by the standards of a later time, and her own relative position as a writer has risen rather than declined. But one aches with pity to see the paucity of tools, of training, of opportunity, and of appreciation under which a creature of so

much power had to find expression.   Self-made
and marvelous she was, indeed, but perverted and
far short of her best ability for want of a normal
medium.   What was said of her might well be
applied to most of the talented women of that
time:

> " Literary work being as yet crude and unorganized in
> America, the public takes a vague delight in seeing one
> person do a great many different things.   It is like hear-
> ing a street musician perform on six instruments at once;
> he plays them all ill, but it is so remarkable that he
> should play them together."

Whatever controversy there may be about the
incubation of genius, the conditions necessary to
the development of talent are tolerably well
settled.   Among men, literary achievement has
usually had a prepared, one might say a
prophetic, atmosphere; it has found somehow its
opportune moment; for, as Professor Lester
Ward long ago pointed out, there may have been
many Napoleons born, but the capacity of all but
one remained latent for want of the right conjunction of circumstances.   Talent, indeed, needs
training in technique and the habit of mental
concentration, while literary gifts, above all,
need emotional stimulation and experience of
life.

Of all the literary women before the Civil

War, Harriet Beecher Stowe attained the highest
mark; yet the conditions under which her talent
came to fruition were by no means favorable.
Born in New England, if she had remained there
she would have been an abolitionist, no doubt,
says Higginson; but she would probably not have
written *Uncle Tom's Cabin!*   Although reared
in a cultivated and brilliant family, it was an atmosphere far more congenial to philosophical
discussion than to the creative imagination.
Married early, and heavily weighted with poverty
and motherhood; without any chance for isolation or continuous thinking; she found only one
thing to give her talent impetus—the moral issue
of slavery.   Compare the equipment and the conditions of Mrs. Stowe with that of her distinguished contemporaries, Lowell, Emerson, or
Longfellow, who lived in an atmosphere of highest culture and liberal letters, undistracted by
babies, cooking, dishwashing, and family nursing; who were, moreover, encouraged by their
fellows, and in line with the accepted conventions
of the masculine world!   But for the exceptional
and almost accidental circumstance that Professor Stowe sympathized with his wife's literary
aspirations, it is probable that *Uncle Tom's
Cabin* could not have been written.   Even so, we
are told that it had to be produced " under griev-
ous burdens and disadvantages . . . much of it

actually written as she sat with her portfolio on her knee by the kitchen fire in moments snatched from domestic cares."

But Mrs. Stowe, above all the women of her day, was fortunate in having a subject that burned within her—a topic not purely feminine, but of tremendous and world-wide interest. For this once she emerged into one of the luminous moments of history, and not even her conventional sex limitations could suppress the power of her moral vision. In spite of an uncertain touch, and though her mind was, perhaps, neither very strong nor profound, the conjunction of an artistic impulse and vital emotion with the golden moment of her opportunity makes her still, after more than half a century, one of the foremost literary figures of her time. Nor does it lessen her preëminence that the picturesqueness of the negro and the evangelical flavor of her chief story have carried it among readers to whom the moral issue of slavery was of minor interest. Cooper and Helen Hunt Jackson both owed as much to the Indian; and many a best-seller of modern times would drop dead on the market but for its conventional religious appeal.

The majority even of the best equipped women of that earlier day had so little intellectual stimulus and so little experience of life outside of domesticity, that they were perforce confined to

purely feminine topics or to the current platitudes of ethics and religion.   The tradition that
a thinking, and still more a speaking, woman was
dangerous to society, checked any natural tendency to choose more vital and picturesque subjects.   While educated men in the more refined
circles sometimes encouraged their women friends
to write, they rarely urged them to go farther
than the fields of harmlessly " pure " literature.
Indeed, one of the striking and almost uniform
characteristics of these early literary amateurs,
is their dependence upon a father or a husband
for their " atmosphere."   Those who married
educated men—like Mrs. Sigourney, Mrs. Lamb,
Helen Hunt Jackson, Mrs. Howe, Luella Smith,
Maria Child—found in the backing given by their
husbands something to neutralize the unfriendly
attitude of a world which still looked coldly upon
an unprotected woman who undertook any unusual work.

The married woman whose husband was sympathetic and encouraging to her intellectual aims
was, by so much, better off than those who faced
the disapproval of the world alone.   For self-
doubt is infinitely more dangerous to the creative
faculty than any public censure, and the women
of the Nineteenth Century were brought up in
the belief that for a woman to compete with
credit in the world of art and intellect was as ab-

normal as for a dog to walk erect—and far less possible.

"The literary women of America before Margaret Fuller," says Professor Bates, "pursued their quest of truth or beauty with all feminine timidity;" and then, with humorous touch, she describes "the craven air of Hannah Adams, who had toiled over bookmaking all her apologetic days, who, with eyes grown dim, was looking wistfully toward heaven as a place where she might find her thirst for knowledge fully gratified." Anything was easier for the unprotected woman than to combat the age-long standards of her world, and therefore only those driven by irrepressible talent or by economic necessity were likely to make a venture into fields hitherto untraversed by their sex. It is a striking fact that a very considerable number of the first feminine attempts in American literature were made under the menace of poverty into which women of talent were thrown by the loss of a father or husband. The avenues of self-support for cultivated women were so thorny and so few that plain necessity drove such as Mrs. Southworth, Amelia Barr, Mrs. Mary Mapes Dodge, the two Carys, Maria Wright, and many others, to writing as a means of livelihood.

Sometimes women of ability were diverted into writing merely because they could get no training or opportunity for the development of less common talents; as in the case of the energetic and versatile Amanda Douglas who, after a hard life on the farm and without a chance to study designing and engraving which she loved, wrote a lot of poor novels and stories. Or, like Mrs. Dodge who, diverted by marriage from the study of sculpture, afterwards produced a children's classic in the little book, *Hans Brinker,* and, while editor of *St. Nicholas,* much other prose and verse.

The current histories of American literature, dealing chiefly with the writers who attained distinction before the last quarter of the Nineteenth Century, differ widely both quantitatively and qualitatively in their estimate of the place of women; but they are substantially agreed that no woman had reached first rank in any line of literature at the National Era. One author mentions only a scant half-dozen in seventy-five years, granting to two of them, Margaret Fuller Ossoli and Harriet Beecher Stowe, exceptional merit; another expands the list to a dozen, giving them a creditable place in the second and third ranks of literary achievement. A third, both more inclusive and more discriminating, finds no more than thirty women before 1890 whose productions contributed anything of real significance to the history of American Letters.

Measured quantitatively, women writers were from one-tenth to one-fourth as many as men; qualitatively, few reached even the secondary rank, and none at all the first. Among the greater names in the National Era of our literature—Bryant, Longfellow, Lowell, Holmes, Emerson, and Whittier—no woman appears; and yet fifty years afterward there was scarcely a field of writing in which some woman had not attained an excellent secondary rank, and in a few they were standing side by side with men.

Looking back over that period in which the domestic-feminine traditions were being broken down, it is easy to see why amateurs of both sexes produced at first so much that was crude and trivial, sentimental and unreal, stilted in tone and lacking in form. All the criticisms on the writings of women before 1875 had been applied with equal force two generations earlier to the productions of American men of letters. English and American critics vie with each other in pointing out the provincialism, the lack of originality and power. In truth, precisely the same causes which had delayed the development of men in literature, operated through a longer period and with greater force to prevent women from producing anything of permanent value. It was said that American men lacked contact with the great minds of all ages—but women experi-

enced the lack to a far greater degree.   Harvard
College alone educated three out of five of the
foremost literary men of the Nineteenth Century,
and opened the door into the wider atmosphere of
universal thought to a thousand more, long before any woman had so much as put her foot upon
the threshold of any real seat of higher learning.

Although nearly all the women writers were
credited by their biographers with an unusual love
of books, their writings show, as did those of men
who made the first attempts, a painful deficiency
in literary technique. It is certainly not without
significance that only sixty of the four hundred
and eighty-seven women authors who attained
mention in the *Who's Who* of 1901-2 had a college training, while among the distinguished men
of every class, two-thirds had taken college de-
grees. The literary women, therefore, must
have been educated—if at all, beyond the grammar grade—by self-trained teachers in inferior
schools, where the " ornamental " were substituted for the " solid " branches. Most of
them satisfied their intellectual hunger by miscellaneous reading and study, and missed entirely
the give-and-take by which men whetted their
minds on each other's knowledge. The taste for
serious reading and culture which must be acquired early in life, if at all, was encouraged in
boys destined for a profession—but never in

girls. We are told that Emerson, Longfellow, Holmes, and Lowell were "bred to cultivation by cultivated parents," and had "tumbled about in libraries." It illuminates, if it does not wholly explain, the voluminous and relatively feeble results achieved by the earlier women, to remember that the very few who attained a place, also lived in the atmosphere of higher culture. Margaret Fuller and Lydia Child shared to some extent, though indirectly, the inspirational influences of Cambridge; Harriet Beecher was reared in the stimulating circle of a brilliant family and an intellectual coterie; and Emily Dickinson, recluse though she was, could not escape the mental impetus of a professor's household.

They were all deficient in technique in proportion to their deficiencies in mental training; still more, in breadth of view in consequence of their narrow life experience. "Words wait on thought and thought on life." The difference between the occasional woman who reached a kind of literary eminence, and the larger number who are quite forgotten now by all but the literary historian, seems to lie rather in the degree of culture and of life experience than in any perceptible difference in native ability. It may be that we owe *Uncle Tom's Cabin* to the fact that a New England woman was transplanted to a Western border state, and set down where the tragedies of

the fugitive slave law gave her talent a concrete
impulse; and, perhaps, the accidental circumstance of life in California gave to the author of
Ramona her first effective contact with the real
life of the world.   Certain it is that, in addition
to the artistic gift and the hunger for ideal expression in words, there must be the stuff of
vital experience with which to work; and of this,
women, by the very stationary and domestic condition of their lives, had almost nothing as compared with men, and even yet have immeasurably
less.

The early female writers were, too, like their
masculine forerunners, caught fast in a saccharine
slough of sentiment and piety which in itself destroyed all freedom of thought and originality
of method.   The cheerful Carys wrote dismal
stanzas of death and despair, affecting what they
could not feel.   The " exemplary " Mrs. Sigourney, " phenomenon rather than an author," composed verse—while knitting socks for the family
—in which were commemorated in the approved
lachrymose phrases, the funerals, baptisms, and
weddings in the circle of her friends.   The most
successful of the women story-writers invariably
combined sentiment and religious emotionality
upon a commonplace domestic background.   As
Professor Trent has pointed out, there was not a
trace of romantic interest, and the style was in-

evitably mediocre and didactic; but whether they portrayed the fortunes of an orphan girl rescued from low life, or the conscientious struggles of a schoolgirl vibrating between tears and prayers, such fiction could be safely recommended by pastors to their flocks as proper mental and spiritual pabulum.

Though women writers had no monopoly of this "milk and water" literature, the middle-class standard set for them was one more weight to hold them back from beholding or attempting better things. In writing, as in every other effort, though less consciously, they were coerced by the tradition of the inferiority of the feminine intellect. Since the province of womenkind was feeling rather than thinking, they felt themselves incompetent outside the realm of didactic poetry and fiction. The literary men of an earlier time had been under a similar thrall through Puritanism, but they had been sooner emancipated into the air of world-culture without which literature is seldom created.

In addition to all the other limitations of superficial education, and absence of intellectual atmosphere, opportunity, and stimulus, women of the Nineteenth Century had still another, self-distrust, which in itself would almost account for their meager representation in the literature of the national era. To man all things are sup-

posedly possible, but nothing intellectual was then
believed to be possible to woman; and when, here
and there, against great odds, some woman rose
above her sex-limitations, compelling recognition,
it was set down as merely exceptional, not characteristic nor attainable by her kind. The very
essence of genius is supreme confidence in what
one has to say. A distinguished actress, in discussing the fact that plays are generally written
by men, has lately said:

" Because they are so tremendously clever and such tremendous egotists—that's why men write greater things
than women—they are capable of such limitless belief in
themselves. All the great creators were so—egotists all."

To all the disadvantages under which men of
literary talent had risen and sunk in America,
women added self-distrust created by the hostility of a society pervaded by the strict domestic
traditions of femininity. And, moreover, the
woman of talent was often paralyzed not merely
by the common assumption that her mind must
be inferior, but by her own fear that she was
morally wrong in feeding her slender flame.

No sooner had the tradition of mental inferiority been broken, the doors of culture opened
into the universe, and the attention of a reading
public attained, than there appeared talented
women by the score who, in a single generation,

and though still handicapped, earned a wide and creditable reputation for serious literary work. As yet, it does not appear how far they may go, nor to what degree their achievements will be colored by sex-experience. But in the space of half a century they have gone so far that the tale of such crude, effeminate, and imitative efforts as their sex once timidly made, already sounds far off and strange.

SECTION IV

FROM FEMININITY TO WOMAN-HOOD

297 SIGNIFICANCE OF FEMININITY

women by the physical and mental standards of
men quite frankly admit that, beyond the primary
sex differences, and a very few permanent secondary qualities, there is a vast debatable area

CHAPTER XIV

THE SIGNIFICANCE OF FEMININITY

"I consider it presumptuous in any one to pretend to decide what women are or are not, can or cannot be, by natural constitution. They have always hitherto been kept, as far as regards spontaneous development, in so unnatural a state that their nature cannot but have been greatly distorted and disguised, and no one can safely pronounce, that if woman's nature were left to choose its direction as freely as men's, and if no artificial bent were attempted to be given to it except that required by the conditions of human society, and given to both sexes alike, there would be any material difference, or, perhaps, any difference at all, in the character and capacities which would unfold themselves."—JOHN STUART MILL.

"We are probably in about the same position and stage with reference to the questions of sex as were the men of the eighteenth century with reference to the question of evolution."—
LESTER F. WARD.

IN discussing the difference between men and women, the words " male " and " female " are perfectly definite, but in the related terms " masculine " and " feminine " there is included a large number of physical, mental, and social characteristics which are variable and unstable, sometimes capable of a precise description, but oftener as accidental and temporary as the fashions of the times. The scientists who have tried to measure

women by the physical and mental standards of
men quite frankly admit that, beyond the primary
sex differences, and a very few permanent secondary qualities, there is a vast debatable area
of variation which must engage the attention of
future investigators. There is no debate about
the significance of a smooth face in women and
of a beard in men, nor about the contrasting
timbre of their voices, but whether the fact that
women have fewer red corpuscles than men sig-
nifies that they are a feebler race, or merely less
developed than men in our age and time, is an
open question.

Whether less sensitiveness to pain and greater
sensitiveness to emotions on the part of woman
indicates an ineradicable difference of nerve
centers, or merely of conventional training;
whether she was born unstable and changeable,
or made so by the limitations of her life—these
and similar disputes have been settled, only to be
unsettled soon afterward by equally scientific
authority. In such a conspicuous matter as mentality the dogmatisms of research with regard
to the inferior brain capacity and intellectual
products of women, were scarcely uttered before
they became untenable by reason of the achievements of women themselves—at first of a few
brilliant exceptions only, and shortly afterwards,
of an increasing number as education and oppor-

tunity were extended to them. As a current journal humorously puts it: women have lived to do everything that it was said they could not do, except grow whiskers.

It is only a short time—as progress goes—since men as far-seeing as Darwin and Huxley held that the " intuitive " or " womanly " quality of mind, the quick perception, and rapid imitation characteristic of women, put them in the same category with bygone civilizations and the lower races. But from the time that Buckle showed that the most important discoveries of modern time have resulted from the deductive method, that is, from the feminine habit of mind, there has been an increasing tendency to believe that imagination and intuition were effecting quite as much progress as the logical understanding. Certainly there is a consensus of opinion among modern psychologists and sociologists in placing higher value upon the very mental quality which was not long ago held to establish finally woman's inferiority.

The ground of the disputes over the qualities and capacity of women has come to lie quite outside the primary sex-functions, or even the secondary sex characters, which were evolved apparently to insure reproduction. Indeed, the characteristics in dispute range from the significance of the larger thyroid gland in the human female to the effect of voting on her loyalty to domestic duty—from the investigation of her senses to the causes of divorce. In short, it is no longer a question of what women could or could not do if they had an equal chance, but of what is likely to be the effect of their trying to do, under a handicap, whatever they have the courage to attempt. In our present stage, the conclusions as to the permanence or significance of any feminine peculiarity at which any observer will arrive are in accordance usually with his habitual anti- or pro-feminine bias. In this respect, the discussion resembles the attempt to determine species and sub-species in natural history. In any large number of specimens there are always some on the border-line; whether these will be named as new species or relegated to a lower place as sub-species or varieties, depends almost wholly on the personal idiosyncrasy of the naturalist.

In some aspects the woman-questions are analogous to race questions. We know tolerably well what degree of civilization the darker races have attained in their native habitats; but there is very little accurate, unbiased information as to the degree and conditions of the progress which any of these races has made in other climates, and under the stimulus of new environments. Only two decades ago it was confidently predicted on scientific grounds that the Hawaiian race would shortly die out; but their increasing birth-rate and decreasing death-rate may now portend a chance of survival. Nor has the last word been said concerning their ultimate contribution to civilization, since the Hawaiian-Chinese half-breed youth have lately surpassed all others in the local schools.

An even more striking instance of premature condemnation of an apparently static race is afforded by the Chinese. It is scarcely half a century since China was an unknown country, and the Chinese—to our complacent view—a weird, incredible, uncivilized people; yet in that time China has risen to be one of the greater powers, and is, moreover, on the verge of developing suddenly, out of her village democracies, a modern constitutional government or republic. The guesses as to the Chinese capacity for progress have been favorable or unfavorable according to the critic's degree of instinctive race prejudice, and his equipment of hearsay or first-hand information. Surely, if in so short a time the " Heathen Chinee " can rise to be a progressive human being in our estimation, it is not impossible that women may become social entities, whose acquired " femininity " may be modifying faster than the carefully digested ideas of scientific observers.

After a round century of discussion and investigation, the real crux of the woman question is still whether some of the so-called secondary and all of the tertiary sex characters are inherent and relatively permanent, or whether they are merely temporary variations due to environmental and social causes. Granting that maleness and femaleness are fundamental and, in the higher orders of life, unchangeable after birth, are the peculiarities comprised in what is called "femininity" and "masculinity" equally fixed? For a good many hundred years it has been assumed that they were unalterable, but the discoveries in biology and the rise of democratic theory have together undermined this as well as many other dogmas.

One of the most surprising results of this change in thinking about women is, that while the number of qualities denominated "strictly feminine" has been rapidly diminishing, masculinity has remained in the minds of most people, until quite recently, a fixed congeries of characteristics. Yet one has only to catalogue the men of his acquaintance to realize that manliness is scarcely a more definite conception than womanliness. Professor Sargent of Harvard University is quoted as having said recently that the modern youth is rapidly approaching effeminacy and the modern girl masculinity, in their physical type. Professor Gayley of the University of California about the same time characterized the male college student as follows:

" Busy to no purpose, imitative, aimless; boastful but unreliant; inquisitive, but quickly losing interest; fitful, inconsequential, platitudinous, forgetful; noisy, sudden, ineffectual."

Curiously enough, the adjectives—with, perhaps, the exception of " boastful "—are precisely the ones applied to women. Professor Woodworth, the entomologist of the University of California, goes much farther in his views of the possible changes in sex-function. He suggests that we may be approaching a new social adjustment like that of the ant-colony, where, in certain members of both sexes, the reproductive function will be subordinated to other forms of efficiency. Altogether, the present views of scientific men are so contradictory and so revolutionary, and the type of domestic womanhood is differentiating so fast and in so many unexpected directions, that no one can safely commit himself to any dogmatic statement beyond the fact that whatever babies are born in the future will still be born of woman.

To the discussion of feminine possibilities the evolutionary scientists have made, so far, the most important contributions—perhaps because they may know better than other thinkers the stultifying nature of dogmatism and the danger of prophecy. The feminist movement, though begun in a period when it was expected that science would prove that woman had been and eternally must be inferior to man, has ended by showing that most of the things formerly assumed are either not so or, at any rate, questionable. Starting at this point, the Twentieth Century observer must ask: why are women as they are? The thoughtful person who sees what the semi-feudal, almost unreasoning peasant of Eighteenth-Century Europe has become in this country, under the stimulus of wider economic opportunities, and relieved from the pressure of militarism, may properly hesitate to predict what womankind might be with an equal liberation and as strong an impetus.

It might, perhaps, be asserted that the distance between the two extremes of opinion as to sex capacity is now generally in inverse proportion to the amount of exact knowledge of its manifestants. Certainly the sociologists who have taken the most pains to test out their material carefully are the least dogmatic as to what may be expected of women. Mr. Havelock Ellis, after a thorough examination of all the available data on sex characters, reached most inconclusive results, as may be seen from the following paragraphs:

"We have to recognize that our present knowledge of men and women cannot tell us what they might be or what they ought to be, but what they actually are, under the varying conditions of civilization. By showing us that under varying conditions men and women are, within certain limits, indefinitely modifiable, a precise knowledge of the exact facts of the life of men and women forbids us to dogmatize rigidly concerning the respective spheres of men and women. It is a matter which experience alone can demonstrate in detail. . . . The small group of women who wish to prove the absolute inferiority of the male sex, the larger group of men who wish to circumscribe rigidly the sphere of woman, must alike be ruled out of court. . . .

"The facts are far too complex to enable us to rush hastily to a conclusion as to their significance. The facts, moreover, are so numerous that even when we have ascertained the precise significance of some one fact, we cannot be sure that it is not contradicted by other facts. And so many of the facts are modified under a changing environment that in the absence of experience we cannot pronounce definitely regarding the behavior of either the male or the female organisms under different conditions. There is but one tribunal whose sentence is final and without appeal. Only Nature can pronounce the legitimacy of social modifications. The sentence may be sterility or death, but no other tribunal, no appeal to common-sense, will serve instead."

The contemporary psychologists, as well, speak in a very different tone from those of a generation past—both less dogmatically and more hopefully as regards what the feminine mind is capable of. Quite recently, in a discussion of co-education, Professor John Dewey wrote:

" Upon no subject has there been so much dogmatic assertion, based upon so little scientific evidence, as upon the male and female types of mind. We know that traits are transmitted from grandfather to grandson through the mother, even the traits most specific in nature. This, with other accessible facts, demonstrates that such differences of mental characteristics as exist are those of arrangement, proportion, and emphasis, rather than of kind and quality. Moreover, it is scientifically demonstrable that the average difference between men and women is much less than the *individual* difference among either men or women themselves."

As the conclusion of a recent examination into " The Mental Traits of Sex," Helen B. Thompson says:

" The point to be emphasized as the outcome of this study is, that, according to our present light, the psychological differences of sex seem to be largely due, not to difference of average capacity nor to difference in type of mental activity, but to the difference in the social influences brought to bear on the developing individual from early infancy to adult years. The question of the future development of the intellectual life of women is one of social necessities and ideals rather than of the inborn psychological characteristics of sex."

In the examination of female sex characteristics, the working hypothesis of the early Nineteenth Century was that these were nearly all
fundamental, and, therefore, unchangeable; but
the scientists, in the course of developing the evolutionary theory, have compiled a great array of
facts, showing that some of these are much less
fixed than others; and that some, once supposed
to be immutable, never existed except in abnormal
persons. Take, for instance, the conspicuous
case of women's respiration, declared by Dr.
Hutchinson in the Eighteenth Century to be
costal, and, therefore, quite different from the
abdominal type of man. For a hundred years this
was taught as a physiological fact; and yet, in
1896, Dr. Clelia D. Mosher of Stanford Uni
versity, and Dr. Fitz of Harvard, overturned
simultaneously this " fact " by more accurate
data, and the physiologies now state that,
normally, women and men breathe alike.

The views of physiologists with regard to so
deep-seated a limitation as the menstrual function are rapidly changing. The idea of the
" curse upon woman," as developed by religious
dogma, and the vulgar superstitions arising from
it, have been displaced by the acceptance of menstruation as a perfectly normal function; and the
incapacity which has often accompanied it in civ-

ilized woman is—according to the latest medical dictum—as remediable by education and correct habits as other functional disorders.

Between the Eighteenth and the Twentieth Centuries, the ground of debate regarding women has been gradually shifting from sex characteristics to the effect of the social environment upon women in producing perversion and limitation of character. Now, in all this series of assumptions, re-examinations of data, discovery of new facts, and making of new hypotheses, only a few women have appeared to give direct testimony. It has been an examination by men of phenomena relating to women as they appear to men to be. In the present state of conventional relations between men and women, men certainly know more about their own sex than about women; and if women are, in truth, the inexplicable and inconsistent creatures that they are commonly represented to be, they must know far more about each other's processes than any man could hope to find out. Only a human being combining all the experiences of man's and woman's life could really accurately describe the life history of either sex. Weiniger, a morbid but keen observer, has pointed out that every man has some feminine, and every woman some masculine, attributes. However true this may be, the differentiation of sex habits and thought is so extreme that each sex has lost in great measure the power to understand the other.

In the discussion now going on—of what women have been, should be, and should not be—there is a missing factor. Not many men and, perhaps, only a very clear-thinking woman, can analyze and visualize the lives of women as they are on the inside. While a few notably sympathetic scientists, like Professor Ward and Professor Thomas, have brought out the effect of restriction and environment upon women, the full weight of social tradition in over-developing some of the superficial feminine qualities, and suppressing other deep-seated ones, has not been measured. Take, for instance, the assumption that most women think superficially and with less logic than men, which is probably a fact. Ward says they reach conclusions by intuition, a sort of short-cut method evolved by the emergencies of their lives. Yet any woman knows from her childhood that men prefer to do her thinking for her, and will disapprove of her if she sets up an opinion against theirs. In primitive ages not only was thinking unnecessary for a woman beyond the narrow range of her traditional duties, but it was an actual impropriety. Now only a genius, a reformer, or a mad person does what will be disapproved of. Until the last half-century, marriage was the only career open to women—a thinking woman was not attractive to men—therefore the astute young woman either stopped reasoning as far as possible when she came to years of discretion, or concealed her mental operations. Many a woman who attains her ends by coquetry and hysteria is, like the parrot who couldn't talk, keeping up a " devil of a thinkin' " all the while; and will confide to another woman, who is in the secret, a keen analysis of the issue involved.

At the same time a sort of compensatory habitude has been acquired in her extraordinary capacity for emotion. Many a man yields to unreasonable demands on the part of some woman because he is afraid she will cry or fly into a tantrum. Women, not being so illogical as they often seem, have concluded reasonably enough to use the easiest method of getting what they want. Indeed, throughout the ages there has been as high a premium on tears and temper in one sex, as on fighting and profanity in the other. On the other hand, although men are as a rule more self-controlled than women— mothers rarely find marked differences in this respect between little boys and girls, when held to identical standards of self-restraint.

In short, tradition and convention have operated with much more force upon women than upon men; and, until the Nineteenth Century in

America, the opportunity for self-expression on the part of women has been much less. So long as a man was law-abiding and self-supporting, he might be as eccentric as he chose in minor social matters without incurring any disastrous social penalty; but non-conformity to social conventions on the part of women has always carried with it a disproportionate disgrace.

The loosening up of all conventions and dogmas, social and religious, in the Twentieth Century, is releasing an extraordinary variety of human nature; but the predominant type of womanhood still remains that of the middle Nineteenth Century, produced by a purely domestic life and the now fast-vanishing standard of what is properly feminine. Men are a sex and something more. If they were judged historically, merely by their achievements in paternity, and if their opportunities in life had been limited for an incalculable time to the field of domesticity, they also might show the marks of a confined and stunted existence. This explains, from a woman's standpoint, why women have been until recently *The Sex,* and so little more. For women are pretty much the product of what they were taught they should be, modified by the opportunity they have had to be otherwise.

Quite recently there have been a few serious books by men in which women are examined from

the research standpoint: in which they are compared with men, biologically, psychologically,
ethnologically. But, however useful as contributions to the natural history of the human female, they tend almost inevitably to over-
emphasize the sex characters and to revert to
them as the obvious explanation of feminine
character and conduct. It is plain that the study
of women by men alone is as one-sided and in-
complete as the studies of animals by the laboratory zoölogist, when uncorrected by the field col-
lector and the observer of their habits in the
open. It may certainly be taken for granted
that to men the processes of womenkind seem
more complex and less consistent than their own;
and there is, in fact, a whole area of thought and
feeling in women of which not even husbands
catch more than a glimpse now and then, and
which has been described only indirectly, and
often morbidly, in the " problem " fiction, which
men as a class avoid reading.

Having assumed that women are inexplicable,
most men approach such subjects as woman's education, or her economic status or suffrage, in a
confused state of mind, which is a mixture of
tradition and instinctive prejudice, modified in
each particular case, by the few female types they
happen to know most intimately. The most just-
minded, even, find it difficult to reason impartially

about any woman question as they would about other purely economic or sociological problems, because it is most closely allied to race questions, and, therefore, involves the more sensitive human relations; perhaps, also, in some cases, because they find a personal application which is unwelcome.

Again, although men may recognize among themselves a thousand shadings in masculine efficiency and morality, they put the women whom they respect and admire in one class, and those whom they use or " have no use for " in another; and, without reasoning at all, are apt to set down those whose deference flatters them as " womanly," and those who do not always agree with them as " strong-minded." This men continue to do in spite of the obvious fact that there have been evolved in the last century many differentiations from the original domestic and compulsorily chaste type,—types whose desires and functions both in the home and in society are correspondingly varied.

Chronologically, the Nineteenth Century covers the lives of three distinct types of women: the Colonial, born after the Revolution, but strictly adhering to the traditions of pure maternity and of domestic manufacture; the mid-century type, born before the Civil War, and in process of transition from a producing to a semi-ornamental class; and the later, transitional varieties, who, though inheriting earlier traditions, were unconsciously forced to break away from them by industrial and social changes which they did not comprehend.

The grandmothers of the middle-aged woman of to-day of American stock belonged to the first or left-over Colonial type; their mothers to the mid-century transitional generation; while they themselves are of many differentiating classes— some still purely domestic and clinging to the handicrafts of home production; others nominally domestic, but largely ornamental; still others struggling for a foothold in an economic world for which they have had no adequate preparation; and, finally, a few, better educated or more fortunate in their opportunities, who have successfully reached a degree of distinction under physical and conventional handicaps far greater than those usually suffered by their masculine models. All of these and many other variants were maternal in greater or less measure as temperament and fate determined. To the earlier type, marriage, maternity, and domesticity were inevitable and inseparable. The confusion of thinking in which both men and women now find themselves arises in part from the fact that many women in our day are seen to be maternal without being in the least domesticated; while a smaller number are essentially domestic without being in the least maternal; and a third group, both domestic in taste and maternal in instinct, are, nevertheless, making a place in the industrial world.

The fear which many intelligent men display at any proposal to alter the sphere of women comes, in some measure, from paucity of ideas. They have not studied the feminist movement, and they see the difficulty of readjusting the current ideas of family duty and marriage relations to admit women to larger liberty. They find it easier, therefore, to continue to assume that, men having made the world largely as it is, they should know what is best for women, and that no reconsideration is necessary.

Furthermore, the conditions of modern social life overstimulate the sexuality of men, and any change in the lives of women which might result in the limitation of their sex function is resented. Modern women, on the other hand, resent equally the pervasive belief that their sex functions represent their only really useful contribution to society. Half a century ago Thomas Wentworth Higginson voiced the views of a few whose number has now become legion:

" Every creature, male or female, finds in its sexual relations a subordinate part of its existence. The need of food, the need of exercise, the joy of living, these come first and absorb the bulk of its life whether the individual be male or female. . . . Two riders pass . . . my window; one rides a horse, the other a mare. The animals were, perhaps, foaled in the same stable, of the same progenitors. They have been reared alike, fed alike, trained alike, ridden alike,; they need the same exercise, the same grooming; nine tenths of their existence are the same, and only the other tenth is different. Their whole organization is marked by the distinction of sex; but, though the marking is ineffaceable, the distinction is not the first or most important fact. . . . This is not denying the distinctions of sex, but only asserting that they are not so inclusive and all-absorbing as is supposed. It is easy to name other grounds of difference which entirely ignore those of sex, striking directly across them, and rendering a different classification necessary. It is thus with distinctions of race or color, for instance. An Indian man and woman are at many points more like one another than is either to a white person of the same sex. A black-haired man or woman, or a fair-haired man or woman, are to be classed together in these physiological aspects. So of differences of genius: a man and woman of musical temperament and training have more in common than has either with a person who is of the same sex, but who cannot tell one note from the other. . . . Nature is too rich, too full, too varied, to be content with a single basis of classification; she has a hundred systems of grouping, according to age, sex, temperament, training, and so on; and we get but a narrow view of life when we limit our theories to one set of distinctions."

The over-emphasis of sex functions, and the domestic and family traditions which grew out of it, found expression chiefly in the Nineteenth Century in America. The lives of hundreds of women of the great, typical, middle, comfortable classes, both living and dead, have been studied, and are here interpreted as showing how coercive the belated conventions of feminine duty and behavior have been. They serve to explain the inconsistencies, the futility, the narrowness of the great mass of such women at the present time. To women who are struggling in the meshes of their own mixed temperaments, and the fast-changing conventions of the feminine world, here is encouragement as well as revelation. When men are able to free themselves from their traditional opinions about women, and to give as dispassionate thought to the efficiency of women as to other social problems; and when women as a class acquire the same belief in their own abilities as men now possess, the " woman question " will solve itself; for it will have become merely a phase of general progress, in which both sexes necessarily rise together.

CHAPTER XV

FAMILY PERPLEXITIES

"Modern conditions and modern ideas, and in particular the intenser and subtler perceptions of modern life, press more and more heavily upon a marriage tie whose fashion comes from an earlier and less discriminating time. When the wife was her husband's subordinate, meeting him simply and uncritically for simple ends, when marriage was a purely domestic relationship, leaving thought and the vivid things of life almost entirely to the unencumbered man, mental and temperamental incompatibilities mattered comparatively little. But now the wife, and particularly the loving, childless wife, unpremeditatedly makes a relentless demand for a complete association, and the husband exacts unthought-of delicacies of understanding and co-operation. These are stupendous demands. . . .

"No contemporary woman of education put to the test is willing to recognize any claim a man can make upon her but the claim of her freely-given devotion to him. She wants the reality of choice, and she means 'family,' while a man too often means only possession. This alters the spirit of the family relations fundamentally. Their form remains just what it was when woman was esteemed a pretty, desirable, and, incidentally, child-producing, chattel. . . ."—From *A New Machiavelli*—H. G. WELLS, 1910.

THE Twentieth-Century woman is in process of transition from hyper-femininity to balanced womanhood. This movement, represented in the middle of the last century by sporadic, exceptional types; and since then by larger groups, such as the college alumnæ on the one hand, and women in industry on the other, is steadily gathering momentum.   Of all the vocations listed in the current census, there is not one which women have not attempted.   At the same time, household management is rapidly becoming an applied science; and motherhood and the rearing of children are taken with infinitely greater seriousness and are measured by a rising standard of devotion and intelligence.

While social conservatives point out—what cannot be denied—that women grow less and less domesticated and feminine in habit; and, while the prophets of the feminists reply that they are, nevertheless, more womanly and humane; plain, thoughtful men and women are puzzled and apprehensive in the face of the problems raised by the change.   The proud father who, at some sacrifice, sends his clever daughter to college, is surprised to find that when she returns home she is not satisfied to be merely the ornament of the house and the comfort of her parents until she marries.   He is troubled by her critical attitude toward her suitors, her disdain of protection, and her reserve toward marriage.   The sweet, domestic mother, whose whole life has been absorbed in domestic detail and in childbearing, grieves that her daughter, just out of school, insists on going to a business college, or to a training-school for nurses, to learn to earn her living " when it is quite unnecessary."

At the other extreme are the " emancipated " parents who, because of their own limitations and mistakes, have an intense desire to plant their girls in a larger life than the old conventional domesticity. They are often astonished and disappointed to find their daughters relapsing into traditional femininity under the fundamental impulses of maternity. All the advantages of education seem to have been thrown away; for the higher culture seems to bear no essential relation to the inevitable duties of the domestic woman.

After all, the confusion and doubts of parents are of less account than the perplexities of the marriageable young woman of this transitional day. She sees that older women accepted as right—if not satisfactory—the peculiar status which was half-domestic, half-dependent; but she has somehow acquired an instinctive sense, from the social atmosphere, from the newspapers, from the example of women who have " done things," that she ought not to accept unquestioningly such a plane for herself. She wants to marry, but does not dare to say so, and must, therefore, practise the ancient arts of concealment and coquetry; or, scorning to do so, is likely to remain unmarried.

If she marries under the impetus of natural

passion and maternal instinct—nothing having
been said to her of the real meaning of marriage or the nature of men—she invariably begins with a romantic and unpractical idea of what
she ought to give and receive. The women of
former generations had to marry or fail utterly
in life, from the standpoint of their world. They
took, consequently, any kind of man, the best that
offered, blindly accepting whatever fate the al-
liance brought them. They considered themselves fortunate if the master of their destiny
was a good provider and a kind father to their
children. However mismated, they could not
face the horror of divorce; nor could they support themselves and their children in an industrial world which was not yet in need of untrained women. Duty to their husbands and religious sanction made child-bearing—regardless
of the quality of the child or the need of population—inevitable and involuntary. Although
purely instinctive parenthood produced large
numbers of undervitalized, defective human beings that ought never to have been born, the
belief that these were providentially sent and
were useful to the state relieved the parents from
all responsibility for their uncertain quality.

The intelligent young parents of to-day, however, after a child or two has arrived—if not before—begin to calculate the cost and, perhaps,

the inconvenience of children under the more exacting standards of modern life. Professor Amos G. Warner once calculated roughly that even in a laboring man's family a baby two months old cost not less than one hundred dollars; while in fairly well-to-do families the expense of extra service while the mother was incapacitated, of nursing, of doctor's attendance, of the layette, and of petty incidentals, amounted to five hundred and sometimes to a thousand dollars. With an ever-increasing emphasis on the hygienic care of children, modern parents cannot but count the cost of them in personal sacrifices as well as in money. The more intelligent the population becomes, the more will married people comprehend that society is not so much in need of mere human beings as of well-born, well-nurtured, competent, moralized citizens. Some people may develop a larger paternity, like that of Leland and Jane Stanford, who, when they had lost their delicate only son, founded a university with the motto: "The children of California shall be my children."

Perhaps there is nothing which the thoughtful married woman of the younger generation resents more than the assumption on the part of theorists that the decline in the birth-rate is due chiefly to her selfishness and failure in maternity. She knows, but cannot publicly explain, that in

not a few cases husbands are unwilling to subordinate their careers to unregulated instinct;
preferring few or no children, with a care-free,
comely partner and a quiet household. Some
modern men value their wives for companionship more than for child-bearing, and it sometimes happens that the wife is only allowed to
have her baby as a sort of concession to
what the husband regards as an overdeveloped
maternal craving. And other men have a conscience toward the unborn child and toward society, wishing to bring into the world only those
that are fit and that can be properly brought up.

If husbands of these exceptional types were
men of dissolute habits and extreme selfishness,
or unintelligent, they might be set down as merely
abnormal; but they are, in fact, as a class, the
physically and morally fit, who would make good
parents. That they hesitate or decline to be
fathers of large families points not to the deficiencies of women, but to a racial change which
is going on toward the whole problem of population. By far the larger part of mankind are
fathers, not because they are consciously paternal,
but because they wish a home and a woman, and
must take its consequences. Even among these
families the onus of the childless household or
the single-child family no longer rests upon
women alone. Within a decade scientific medical

research has transferred it largely to men. The revelation of the direct causal relation between venereal diseases among men and sterility and physical degeneration among married women has only just begun to take effect. In time it must afford that new " sanction for pre-marital chastity" in men which a modern German scientist urges as the absolute essential of a self-renewing and healthy population.

All this recent agitation against " the conspiracy of silence," this criticism of the childless married woman, this modern emphasis on child-care, this exposé of the unchastity of the average young man, cannot but reach in some form the girl who thinks of marriage and children, however carefully she may be guarded. The girls of leisure, who fill up the interval between school-days and marriage with friendly visiting, hospital and charity labors, church and settlement work among the poor, must come upon the tragic origin of defective children; and cannot fail to see how many children are undesired and neglected. Unlike the secluded and ignorant young creatures of former times, who became wives before they were physically grown, the modern young woman sees and fears and questions the facts of sex; and by so much as she does so, will wish to know more and to exact more of any man who offers himself to be the father of her children. Herein will lie many tragedies both for the man and the woman.

Under the influence of contradictory impulses many girls now go into wage-earning. The ranks of school teaching and office workers are filled up with young women of the comfortable middle-class, who, in a former day, would have remained at home waiting to be married. Since these workers are likely to have more self-respect and more initiative than those who accept dependence without question, they are a strong and selected class; and by that fact, therefore, they are more fit to be mothers. The office women, in the course of their work, are likely to meet men of similar tastes and aims, and to marry with every chance of happiness. But the school teachers are, by the very conditions of their trade, an isolated class; and thus it comes about that thousands of young women of exceptional education and capacity find an outlet for their maternal instincts in the task of doing for children what their parents cannot do.

Nature, indeed, may have no use for childless people; and a society that is under the necessity to breed vast numbers of soldiers abhors them. But in the American world, where militarism plays small part in the lives of ordinary citizens, and where there is an increasing effort to preserve child-life, there is an immense need of those who have strong childward instincts, and who can be satisfied with vicarious parenthood. The tenderly maternal, patient women who carry on the kindergartens, the orphan asylums, the hospitals for crippled children, and the homes for defectives; or who spend their lives among the poor in settlements, have compensations for their childlessness such as many unthinking parents who take their children impatiently, in the course of nature, never knew.   And if there are still some who cannot be fully satisfied to hold in their arms any child except one of their own fulfilled love, even such enforced denial is not so great a tragedy as the mother who brings into the world infants she cannot wish for and perhaps finds it difficult to love.

Historians have pointed out that the Christian celibacy of the Middle Ages prevented the reproduction of the most refined and the most intellectual class in Europe; yet it was the monks and nuns who kept alight the shrines of Faith, who trimmed the lamp of learning, who preserved the gentleness of unselfish, humane religion. While the whole Continent of Europe was drenched in blood and devastated by religious wars, while plague and ignorance mowed down the helpless people, the scholar and the devotee cherished the seeds of civilization.   So in our day the childless, whether single or married, may find a larger duty to their kind than the easy gratification of instinct; and may make as great contributions to society as those who follow nature without question.

Undoubtedly the higher ideal of love as well as of parental duty in our day prevents the marriage of some of the best individuals, because " it differs wholly from localized passion in being selective." Although, in the readjustment of higher ideals, there are now some women unmarried who would make superior mothers, and many others, undeveloped and uneducated, who make very poor ones, there are a few—prophetic of the many soon to come—who deliberately and joyously choose motherhood. At the time when the women's colleges were founded and the co-educational method was established in the state universities, two main objections were made by the conservatives. It was said that girls who were to marry did not need such an education; and that, if they took it, they would not wish to marry. But in the forty years since then, thousands of college women have disproved both of these contentions, and have, besides, borne as many and as vigorous children as the women of the same social class who were educated in the traditional feminine ways. Although they found it extremely difficult to apply a classical training —devised by men for men of a special class—

to domestic needs, their mental culture has been
by no means wasted. They could, at any rate,
grasp the problems of their children's education.
To their experience and their effort is due, in
great measure, the demand for domestic training for girls in schools as well as colleges; and
also the growing emphasis upon sanitation,
hygiene, physiology, and physical training, to the
neglect of piano-playing, fancy needlework, and
the purely ornamental requirements for girls.

There is an increasing number of young women
who, in spite of a purely masculine culture, have
survived to be exceptionally happy and fortunate
mothers of strong, clever children. I have in
mind one who, after attaining the Phi Beta
Kappa, and making a brilliant record as a
teacher, married a college man, and is now the
mother of six fine children. When the third of
these was born within fifteen months of the second, a friend suggested that this was rather too
precipitate. The mother smilingly and content-
edly replied: "But I married so late—if I am
to have a family I must be quick about it." Yet
she had been a rich girl, had married a poor man,
and has never had more than eighteen hundred a
year to spend for the family. As the expense
of higher education for the children comes on,
she is returning to tutoring as a means of fulfilling her parental ambitions. When they shall

have been launched in life, she will yet have many years in which to recoup herself for all her sacrifices, by personal culture and in public service.

If it be thought that such a woman is exceptional, let it here be set down as a fact that there is a daily growing roster of voluntary mothers. Out of the confusions of domestic readjustment there is emerging a new and higher ideal of motherhood and family life. As the delicate, prudish, ignorant girl of a former time is replaced by those more robust, more sensibly dressed, and more practically educated, more and more of them will choose to marry poor young men, not at all to be supported, nor solely under the glamor of romantic love, but for the sake of equal comradeship and for the sacrificial joys of motherhood. They are neither afraid nor victimized, but choosers of their fate and adequate to meet it.

The most hopeful signs of our times are, on the one hand, the increase of voluntary, conscious, intelligent parenthood in the middle stratum of society; and, on the other, the tendency to limit degenerate procreation both by public sentiment and by law. The marital tragedies of our time are, to a considerable extent, due to the fact that men are as yet lagging behind women in their racial conscience. The more refined nature and the intimate personal relation of women to posterity give them a clearer vision of the consequences of indiscriminate and unregulated sexuality. Men still associate sex-vigor with manliness, and, having been brought up in the conventional theory that the sex appetite is beyond control, and its gratification essential to health, they have, as a class, no adequate motive for chastity before marriage, nor for self-restraint afterwards.

Since even engaged persons rarely have any understanding on this fundamental matter, they begin their married life in entire ignorance of each other's views, and often with widely differing standards. The specious terms of the divorce court, in a very large number of cases, cover the tragic incompatibility on this primary relation, which both partners have too much decency to confess. The very innocence in which girls are still enshrouded makes them, as wives, unjust to their more primitive partners; and the atmosphere of vulgarity in which the average boy grows up makes it impossible for the man to understand the shocks that the commonplaces of sex experience bring to the idealistic woman. Formerly, the woman had no future but marriage, and no recourse after marriage but endurance; but the modern woman who goes into social work or wage-earning, senses dimly, if she does not fully know, the animality of certain types of men, whom she will not marry, while these men themselves instinctively prefer a less critical and more sensual partner. And if a refined woman should marry such a man, it is evident that no woman, however vital, is likely to satisfy one who has acquired the habits of promiscuity.

A partial explanation of the changing attitude of young women toward marriage must be sought in the entirely altered conditions of courtship. The girls of two and three generations ago were courted briefly and married promptly before their physique was mature or their characters crystallized. It was far easier for a semi-child of eighteen or less to accept a husband's rule than it is for the modern woman, who marries at maturity, and who has already had some life of her own. In our day nearly two-thirds of all girls in the whole country between sixteen and twenty years of age are engaged in some gainful occupation. The period of courtship, and even of betrothal, is greatly prolonged, and marriages are far less likely to be hastily made. If the marital adjustments are more difficult because the habits of the partners are more fixed, there is compensation in the fact that they marry less blindly and with better judgment.

Moreover, the conditions of courtship are rapidly changing. It is less the game of pursuer and pursued; more a preliminary excursion in which the young pair who are mutually attracted try out each other's characters. Formerly courtship was carried on under abnormal circumstances, at parties, and when both boy and girl were on their best behavior. But nowadays they grow up seeing each other every day, in school and college classrooms, in stores and offices, on boats and cars, as they travel to and fro about their work. There is constant opportunity for them to learn each other's essential qualities, and time enough for one or more trial engagements before marriage is possible.

So far from this freedom resulting in laxity of morals, it seems to operate the other way. Jane Addams has pointed out that, in spite of this modern army of girl wage-earners, whose wages are below a decent living standard, the price of " white slaves " is constantly rising, and the procurers find it more and more difficult to supply the market. It is certainly encouraging that girls so hardly pressed in an inhuman industrial world, sell themselves less readily both into marriages of convenience and into body-slavery than ever before. With economic independence there has come a higher degree of self-respect.

In this period of transition the financial aspects of married women's lives are certainly perplexing. Although the law still entitles a wife to support, there is an increasing group of thinking people who believe that that right should be qualified, or made in some degree reciprocal between husband and wife. Some believe that childless women ought to earn their own living, whether married or single; or, at least, to give their leisure to philanthropy and civic service. Others go as far as Charlotte Perkins Gilman in requiring even child-bearing women to definitely contribute other services to society, except during the small part of their lives when they are actually bearing and nursing children. They point to our grandmothers who, even with large families, gave more than half their time to domestic production. For the present, however, most thoughtful people will feel that it is for the best welfare of children, and therefore of society, that mothers should be supported either by their husbands or pensioned by society temporarily, until the children themselves have been fitted for some vocation and are old enough to earn a living.

With the elimination of many processes from the household, and the application of scientific invention to others, the simple housekeeping necessary to family life becomes steadily less and the attention bestowed upon children constantly greater. Domesticity is becoming relatively unimportant, while motherhood and child-nurture are rising in value. This change of emphasis points to a fundamental modification of the ideals of wifehood and motherhood. It is at last conceivable that a woman may fulfil both duties acceptably without being able to darn her husband's socks, to make buttonholes, or produce mince pies. One of the most successful mothers of my acquaintance—judged by the product of her life, two capable and morally superior sons—can do none of these things, and never did do them, although she had only a moderate income. Left a widow when she was scarcely more than a girl, she concentrated her attention, not on feeding and indulging her boys, and practising exhausting economies to pamper their selfishness, but on guiding their minds and morals. As she herself says: " I had to be father as well as mother to them," and her interpretation of that was to make herself a delightfully sympathetic companion in every thought and impulse of their lives, interested in their school and athletic activities, and even in their sex problems. She is still their chosen confidante in manhood, while devoting herself to the personal culture for which she had scant time formerly.

In proportion as the meaning of the family centers in the needs and companionship of children rather than in physical luxury and wifeservice, the mentality of women is stimulated.

It has already been pointed out that for the proper nurture and guidance of children something more is required in the mother than an ornamental education and perfection in superfluous domestic detail. We are at the beginning of a movement to adapt public education to the needs of ordinary men and women. The culture of common things is beginning to take precedence of learning, which has often existed solely "for its own sake," as a sort of personal luxury, like diamonds or antiques. In this progress women will share, and, in so doing, motherhood will become something more than a blind obedience to nature and mankind. It will become— what it has always been potentially—a high vocation worthy of the best preparation and the profoundest devotion. At the same time it will not demand, as it used to do, the absolute surrender of all personal life and liberty. It may even happen very soon that nothing will be too good for those whose chief task it is to raise the quality of the race. And self-sacrifice, which has long been the excessive virtue of maternal women, may be reduced to a normal minimum, leaving just enough to keep feminine conceit within bounds, and masculine selfishness as well. The time has certainly come when maternity is no longer an excuse for keeping women within "their sphere," but is rather an imperative reason for compelling them to enlarge it to the periphery of the world.

Just now, the most serious perplexity of the intelligent married woman of middle age is what to do with herself when her children are gone from home, and when housekeeping, properly systematized and modernized, ought not to engage more than half her working-day. Dreading the atrophy of premature age into which many women fall for want of tasks commensurate with their powers, she seeks to contribute something more than mere manual busyness and social chitchat and hospitality to her neighborhood. She is, however, seriously handicapped by the superficial education of her youth, her lack of experience of the world, and by the disuse of her intellect during the twenty or twenty-five years given to family duties. While she may be strong and capable, she has no vocation, and does not know where to take hold on life. A large body of women in this situation are trying to solve it by the cultural opportunities of women's clubs, where they are often led by those only a little better equipped than themselves. Others devote the time to charity councils and committees, and to a thousand other unpaid social services. Yet even for these tasks of citizenship their training has been quite insufficient. Many, in default of any proper chance for a belated education, and without any necessity for self-support, relapse into the conventional social pleasures in order to fill up the time till old age comes upon them.

The loss to society by this waste or partial use of released human capacity is incalculable—comparable only to the waste of human life in prisons. It is a curious fact that we still cling to the notion that education must be formal, and that it is properly confined to the first third or quarter of life. Whenever middle-aged persons attempt to remedy the defects of earlier years, they are commonly regarded with a mixture of pity and amusement, instead of with the admiration which their aspirations deserve. Formal education in youth is in reality a sort of skeleton to be clothed and filled out by personal experience and continuous accretions. It is more convenient to begin life with a skeleton to work upon, but there is no reason why education should not be co-extensive with the whole mental development. When a house has been well built and the foundations rot out, it is possible and very good economy to jack it up and put new supports underneath—it need not be left to decay. When repaired, enlarged, and perhaps refurnished, it is often more interesting and comfortable than a new one. So is it, likewise, with human beings.

These difficulties of the middle-aged woman

point unquestionably to a reconstruction in women's education.   Since parents cannot know whether a daughter is to marry or not, they must prepare her for marriage certainly, and for self-support as well.   No woman, even when married, can be sure that she will never have to support herself.   These two aims are by no means incompatible, if the *order* of studies in the present curriculum were readjusted so as to give first the essentials and afterward as much culture as there may be time for.   There is really very little dispute about what the ordinary girl needs to know—none at all, except with regard to sex matters—and since the majority of girls leave school before they are sixteen years of age, there is approximately only ten years in which to prepare them for life.   Yet our present program takes this hardly at all into account, but assumes that education is to make conventional gentlemen and ladies rather than efficient citizens.   It is in thrall still to a tradition as strong as that which has imprisoned women—the idea that the object of education is to attain gentility rather than to develop industrial and moral capacity.

For the daughter of the laboring man, wage-earning is usually imperative until she marries, and, in many cases, afterward, since her husband is liable to be out of work, to be ill, or to become disabled.   But she rarely stays in school long enough to get training for self-support, even were it offered. Among young women somewhat better off, self-support is rapidly becoming the rule, because they like the sense of economic independence; but as yet the common schools, and even the high schools, only afford inadequate training in a few limited lines. Vocational training is, therefore, an expensive luxury, instead of an essential preparation provided by the state. This has brought about a terrible competition in all the lines of work open to girls, which require only a short apprenticeship, and from which there is no possible promotion.

But when the readjustment of educational methods to the real needs of youth shall have been made, there will still remain the problem of what to do with the married women when they shall have fulfilled their maternal functions. They must, somehow, begin to educate themselves over again, and it is an interesting fact that the agricultural colleges point out the way in which it may be done. The " short courses " offered at Cornell, Wisconsin, and other colleges, set a model for the coming schools for re-education, for the education of the middle-aged. Already there are courses of reading and study for the farmers' wives, and the time may come when the ambitious mother and wife, partially liberated from family cares, will neither be " laid on the

shelf " nor be an object of jest when she under-
takes to develop her latent abilities.

The case of the able-bodied woman of fifty is
clear—she ought to have something more to
do than that which housekeeping usually requires
in modern life—but the solution of the restless-
ness of younger wives is not so easy.   More and
more, trained nurses and nursemaids, mothers'
assistants, kindergartens, playgrounds, nurseries,
and primary schools remove children from their
mothers' care during several hours a day.   The
preparation of many foods and the making of
garments are better and, oftentimes, more
economically done outside the home than they can
be in it.   The pleasures of the family, which once
involved much labor for the housewife, are found
outside the house.   Industrial changes on the one
hand, and household conveniences on the other,
continually release more and more domestic
women from really necessary and satisfying
labor.   Thus the age limit of partial leisure for
this class is pushed back to, perhaps, thirty-five
or forty years, if there are not more than three
children in the family.

Not only does the intelligent married woman
of small family have more time in which to think,
but the ideal of the family bond itself has been
altered since women were exclusively domestic.
Until quite recently marriage had only two aims:

offspring and the regulation of the sex instinct. It has now come to have another of profound import: the comradeship of congenial temperaments. At present this third motive is demanded by the wife more than by the husband, partly because she has time to think about it, and more probably because the man's gregariousness finds satisfaction in business association with other men. Professor Thomas has expressed this admirably in the following paragraphs:

"An examination, also, of so-called happy marriages shows very generally that they do not, except for the common interest of children, rest on the true comradeship of like minds, but represent an equilibrium reached through an extension of the maternal interest of the woman to the man, whereby she looks after his personal needs as she does after those of the children—cherishing him, in fact, as a child—or in extension to woman on the part of man of that nurture and affection which is in his nature to give to pets and all helpless (and preferably dumb) creatures. . . .

"Obviously a more solid basis of association is necessary than either of these two instinctively based compromises; and the practice of an occupational activity of her own choosing by the woman, and a generous attitude toward this on the part of the man, would contribute to relieve the strain and to make marriage more frequently successful."

For any one to suggest a solution for all these family perplexities would require the assumption of omniscience. It is sufficient here to show that many types of family and marital relations are being evolved which give promise of greater justice and more content to all concerned. Lester Ward remarks that, while most persons suppose that nothing is so certainly fixed by nature, and even by divine decree, as the particular form of marriage which happens to prevail in their own country, there is, in fact, nothing which is so purely conventional as just the way in which men and women agree to carry on the work of continuing the race. Professor George Elliott Howard boldly declares that the problems of the family should be studied in connection " with the actual conditions of modern social life;" that it is vain to appeal to ideals born of old and very different ones; and he urges that the moral leaders of men should preach " actual instead of conventional righteousness."

There can be no doubt that, with relative economic independence, and with a broader and more practical education, women are rapidly passing from purely instinctive to conscious and voluntary motherhood; nor that, as they do so, they will set a higher standard of sex morality for men. In this process there will inevitably be some mal-adjustment and some unhappiness— whether more or less than our forbears endured when conditions were even farther from the ideal than now, there is no means of knowing. So far as women are concerned, this growth means a larger life, a life not exclusively domestic and maternal; and by so much as mothers are more than instinctively maternal, their children will be better born and more intelligently nurtured.

CHAPTER XVI

THE LARGER LIFE AND CITIZENSHIP

> "We're hungry . . . and since
> We needs must hunger—better for man's love,
> Than God's truth! better, for companions sweet,
> Than great convictions! Let us bear our weights,
> Preferring dreary hearths to desert souls."
>
> ELIZABETH BARRETT BROWNING.

"We are discovering women . . . our modern world is burdened with its sense of the immense, now half-inarticulate, significance of women. . . .

"Woman insists upon her presence. She is no longer a mere physical need, an æsthetic by-play, a sentimental background; she is a moral and intellectual necessity in man's life. She comes to the politician and demands, Is she a child or a citizen? Is she a thing or a soul? She comes to the individual man . . . and asks, Is she a cherished weakling or an equal mate, an unavoidable helper? Is she to be tried and trusted or guarded and controlled, bond or free?

"For if she is a mate, one must at once trust more and exact more; exacting toil, courage, and the hardest, most necessary thing of all, the clearest, most shameless, explicitness of understanding. . . .

"The social consciousness of women seems to me an unworked and almost untouched mine of wealth for the constructive purpose of the world."—From *A New Machiavelli*—H. G. WELLS.

THE survey of the life of the ordinary domestic woman of the past century has brought us to the conclusion that excessively feminine habits were the most serious disadvantage under which women struggled. By implication, also, men were as much too " masculine " as women were too " feminine " for the uses of modern life, and the gulf between them made the adjustments of marriage unduly difficult, besides reacting injuriously upon the children. With the definite decline of militarism and paternalism at the beginning of the Nineteenth Century, new types of domestic relations began to appear; but the traditional habits characteristic of the earlier régime still persisted.

The restrictive theory of a female sphere ordained by God and controlled by men, culminated in America about the time of the Civil War, and was afterward rapidly broken down by vast changes in industry and in religious thought, and by the applications of science to common life which have taken place since then. Yet even now the conventional behavior associated with hyper-femininity and hyper-masculinity is still affected or unconsciously imitated in childhood, and is deemed essential—at least in women—to respectability. Evidently, so long as the standards of religion and conduct devised by men continue to be revised largely by them, progress toward a common human—as distinguished from a bi-sexual—basis of morals will be slow.

No thoughtful person will deny that the average man needs refining and moralizing, nor that the ordinary woman is lacking in strength and largeness of mind; yet the vestigia of old social ideas remain to make girls more foolishly girlish and boys more brutally boyish from their childhood up. Though we know that half the misery of modern life comes from living in daily intensity, from sex-suggestion and indulgence, there is yet very little intelligent attempt to abate it, except by the negative process of suppression. There is certainly nothing which the world needs less at the present moment than emphasis on sex and sex differences, nor more than preparation for family duties.

Although co-education has now been established in schools and colleges for more than a generation, it is still regarded by most people as a matter of convenience and economy, rather than as an effective and rational opportunity for preparing the young for family life. The entrance of young women into industry is deprecated as diverting them from marriage and motherhood, rather than accepted—as it should be—as one of the suitable means for marriageable young people to become acquainted with each other on a self-respecting basis of business association. Although low wages, excessive hours of labor, and unsanitary conditions threaten every young person in industry, let us not forget that the girls of two or three generations ago were physically even less fit to be mothers than many modern workers, in spite of the protection of a home. If the health of girls is menaced by the inhuman exactions of many occupations, it obviously points to the alleviation of working conditions rather than to a denial of the right of economic independence.

The problems precipitated by the escape of women from the purely domestic sphere are, indeed, not capable of immediate solution; but they are relatively easy as compared to keeping them within it. It would be too bold, perhaps, to say that one of the best remedies for domestic infelicity is the feminization of men and the masculinization of women; but if men could be domesticated just a little more, and if women could be persuaded to be a little less feminine in their habits and more masculine in their minds, marriage would be more practicable and the family life somewhat nearer the ideal.

There is some alarm nowadays about the "feminization" of the schools by women teachers, but very little, apparently, about the "feminization" of the family through the inattention of men to their family duties. Yet, in practice, the ordinary father—an artisan, a clerk, or a business man—does very little fathering beyond providing support and playing with the children a little, nights and Sundays. The constructive work of bringing up the family is left largely to mothers, whose education and experience are very limited. As the hours of the working-day decrease, and as transportation facilities make it possible for men to be more at home, it should be possible to revive in a better form the coöperative family, somewhat after the old-fashioned rural type. Parents and children may come to share not only the proceeds of their joint labors, but educational opportunities and pleasures as well.

It is one of the most hopeful signs of our times that a certain class of men—though only a small and selected class—take it for granted that their paternal duties are as important as their business. In every community, and particularly in college towns, there are a good many young husbands who spend at least a part of their leisure in baby-tending, in dishwashing, and the heavier kinds of household labor. They do these things in order that their wives may escape the confinement and monotony of domesticity for a part of each day; they even help that their wives may have time for culture clubs and social reforms. There are families where the husband and wife divide the household labors between them, and both go out to work every day to earn and to share the common income. In one family, the educated wife, after having borne several children, left them when they were out of babyhood to a relative of highly domestic traits, and herself accepted a salaried position. So far from disrupting the family, this unconventional procedure has made fine men of these boys, men who have a strong attachment to their home and their parents, and who are peculiarly considerate toward their young wives. This wife was maternal, but not domestic; but so reasonable an arrangement would not have been possible, had not the husband possessed highly paternal qualities, and been willing to take his full share in bringing up the family.

There are, in truth, a thousand different adjustments of maternal and paternal relations, and as many redivisions of domestic labor and family finance. Perhaps the happiest as well as the most uniformly competent family of my acquaintance consists of ten persons. The parents, both graduates of a good small college in the Middle West, came to California for the husband's health, and the wife for a time, and in addition to child-bearing, chiefly supported the family. They have always lived simply and on the principle of all members of the family, regardless of age and sex, sharing all there was—whether of labor, drudgery, domestic care, pleasure, or money. When the family grew too large for the mother and the elder children to do all the work, they brought in a young girl from the Indian reservation near by, who is now, at middle-age, almost as intelligent and as much a member of the family as the adopted daughter. For, in addition to raising six children of their own, these warm-hearted people adopted another who needed a home.

The children, one by one, have gone to college, partly earning their own way; and the older ones, as they got into the world, helping the younger. Now the parents, at their prime of life, occupy jointly a conspicuous public position. The eldest daughter, who is of a maternal disposition, runs the house and looks after her younger brothers and sisters, and is compensated therefor by her parents. It is, indeed, a very plain establishment, but altogether sanitary and comfortable. Every person in it is well fed, well clothed, industrious; and nobody is drudging to give other members of the family something they have not earned and do not need. Every member of the household is useful, happy, and loyal to the rest; and, unitedly, they make sacrifices in order to contribute service to the public welfare. Their hospitality is proverbial, and seldom do their guests hear elsewhere more interesting conversation than in this jolly, coöperative family.

This might be called the ideal American family, yet the parents were not exceptional, perhaps, except in their sincere and simple insistence upon the principle of family unity, regardless of the sex, age, and condition of servitude of its members. Consider the difference in the results if the women had all stayed at home keeping a conventionally elaborate house; pinching their pin-money to be well-dressed, and hanging like dead-weight on the males of the family. Suppose the daughters, instead of working their way through college with some help at home, had attained a merely superficial education, and contributed nothing to society but " good looks " until they were married! As it is, there are ten persons, eight of whom are already self-supporting and well-educated, while the two younger ones give promise of meeting the family standard. All of them have had a larger life, all of them are better citizens than under the old system of sex-spheres and sex-duty; and even the head of the family has had an easier time—not to count in the spiritual compensations of profound family affection and the close comradeship of the husband and wife.

Still another significant tendency of our time is the emergence of a considerable class of men whose personal ideals are neither patriarchal nor military. In America, at any rate, the fighting man—the bully, the pugilist, the war hero, the fire-eater, the tyrannical husband and father, the man who expects to be waited upon by all women —holds a much less honorable place than in Europe. The predatory and the parasitic— whether men or women—are slowly being discredited. There is a reclassification going on which tends somewhat towards that among the Chinese, who rate people in the order of their contribution to society: scholars, producers, merchants, soldiers, et cetera. The humanitarians, once so exceptional, are a growing class of men of personal cleanliness, abstemious habits, fond of family life, and interested in political and social reforms, and by no means physically effeminate. They are, rather, men of a refined but powerfully muscled athletic type, whose fighting instincts find expression in the protection of the weak by the exercise of their higher mental shrewdness. These are the attorneys who fight for poor clients and for just but unpopular causes; politicians who wade into the muck of partizanship, not for personal gain, but for the joy of cleaning things up and making a better world to live in; employers who try industrial experiments for the solution of labor disputes, and the lessening of unnecessary drudgery; doctors who give as much time to unpaid preventive work as to building up a lucrative practice; men whose religion takes the form of settlement club work for boys, or probation and prison reform; and many others to whom some form of social service is as necessary as the fulfilment of their worldly ambition.

The relation of these new kinds of men to this discussion lies in the fact that these are the men who want wives as companions rather than domestic subordinates; who call in women to help them solve social problems; who join hands with them in their efforts to obtain the guardianship of their children, the control of their persons, property, and earnings; to protect young girls and boys; and even, and last, to help them secure equal political rights. Unquestionably there is an increasing number of thoughtful men to whom the acceleration of progress seems to depend largely on the emancipation of women from pettiness, ignorance, idleness, and social pauperization. At one end of our social scale there is a great body of idle, dissolute men; at the other, a group of selfish, luxuriously clothed, and economically dependent women. The men flock into the cities and hang about the " slum " districts; the women parade the fashionable quarters, exhibiting themselves and their finery. The imagination can hardly compass what would happen if such men stopped drinking, and such women stopped talking about clothes, and all of them went to work at some really useful occupation.

Too often the arguments for the social liberation and political enfranchisement of women are based merely on what might happen if they were achieved. There is scarcely anything which was said in favor of the enfranchisement of the common man a century ago; or of the negro and the foreigner in more recent times, which does not now apply equally to women. But, aside from the justice of it—an unanswerable argument in our day—and without regard to the specious cry of expediency, and omitting all prophecy, women need and must have a larger life. Even when motherhood shall have become, for all except the most ignorant, a high and chosen vocation; and even with every scientific assistance in the household, the life of the exclusively domestic woman will still be too narrow. Although during the earlier years of child-bearing the life of a mother is necessarily confining, there remains to the average woman from a third to a quarter of her whole adult life in which these primary duties occupy relatively very little time, and when, therefore, she might be a producer, or of public service.

It is customary for many conservative persons who are willing to grant so much as this, to point out the unpaid honorary services in philanthropy and charity in which women may now properly engage, and to which they think it wise to limit them. Let it be remembered that all philanthropy was once the province of the great lady, the priest, and the religious orders who received no pay, but it was not the more efficiently done on that account. Consecration may reduce the selfishness of the charitable, but it does not eliminate the human instinct to do that which brings compensation better than that which does not. The most faithful wifehood and motherhood on the part of members of a woman's board do not necessarily prepare them to solve the business of charitable institutions and societies, nor to comprehend and prevent the causes of poverty and family desertion, of sickness and unemployment. The merely palliative, hand-to-mouth methods of the charities of past generations were, in a measure, due to the fact that they were carried on chiefly by clergymen and domestic women. The gulf between the old-time, classically trained minister, and the modern clergyman, whose preaching and praying are only a part of many social and civic duties, is no greater than that between the old-time charitable lady and the trained charity worker of our day.

Nor are the men chosen for honorary service boards those living at leisure, devoting their time to clubs, personal culture, amusement,

travel, society; but almost invariably those who
have made a conspicuous success in some other
field, and who, at the same time, are willing to
give their scant leisure for the public welfare.
The accepted measure of economic usefulness is
money; and the public justly values honorary public service at what the giver would be valued at
in his industrial capacity. Many women of small
earning capacity are performing the honorary
services for their husband, and are measured
rather by the status of the man who supports
them than by anything they have done themselves. But more and more the services of
women, whether to the individual household or to
industry, or to the public welfare, must be reck-
oned in terms of money before they will be
thoroughly respected either by men or by other
women.

Women are demanding in their own leaders
intelligence and competence rather than wealth
and social position, and are beginning to be willing to pay for them. The charity organizations
are officered largely by trained and salaried
women secretaries, and supported by wealthy men
and women, who recognize their superiority over
volunteer workers. The woman suffrage movement illustrates the appreciation which domestic
women and women of leisure have of the abilities of others who have held a place in the wage-

earning world. The campaign of political education, financed by women of wealth, is carried on
almost wholly by speakers, writers, and organizers who have established their social value
in competition with men.
The financial measure of human ability may
not be the ideal one, but it is a necessary stage
before a higher one can be applied. The woman
who has earned a salary of a hundred a month
before her marriage, can accept support with self-
respect only if she does a hundred dollars' worth
of necessary labor afterward; or contributes a
child to society of a quality which justifies
her temporary release from labor. She can no
longer shilly-shally with her conscience by assuming that, in managing servants, paying calls, dressing herself becomingly, and making herself a
charming wife and hostess, she is fulfilling all
that society has a right to expect of her—even if
her husband be satisfied. The efficiency test
alone is rapidly discrediting a class of personally
lovely women who spend their lives in consuming
rather than in producing; and, on the other hand,
it is setting a higher valuation on competent
mothers and on women workers.

From another aspect, the entrance of young
women into the economic world has an important
relation to marital happiness. Until girls have
as good an education and are as capable of self-

support as young men, it will continue to be assumed that a suitor does his fiancée a favor in marrying her and relieving her of the necessity of proving herself in serious competition. The man who marries a woman who has already proved herself in work as exacting as his own, does not regard her as "a weaker vessel," but instinctively respects her competence and her opinions as he would those of another man. Both she and her children rise in value in his eyes, by so much as he is compelled to recognize the pain, the peril, the limitation of life, and the incessant labor which good mothering involves.

Jane Addams, in her *Newer Ideals of Peace,* points out how women's lives have been restricted by the arbitrary assumption that their contribution to society must be made solely through children and the home:

"From the beginning of tribal life women have been held responsible for the health of the community, a function which is now represented by the health department; from the days of the cave dwellers, so far as the home was clean and wholesome it was due to their efforts, which are now represented by the bureau of tenement house inspection; from the period of the primitive village, the only public sweeping performed was what they undertook in their own dooryards, that which is now represented by the bureau of street cleaning. Most of the departments in a modern city can be traced to woman's traditional activity, but, in spite of this, so soon as these old affairs were turned over to the care of the city, they slipped from women's hands, apparently because they became matters for collective action, and implied the use of the franchise."

Miss Addams shows, further, that these outside occupations develop in the immigrant workers " an unusual mental alertness and power of perception " which results in their breaking through custom and habit, and in their acquiring the power of association.

These are qualities which women as well as immigrants need, and the domestic woman must somehow be brought in touch with a larger life —for her own sake to liberate her from conventional pettiness; for the children's sake that she may be their intelligent guide; and for her husband's sake, to relieve the marital tension which inevitably rises between a man and woman so far apart as the conventional married pair. Because of the intensely personal view which the wifely and maternal life engenders, women are emotionally exacting and expect of matrimony satisfactions which only a connection with outside realities can give. Their problem is, then, how to widen their view, how to keep abreast with the great currents in which men are caught by their very occupations, and yet how to remain the center and the mistress of the home and family.

One solution is already suggested in the fact that girls now generally remain at school longer than boys. There can be no question that the woman who is to marry and, by her motherhood cares, to be sequestered for a period of her life, needs a better education—a sort of anticipatory fund of resources, as it were—than the man whose daily contact with the business world is a continuous education in itself. The earlier years of motherhood develop the emotions to the neglect of the mind; and, because they must be filled with a monotonous succession of petty and imperative duties, tend to rob the woman of the power of systematic thought. The early mental training of girls should anticipate this heavy draft, so that the mother may keep alive her mind and soul in after years. It is necessary not alone for herself, but for the children whose friend and counselor she is destined to be through the years when they will question her competence and her authority.

It is curious that those who are quite willing to grant the necessity of a broader education and better physical development for girls who are to marry; who acquiesce in their employment in charities and the politer social reforms, balk just at the barrier of suffrage. It is, no doubt, because they are still unconsciously in thrall to the rub-off-the-bloom theory of the past century.

The tradition that the essential qualities of womanhood, like the veneer which has been called " femininity," would somehow be destroyed by the larger life, and particularly by the exercise of political rights, is still lingering in the minds of a majority of men. While they are clinging to this time-worn apprehension, the field of politics itself has come to include nearly everything requiring collective action, and which touches the life of every member of the family.

The chief function of every citizen who votes, as distinguished from the politician and the office-holder, is now to watch, to approve and disapprove by the ballot, their use of power and the measures they promote. The regeneration of democracy now going on in this country, which takes, on the one hand, the form of breaking down the machine, and, on the other, the direct appeal to the people, throws into higher relief the absurdity of refusing to women a share in deciding upon officers and issues which concern them quite as much as any other portion of the people.

Without reiterating the stock arguments in favor of admitting women to suffrage, it is important to note that voting with the occasional interest in political campaigns and large public questions affords just that connection with the larger world which the domestic woman needs; and requires no more of her energy than it does of the ordinary male citizen. Many " strictly feminine " women now spend more time away from home in social teas and card parties, in charities and bazars and aid societies, in clubs and musicales, than would serve to make them intelligent voters and active citizens. They spend their energy, moreover, with less compensation, since they do not need encouragement in pettiness, futility, idleness, luxury, nor even in polite begging to promote benevolences of which they have no personal knowledge. They sorely need the breadth of mind which the discussion of impersonal issues—trusts, tariff, and municipal graft, police, school, and health measures— would tend to produce.

In modern society the common interests of the family group are all too few. The man engrossed in the economic struggle—the children in school and play—the mother in housekeeping, social amenities, and benevolence—though together constituting the social unit, have slight mutual concern in anything except the spending of the income. If politics are discussed at all, it is by the father and son, while the women give a bored and superficial attention. But if the women were conscious of a power in these matters, all would have a common interest in being informed on them, as they already have a common stake in their proper conduct.

What, then, do women need? It must be clear enough to the open-minded reader of the preceding pages that, since the decline of home manufactures, the domestic woman has had less and less means of justifying her existence except through motherhood.

Under the spell of the idea that every woman is a potential mother, whether married or not, many people overlook the fact that at any particular time there are many hundred thousands of women who are not mothers, and who must make their claim to support by men on the ground of being housekeepers. The wife who is doing the work of the household is, at any rate, earning her board and lodging, often something more. And, as the number of children in the family is likely to be in proportion to poverty rather than riches, these working women probably contribute throughout the whole of their lives—as housekeepers, mothers, and grandmothers—more than the equivalent for all they receive; and are, therefore, in a self-respecting position.

But it would be easy to show that there are several hundred thousand women in America whose inactivity or quasi-domestic occupation makes them dissatisfied, while at the same time society is feeding and clothing them. As to the unmarried ones, there can be no question that they

ought either to be preparing themselves for usefulness, or to be giving something definite and
necessary to society. And as to the married
ones, only those who are fully occupied with children and with really necessary—not fictitious—
household tasks, should be regarded as fulfilling
their whole duty. Even mothers of children,
when the children are grown up and gone, should
be able to give a portion of their time in mature
and useful service outside the home. In proportion as women of all classes are transferred
from the consuming to the recognized producing
classes, they will gain in self-respect and content-
ment; while the world at large will be the richer
thereby.

The first thing women need is to see clearly
that it is disreputable to trade wifehood and
merely potential motherhood for the luxury of a
home and the protection of a husband. Indeed,
a very considerable number of women do realize
it, and are driven more and more into volunteer
social service by their discontent with a parasitic existence. Such discontent with the semi-
idle or relatively useless life is highly creditable
to them, and the effort to escape from the tradition which surrounds them should be encouraged
by men. When women have learned not to exchange their beauty and their sex-function for
luxury, and when they begin to try to do some-

thing worthy of their human energies, then they will begin to rate their labor in a truer perspective. Men, as a rule, work harder than women, but they are not half so busy. A woman will tell you she has no time to read—but is meantime doing beautiful and often quite superfluous needlework in all her spare moments. She has no time to keep up her music, which she really loves, and upon which she spent so many years of practice in girlhood, but she will retrim her hats, remake her dresses, taking infinite trouble to propitiate that Juggernaut of womenkind—Fashion.

In proportion as women go to work at exacting, routine occupations outside the home, they are dropping the habit of futile busyness; they buy fewer, plainer, more substantial clothes, and wear them longer. The standard street dress, represented by the separate waist and tailor suit, which became the fashion for the first time about 1890, is a historic landmark in the life of American women. In spite of manufacturers and designers, that type of dress, corresponding to the man's business suit, has remained the standardized dress of the modest woman.

This readjustment of values is in itself making a wide differentiation in the varieties of domestic women. Once all domestic women had the same ideas, and their lives were spent in a continuous effort to attain an ever greater elaboration of clothes and housekeeping. While now there is a larger and larger group of women who are putting their housekeeping under their feet, so to speak—reducing it by appliances, short-cut methods, elimination, systematization, simplification, to a point where it is pleasurable and good exercise, and where it leaves them the greater part of their time and energy for the higher interests of the home and for intellectual comradeship with husband and children.

As soon as girls began to go into industry, they began to learn anew the habits and the joys of thoroughness, which had been the characteristics of their manufacturing grandmothers. They began to test themselves by the achievements of men and to take pride in meeting their business requirements. But, as a rule, as Professor Thomas so justly remarks, women are still to men as amateurs to professionals, for they came late into the economic game. But already the effect upon their habits and modes of thought is strikingly apparent. To do hard things, under trying conditions, and under the supervision of men upon whom the conventional tears, temper, and coquetry have no effect, either by way of excuse or increased wages; is a tremendous corrective to the emotionalized feminine temperament. For a pretty girl to discover that her male employer has no use for her unless she can spell and take dictation correctly, is an education in itself. Instead of depending merely on her traditional sex weapons, she will more and more depend upon competence, and, in doing so, will gain self-control and an independent poise.

The entrance of young women into industry is readjusting all the sex relations and making mutual concealment between man and woman more difficult. Two generations ago the whole education of a girl was aimed to conceal her nature from herself as well as to keep her ignorant of the nature of men. The old-fashioned private school reared girls to a kind of sexlessness, with the result that they were morbidly fearful and yet curious about sex matters. They were inevitably oversensitive, feeling themselves stained, as Marholm says, " by everything imaginable—by the glances of indifferent men, by their own thoughts, by physiological knowledge." Such a state of mind is not possible to young women who meet men daily in business relations. Nor can men much longer conceal from the women whom they meet in business the unsavory facts of their own social habits. Girls who, in the seclusion of the home, might never learn what their suitor's previous life had been, cannot fail to see men somewhat as they are, and to exercise their judgment as never before. The power of selection, so long almost wholly in the hands of men, is gradually being transferred to the potential mothers of the race.

But of all the modifications which economic and political liberation will work in the characters of women, the most important is the development of a social conscience. The women of the past century, having no responsibility for matters outside the home, and no direct knowledge of how money was made, accepted all they could get from their men-folk with a clear conscience. But the woman who earns her own living in our day —however pleasantly—sees young girls by the thousands paid less than a living wage, to supply the luxuries of society at a price below the proper cost of production; or to furnish inordinate profits for men to waste upon other and idle women. The thoughtful woman who does volunteer social work begins to measure her own comforts in terms of others' need. Women are thus acquiring a socialized conscience—they no longer willingly buy sweatshop lingerie; or accept unquestioningly jewels bought with money made in predatory businesses. There is, perhaps, no more touching and hopeful aspect of the growing social conscience of women, than the efforts of rich women to square their awakened consciences by spending themselves and their money in the service of mankind.

Of the unmarried woman, almost nothing has been said in these pages, although there might profitably have been inserted a chapter on " The Superfluous Woman," in order to round out the discussion of the tyranny of tradition. It is enough for our purpose to note that she was once regarded as superfluous: a poor, unfortunate, useless human creature, who had missed the only worthy vocation of woman, and for whom there was no suitable niche in the home or the world. In this better time we need not trouble ourselves very much about her. She is neither superfluous nor idle, as a rule, and, in spite of hampering conditions, is working out her own ambitions. Though often underpaid, as compared with men of the same degree of efficiency, though handicapped by her over-feminized conscience and her conventional habits, her future is solving itself with encouraging rapidity and ease. When she shall have caught up with the game, and when she has acquired the same confidence in herself that the ordinary man has, and an equal opportunity to exercise her abilities, she will be—herself! Not a masculine female, nor a defeminized anomaly, but just a competent, sensible woman, for whose service the world already has unlimited use.

What, then, do women need? Above all, fair play and freedom from interference. Havelock Ellis has expressed the idea finely:

" We are not at liberty to introduce any artificial barriers into sexual concerns. The respective fitness of men and women for any kind of work or any kind of privilege can only be attained by actual experiment; and as the conditions for such experiment are never twice the same, it can never be positively affirmed that anything has been settled once for all—. . . . An exaggerated anxiety lest natural law be overthrown is misplaced. The world is not so insecurely poised."

It is one of the most astonishing vagaries of human thinking that, in spite of faith in God, in the face of the demonstrated power of good, and the progress of humanity, mankind continues to balk at every change. The instinct of motherhood is as old as that of procreation, and more fundamental to life; yet the world is in a state of fright for fear women will forsake their calling. If the last word has not yet been said of the Divine Spirit or of Nature, why should it be supposed that the family relations are finally determined, and the significance of woman to life wholly fixed! Every liberation of women in any direction has, so far in the world's history, tended toward a higher civilization; yet women are still heavily weighted with traditions which obscure

their true nature and which hinder them and
their children. Let every man who has read
these pages ask himself whether he is really a
god, that he should presume to set for women the
limits of capacity and duty; and let every woman
take courage to develop all that is hidden within
her—" for we know not what we shall be."

American Women: Images and Realities
An Arno Press Collection

[Adams, Charles F., editor]. **Correspondence between John Adams and Mercy Warren Relating to Her "History of the American Revolution," July-August, 1807.** With a new appendix of specimen pages from the "History." 1878.

[Arling], Emanie Sachs. **"The Terrible Siren": Victoria Woodhull, (1838-1927).** 1928.

Beard, Mary Ritter. **Woman's Work in Municipalities.** 1915.

Blanc, Madame [Marie Therese de Solms]. **The Condition of Woman in the United States.** 1895.

Bradford, Gamaliel. **Wives.** 1925.

Branagan, Thomas. **The Excellency of the Female Character Vindicated.** 1808.

Breckinridge, Sophonisba P. **Women in the Twentieth Century.** 1933.

Campbell, Helen. **Women Wage-Earners.** 1893.

Coolidge, Mary Roberts. **Why Women Are So.** 1912.

Dall, Caroline H. **The College, the Market, and the Court.** 1867.

[D'Arusmont], Frances Wright. **Life, Letters and Lectures: 1834, 1844.** 1972.

Davis, Almond H. **The Female Preacher, or Memoir of Salome Lincoln.** 1843.

Ellington, George. **The Women of New York.** 1869.

Farnham, Eliza W[oodson]. **Life in Prairie Land.** 1846.

Gage, Matilda Joslyn. **Woman, Church and State.** [1900].

Gilman, Charlotte Perkins. **The Living of Charlotte Perkins Gilman.** 1935.

Groves, Ernest R. **The American Woman.** 1944.

Hale, [Sarah J.] **Manners; or, Happy Homes and Good Society All the Year Round.** 1868.

Higginson, Thomas Wentworth. **Women and the Alphabet.** 1900.

Howe, Julia Ward, editor. **Sex and Education.** 1874.

La Follette, Suzanne. **Concerning Women.** 1926.

Leslie, Eliza . **Miss Leslie's Behaviour Book: A Guide and Manual for Ladies.** 1859.

Livermore, Mary A. **My Story of the War.** 1889.

Logan, Mrs. John A. (Mary S.) **The Part Taken By Women in American History.** 1912.

McGuire, Judith W. (A Lady of Virginia). **Diary of a Southern Refugee, During the War.** 1867.

Mann, Herman . **The Female Review: Life of Deborah Sampson.** 1866.

Meyer, Annie Nathan, editor. **Woman's Work in America.** 1891.

Myerson, Abraham. **The Nervous Housewife.** 1927.

Parsons, Elsie Clews. **The Old-Fashioned Woman.** 1913.

Porter, Sarah Harvey. **The Life and Times of Anne Royall.** 1909.

Pruette, Lorine. **Women and Leisure: A Study of Social Waste.** 1924.

Salmon, Lucy Maynard. **Domestic Service.** 1897.

Sanger, William W. **The History of Prostitution.** 1859.

Smith, Julia E. **Abby Smith and Her Cows.** 1877.

Spencer, Anna Garlin. **Woman's Share in Social Culture.** 1913.

Sprague, William Forrest. **Women and the West.** 1940.

Stanton, Elizabeth Cady. **The Woman's Bible** Parts I and II. 1895/1898.

Stewart, Mrs. Eliza Daniel . **Memories of the Crusade.** 1889.

Todd, John. **Woman's Rights.** 1867. [Dodge, Mary A.] (Gail Hamilton, pseud.) **Woman's Wrongs.** 1868.

Van Rensselaer, Mrs. John King. **The Goede Vrouw of Mana-ha-ta.** 1898.

Velazquez, Loreta Janeta. **The Woman in Battle.** 1876.

Vietor, Agnes C., editor. **A Woman's Quest: The Life of Marie E. Zakrzewska, M.D.** 1924.

Woodbury , Helen L. Sum n er. **Equal Suffrage.** 1909.

Young, Ann Eliza. **Wife No. 19.** 1875.